From Tragedy to Apocalypse in American Literature

Good luck with your reading!

From Tragedy to Apocalypse in American Literature

Reading to Make Sense of Our Endings

Lin Atnip

LEXINGTON BOOKS
Lanham • Boulder • New York • London

Published by Lexington Books
An imprint of The Rowman & Littlefield Publishing Group, Inc.
4501 Forbes Boulevard, Suite 200, Lanham, Maryland 20706
www.rowman.com

86-90 Paul Street, London EC2A 4NE

Maclean, Norman. *Young Men and Fire*. University of Chicago Press, pgs 207-208.

Need for Roots: Prelude to a Declaration, Simone Weil. Copyright © and Imprint. Reproduced by permission of Taylor & Francis Group.

Excerpt from "To Shozo Tokunaga, Jan 10, 1969" from *The Letters of Robert Lowell* edited by Saskia Hamilton. Copyright © 2005 by Harriet Lowell and Sheridan Lowell. Reprinted by permission of Farrar, Straus and Giroux. All rights reserved. UK permission from Faber and Faber Ltd.

From "The Quaker Graveyard in Nantucket," from *Lord Weary's Castle* by Robert Lowell. Copyright 1944, 1946 by Robert Lowell. Copyright renewed 1974 by Robert Lowell. Used by permission of HarperCollins Publishers. Additional permission granted by Farrar, Straus and Giroux.

"Of Modern Poetry," copyright 1923, 1951, 1954 by Wallace Stevens; "The Man with the Blue Guitar," copyright 1937 by Wallace Stevens; "The Auroras of Autumn," copyright 1948 by Wallace Stevens; and "Man and Bottle" from *The Collected Poems of Wallace Stevens* by Wallace Stevens, copyright © 1954 by Wallace Stevens and copyright renewed 1982 by Holly Stevens. Used by permission of Alfred A. Knopf, an imprint of the Knopf Doubleday Publishing Group, a division of Penguin Random House LLC. All rights reserved. Additional permission granted by Faber and Faber Ltd.

British Library Cataloguing in Publication Information Available

Library of Congress Cataloging-in-Publication Data

Names: Atnip, Lin, 1982- author.
Title: From tragedy to apocalypse in American literature : reading to make
    sense of our endings / Lin Atnip.
Description: Lanham : Lexington, 2024. | Includes bibliographical
    references and index. | Summary: "This book argues that imaginative
    literature is essential to comprehending contemporary threats to human
    life. Readings of postwar American works by Robert Lowell, Wallace
    Stevens, Cormac McCarthy, and Norman Maclean show how their literary
    forms educate us to the reality of a new ground of sensemaking-the
    apocalyptic sublime"-- Provided by publisher.
Identifiers: LCCN 2024012879 (print) | LCCN 2024012880 (ebook) | ISBN
    9781666925586 (cloth) | ISBN 9781666925593 (ebook)
Subjects: LCSH: American fiction--20th century--History and criticism. |
    Apocalypse in literature. | End of the world in literature. |
    Fiction--Psychological aspects. | Literature--Philosophy. | LCGFT:
    Literary criticism.
Classification: LCC PS374.A65 A86 2024 (print) | LCC PS374.A65 (ebook) |
    DDC 810.9/355--dc23/eng/20240508
LC record available at https://lccn.loc.gov/2024012879
LC ebook record available at https://lccn.loc.gov/2024012880

To Elder

Contents

Preface

In 2017, David Wallace-Wells announced in his urgently titled article "The Uninhabitable Earth" that "absent a significant adjustment to how billions of humans conduct their lives, parts of the Earth will likely become close to uninhabitable, and other parts horrifically inhospitable, as soon as the end of this century."[1]

I have written this book in the shadow—or rather, in the rising heat—of global warming and our awareness of its present and future consequences, which appear as ever more catastrophic and imminent. This is not the only risk we face. In addition to climate change, the Future of Life Institute lists three other categories of potential "existential risk," defined as "any risk that has the potential to eliminate all of humanity or, at the very least, kill large swaths of the global population, leaving the survivors without sufficient means to rebuild society to current standards of living": nuclear war, biotechnology, and artificial intelligence.[2]

When I first read Norman Maclean's book *Young Men and Fire*, driving across the American West five years ago, it was Maclean's endeavor to write a modern tragedy that arrested my interest. As the project progressed, Maclean's turn at the end toward the apocalyptic acquired ever-greater gravity and eventually became a dominant theme, pulling in the other works I discuss. It is hard to say whether it was my increasing consciousness of crisis—of modernity *as* tragedy—that drove this expansion of the work to include other more explicitly apocalyptic works, or vice versa, but either way, the disturbing currency of my theme has become increasingly apparent.

I would emphasize that I mean not to be speaking (only) of some potential future disaster which may or may not come to pass. It is true that it is the prospect of the human-caused extinction of humanity that makes our situation unprecedentedly apocalyptic; and none of the "lesser" possible catastrophes—the collapse of civilization or the degradation of humanity as imagined in dystopias like *Brave New World* or *1984*—are in the same category. The end is the end—as Clint Eastwood says in *Unforgiven*, "When you kill a man, you take away everything he has and everything he's going to have"; so with humanity. In any other scenario, at least there is some hope: of pockets of survivors persisting, of individuals resisting, of culture rising again. But the perception which underlies and was strengthened in the course of writing this book is that our situation is, in some significant sense, *already* apocalyptic, whether or not we manage to "muddle through"—that we are already well underway in undermining the material and cultural conditions of humanity as we have known it, that we find ourselves collectively incapable of responding to the potential disasters that confront us, that history is being determined not by human reason and goodwill but by the darker forces within us and our institutions. I cannot argue for this directly in the book, but I believe it to be one of the realities to which we are referred by the works I read, especially insofar as they do not explicitly imagine "the end of the world" but rather represent historical and more recent events *as* apocalyptic or as having an apocalyptic dimension.

Alongside my concern about our predicament in its various facets, this study was also motivated by the question of why we find literature—and art more generally—so compelling; why a great novel or poem is an object of eros and of fascination—and an intuition that this eros and this fascination derive from our apprehension in art of some profound *reality* with which our everyday lives does not often put us in contact.

Numerous answers to this question, beginning perhaps with Aristotle's *Poetics*, have of course been articulated, some brilliant and thorough. But it is my perception that the question keeps changing its meaning with our historical situation, and the task of trying to conceive and to demonstrate literature's relation to reality is not a task we can have done with. In our case, I believe, the question takes on a new form and a new urgency in light of modern skepticism and postmodern deconstructionism as well as the existential threats enumerated above.

For the past decade or more I have been working closely with Charles Thomas Elder, whose work articulates and argues for a conception of the normative basis of modern human life as the imperative to consciousness, deriving this imperative from what he calls—in a broadly Wittgensteinian sense—"the grammar of our humanity," with the implication that our engagement with the higher culture is essential both to the development of consciousness and to knowledge of human realities and the conditions of human life. This book can be seen as emerging from and complementary to this work, though it of course intends to be fully convincing in its own right. I articulate briefly how I believe we are educated by literature to the conditions of sense; the bulk of the book then attempts to put this view to practical use in the close reading and analysis of my chosen modern tragic and apocalyptic texts.

This approach could be applied to any work of serious literature. But there was compelling reason to follow these questions out in relation to *Young Men and Fire* because Maclean makes distinctively, perhaps uniquely, transparent the struggle for a sense beyond common sense, a sense that can somehow only be attained through finding the proper literary form. It became progressively clearer in the process of my inquiry, and as I proceeded through the works to which *Fire* led me, that there is a fundamental convergence of the question of the reality to which we are educated in reading and the question of the reality to which we are referred by our readings of these works of modern tragedy and apocalypse: a convergence in the idea of a normative ground of meaning and judgment that has become fractured and dissipated under what Wallace Stevens calls "the pressure of the contemporaneous."

The ultimate point of the book, therefore, is to present a compelling case that literature should be taken seriously as a unique and, in some sense, essential mode of knowing the conditions of sense of human life, and to convey something of those conditions and their precariousness as suggested by the works I read. This is, I hope obviously, not to deny that people uneducated in the humanities are capable of judging and acting humanly (often more so than practitioners of the academic humanities)—but if our species is at a juncture, as it would seem to be, in which inhuman forces are systematically undermining both the material and the nonmaterial ("spiritual" or "ideal") conditions of our humanity, undermining our collective capacity to recognize and act upon normative imperatives and constraints, and if literature educates us to such imperatives and constraints, then it is not too much to say that preserving our humanity depends, or would depend, upon developing our collective capacity to read.

It is not just a matter of "giving literature its due," making sure it gets credit for our moral knowledge so that we as a society continue to teach and fund the humanities. Nor is it simply a matter of reading to expand the range of one's sensibilities. It is a matter of recognizing the need to inhabit a different world—a world structured not, finally, by the calculations of utility or the striving for personal happiness, but by the imperative to fulfill the demands of our humanity—including, fundamentally, the imperative to know what those demands are.

NOTES

1. Wallace-Wells, "The Uninhabitable Earth."
2. "Existential Risk."

Acknowledgments

This book began as a dissertation in the John U. Nef Committee on Social Thought at the University of Chicago, and I am indebted to my advisers, Robert Pippin, Rosanna Warren, and David Wellbery, for their inspiration, enthusiasm, responsiveness, and many stimulating and helpful comments and provocations, and to the rest of the faculty and my fellow students in the Committee for contributing to a collegial, collaborative, and intellectually productive and at times exhilarating community.

Thomas Carlson offered constructive resistance and vital material and intellectual resources for developing my thoughts on apocalypse and human conditions at the Humanities and Social Change Center at the University of California, Santa Barbara. I'm grateful too for the stimulating insights and challenging perspectives of other members of the Center, particularly Andrew Norris, Simon Thornton, and Saleem Al-Baholy.

Jakub Kowalewski invited me to contribute to *The Environmental Apocalypse: Interdisciplinary Reflections on the Climate Crisis* (Routledge, 2023); the process of writing my chapter, Jakub's thoughtful editing, and the response of other contributors expanded and refined the thoughts articulated in the present work.

Jason Frydman, Adena Rivera-Dundas, and the participants of their seminars at the 2023 American Comparative Literature Association conference—"End of World Literature: Genres of Apocalypse" and "'This is You Beyond You': Representing the Present through Speculative Futures," respectively—helped ensure I was current with the scholarly discourse on contemporary apocalyptic literature. Thanks to St. John's College for funding my participation in the conference.

Thanks to Alan Thomas of the University of Chicago Press for general support and for deepening my understanding of the writing of *Young Men and Fire*, and to John Maclean and Jean Maclean Snyder for sharing Seeley Lake and their memories of their father with me.

Mark Halliday generously gave timely, not to say last-minute, feedback on Chapter 3.

Thanks to my family for their love, support, and interest in my work. In particular, the completion of this book was inspirited by the loving memory of my uncle Gilbert Atnip, who said I'd "better get it done."

Finally, my deep gratitude to Charles Thomas Elder, who convinced me of the objectivity of conditions of sense and who set me on this path, and to both Charles and Amy Thomas Elder for sustaining me along the way and for never letting me forget what was at stake.

Introduction

Literature as Apocalypse

From reading the news, one would think that the world was going to end.

The language of apocalypse has become commonplace in recent years, and not without reason. Global warming, perhaps the most common concrete referent of apocalyptic discourse—"climate apocalypse" now has its own Wikipedia page—carries the prospect of mass extinction and is already giving rise to consuming wildfires and obliterating floods. The vision of ecological cataclysm may, for the present, have eclipsed that of a species-ending nuclear war and nuclear winter, but the latter threat is still with us as well. And while the COVID-19 pandemic seems not to have materially endangered the species or civilization, it made vivid the prospect of future plagues that might, and caused enough havoc of its own to count as a kind of apocalypse, a catastrophic revelation of hitherto unseen destructive powers, not only the virus itself but the various social and political forces that impeded a unified and efficacious response to combat it.

We live in an age, that is, in which the end of the world, in one sense or another, seems not only possible but probable—that is, we live not just with the perennial chance of an "act of God," a freak external event like the eruption of a supervolcano or an asteroid hitting the Earth, but with the prospect of catastrophe embedded within human institutions and the trajectory of human civilization. (As has been observed, even "natural" disasters like pandemics are made more likely due to the encroachment into wild habitats, and every kind of disaster is more likely to reverberate globally because of our economic interdependence.)

This book is about what literature can tell us about our apocalyptic situation. In it I will reflect on apocalyptic anticipations in twentieth-century American literature and try to show that only by reading and reflecting upon these works and others like them can we begin to adequately understand—and perhaps resist—our present and approaching apocalypse(s).

Thus broadly stated, my aim is far from original. The awareness of our precarity has flowered forth in literary and cinematic visions of apocalypse and postapocalypse,[1] and inspirited by this zeitgeist both textual and extratextual, literary and cultural critics have devoted considerable labor to analyzing these artistic expressions for insight into the modern apocalyptic imaginary.

I will return later in the Introduction to the recent critical discourse, but a few preliminary remarks on what I take to be the distinctiveness of my inquiry.

First, much of the criticism linking literature to our present crises focuses on the genre of postapocalyptic literature, fiction set in the aftermath of a civilization-destroying catastrophe. Such works address themselves directly to the anxieties of the moment, whether in imagining how a real threat might come to pass or how humanity might respond under conditions of civilizational collapse, and their relevance is obvious. For reasons to be articulated, however, I will focus on works that do not depict such totalizing disaster but which have what one might call an "apocalyptic feel," which present not a literal but a figurative apocalypse, intimating that the world is in some fallen state in which the seeds of disaster are immanent. Indeed, the former may not be a strict subset of the latter; Emily Mandel St. Cloud's *Station Eleven* and Neal Stephenson's *Seveneves*, for instance, depict the erasure of most of human life on earth, but they do not (it seems to me) fundamentally call into question the sense of what we were (are) doing pre-apocalyptically—they are stories of survival, of the attempt to preserve and rebuild what was destroyed. On the other hand, Cormac McCarthy's *Blood Meridian*, one of my apocalyptic linchpins, does not depict the end of the world in this literal sense but nonetheless casts doubt on the human future.

Second, in keeping with the tendency to the focus on depictions of literal apocalypse, criticism of (post)apocalyptic fiction tends to focus on the content of the work—the situations represented, the nature of the crises and the way the characters respond to them[2]—whereas the present book will attend closely to aspects of literary form—structure, narrative perspective, imagery, poetic language. I will try to show that certain aspects of our apocalyptic situation can only be represented "literarily" and only come into view for us in reading and trying to make sense of literary works.[3]

Finally, much if not most of the discussion of modern apocalyptic American literature treats these literary works as rhetorical, transforming real-world events or situations according to the (or a) myth of apocalypse, for good or for ill.[4] I want, by contrast, to consider that our situation really is, in some sense, apocalyptic—that we can only grasp the reality of our situation by seeing it as apocalyptic—and to explore how literature is a necessary partner in our attempt to grasp that precarious reality.

In keeping with the idea that literary works enact their revelations distinctively through their form—and with the intent of making this compelling—this book is not a broad survey but rather a close reading of works in this apocalyptic strain that I find singularly revealing: Norman Maclean's *Young*

Men and Fire, Cormac McCarthy's *Blood Meridian*, and poems by Robert Lowell (particularly "The Quaker Graveyard in Nantucket") and Wallace Stevens (particularly "The Auroras of Autumn"). These works represent modern (American or Western) history as a history of divergence from the normative and material conditions of human life, and in representing this divergence indicate a radically different ground of judgment from which we must understand and judge our situation. In this sense the works themselves are apocalypses, that is, revelations: in making sense of what they represent and the form of that representation, we are directed toward and made conscious of a different ground of sense and judgment.

I begin by considering what it means to "make sense" of our experience, how traditional tragedy and apocalyptic literature have contributed to our efforts at sensemaking, and why we might particularly, even desperately, need the revelations of literature in our present age, in which conflagrations both literal and figurative threaten to consume us.

THE BACKGROUND OF SENSE

It is a truism that we are constantly engaged in processes of sensemaking—sifting the flux of our experience into the comprehensible categories of social reality (*What is happening here?*) which indicate how we are to judge and to respond to what we encounter (*What do I do?*). When I walk down the street or into a party, when I respond to a distraught child or coworker or stranger, when I decide what college to apply to or what kind of job to take or whether and whom to marry—all of these actions depend on the sense I make of the situation in which I find myself. In making such decisions I refer, consciously or unconsciously, to a background not only of meanings and values but of *reality* as I understand it—to "the way things are."

Much of this sensemaking occurs tacitly and automatically, especially within our habitual daily lives—I do not need to make a conscious effort to understand what is going on when my partner enters the room carrying the laundry, when a colleague raises their hand to speak at a weekly staff meeting, and so on. In such cases the sense is given by habit, convention, and institutions—that is, we make sense against a background of social reality, the given framework for sensemaking, judgment, and action into which we are socialized beginning in childhood. This is largely true of wider contexts as well (perhaps more than we'd like to believe).

At times, however, we encounter problems—dilemmas regarding what to do, how to judge what is happening, and how we should respond to it—sometimes to the point of crisis. To the extent that such problems are not to be resolved by utilitarian calculus, they can be seen as problems of sense and coherence, and they compel us to consult more consciously and explicitly the background of sense: is this an act of selfishness or of independence? Is the meaning of my life to be found in my relationships or in my work? Which should take priority in a given situation?

Even such problems can, to some degree, be worked out in reference to the resources of our ordinary language and our institutions—from our workaday concepts of good and bad to commonplace notions of what constitutes a fulfilling life. As most of us have experienced, though, these understandings sometimes prove to be inadequate to our needs for sense, and on occasion radically inadequate. In *The Social Construction of Reality*, sociologists Peter Berger and Thomas Luckmann describe how the schemas according to which we construe the world—from "marriage" and "justice" down to basic categories of gender—are *functional*, that while they are constrained by material and psychological realities (e.g., aging and death, parents' attachment to their children, etc.), they develop so as to support the stability of a particular society and the reproduction of its institutions. More fundamentally, these schemas are necessarily reductive and simplifying, whether for ideological purposes or simply to enable us to operate in the world on a day-to-day basis without being overwhelmed by the variety and complexity of what we encounter.

The background of sense into which we are socialized is, therefore, not always congruent with the realities we encounter, and sometimes an event, experience, or discovery challenges the adequacy of that background: we fall in love with someone unacceptable; we lose someone or something essential to our identity; we learn of enormities committed in the past or present by our country; we find ourselves facing our own mortality—or living in a world that seems to have no future.

Death, as Berger and Luckmann argue, poses the greatest threat to the social order because it seems to call into question the sense of our everyday lives, which are lived with reference to, and in order to secure, the goods of this world. Death must therefore be "legitimated" with reference to some "symbolic universe" that transcends our immediate experience, a conception of a reality that encompasses and abides beyond our individual lives, that "links men with their predecessors and their successors in a meaningful totality, serving to transcend the finitude of individual existence and bestowing meaning upon the individual's death."[5] Whether in the form of honor and glory, as for the ancient Greeks, or Christian salvation and the Kingdom of God, or the idea that one lives on in one's children and one's good works on earth, the sense of our lives seems to depend on the existence of something beyond them. As this would indicate, the actual or anticipated destruction of a community, and even more so of civilization or the whole human race, could create an even greater crisis of sense if the continuation of the community or species is that "something beyond" or at least a condition for it, as it arguably is for the nonreligious.

Literature responds to this need for sense, not so much by legitimation of existing social structures but, as I mean to show, by evoking and reorientating us toward a reality that encompasses and transcends those structures—particularly tragic and apocalyptic literature, if it is tragedy and apocalypse that confront us with death and, more broadly, all those realities and conditions which are most inimical to our happiness and which, therefore, we are most likely, both individually and collectively, to resist knowing or admitting until we have no choice. Such literature acknowledges the reality of death even as it transposes it into a different register. We might say, as Simone Weil did of love, that it offers us not so much consolation as light.[6] (Poet Rosanna Warren relates that someone once asked her, in a rather belligerent tone, "Why read poetry?" compelling her to respond, no less vehemently: "*Because you're going to die!*")

How does it do this?

LITERATURE AND SENSEMAKING

As in "the real world," so also in reading literature we are constantly engaged in making sense and looking for coherence—of the plot or story or structure, and of the images and descriptions—and in doing so we find ourselves having to refer at times to a different background of sense than that which governs our habitual lives. I must just assert without being able to demonstrate here that this belongs to what we mean by *literature*—those works of fiction or poetry which do not just enact some gratifying fantasy but somehow challenge our conventional and habitual frameworks of sense. Thus in the course of making sense of a literary work we are educated to a different—deeper, more complex, more adequate—background according to which we might, or must, make sense of our lives.

In reading (or viewing a film or play) we have to make sense, broadly, along two dimensions—the horizontal unfolding of the plot, and the vertical references of images, symbols, figuration. To the first: making sense of plot or story (or the temporal unfolding more generally, in the case of lyric poetry or other nonnarrative works) means understanding whether and how it is plausible and satisfying that the work should proceed as it does. This encompasses questions about what happens within the story—the characters, their actions and motivations, as well as the selection and sequencing of episodes and the overall arc of the narrative. In reading *Moby-Dick*, we ask, for example: What drives Ahab's quest for the White Whale? What compels the crew to join him? How are we to understand his final failure? Is Ahab a tragic hero or a villain? What drives Ishmael's own pursuit of the whale? Is he transformed in this pursuit? Is the resolution satisfying, right? If so, why? If not, why not? (For even great works of literature may fail in certain ways, and those failures can themselves be educative, bringing to awareness our tacit knowledge of what a proper resolution would be, of the conditions of a proper resolution.)

As the above questions imply, stories are about individuals pursuing certain ends, and understanding them entails understanding those ends and the motivations for and means of their pursuit. The attempt to understand such matters refers us first to human psychology and to social and cultural conditions—why and under what circumstances would people act this way? This itself can be educative insofar as the story shows characters acting in surprising yet plausible and compelling ways.

Understanding what characters do, however, further entails *judgment*—assessing their actions in light of some standard. As a colleague once claimed, "you can't understand what someone did without understanding what they ought to have done."[7] This judgment need not be, and rarely is, as simple as "good" or "bad"—it is often difficult to say what a tragic protagonist "ought to have done," since tragedy frequently deals with situations in which characters are torn between irreconcilable imperatives (for Hegel, indeed, this is the definition of tragedy). Any adequate account of a character's actions, though, even a descriptive one, is inescapably tinged with value. To understand Ahab's pursuit of Moby Dick and its outcome, for example, means determining (among other things) the sense of his quest and the justice or appropriateness of its outcome.

While literary works are sometimes taken as straightforward morality tales—for example, Ahab as insane demagogic villain—great literature is complex and ambiguous, and the actions of literary characters can only be understood and judged by appealing, at least implicitly, to a ground of judgment that transcends the conventional or everyday ground. Compelling works of literature therefore educate by showing the inadequacy of the conventional ground of judgment and implying another ground—a ground according to which the obsessive hunt for an albino whale can be seen to be, if not "right" (even Ahab concedes he is "mad"), at least to have a certain compelling logic that links up to deep and general human concerns—such as the challenge of making sense of and responding to a reality that is incommensurate with human interests and needs. Such a ground might be described as a "grammar of humanity."[8]

Understanding *Moby-Dick* also means comprehending the book's proliferating and often uncanny images—how are we to make sense of the whiteness of the whale, "God's foot on the treadle of the loom," the faintly heard pick of the subterranean miner within, the bearded king beneath the Hotel d'Cluny, and so on and so on? And what of the whale and sea, which of course function symbolically as well as literally?

It should be obvious even without specifying particular interpretations that what metaphors and images generally do is suggest some aspect of our world or our experience which cannot be adequately conveyed or evoked by conventional or literal language—some possibility of "resemblance," as Wallace Stevens called it, which makes us aware of the deeper ground which is the basis for that resemblance. This could be said, too, of the work as a whole, which seems itself to be an image of something—that is, it seems to be about more than what explicitly transpires within it (hence we might say, with Alfred Kazin, that *Moby-Dick* is about *magnitude,* or immensity,[9] and not only about a whaling voyage—and magnitude itself is not just a quality of whales or galaxies, not just something "sensible" but "intelligible" that is essential to the meaning of our humanity).

Thus it might be claimed that the effort to understand the narrative dimension of the work refers us to the conditions of human intentionality, character, and action and the possibilities of human destiny, while the effort to understand the imagistic or figural dimension refers us to a transcendent ground of sense and judgment, to which we must appeal in order to make sense of literary and poetic figures. Together they refer us, at least indirectly, to the normative conditions of our lives—that is, those conditions for our lives being good or full or properly human—as a ground of sense apart from the social facts and realities that make up our everyday world. (In practice, of course, there is and can be no clear separation between these two dimensions: figuration evokes those aspects of the world that help us to make sense of what the characters do within that world, while the unfolding narrative cannot fail to bear on the meaning of specific images and symbols.)

Some works, like *Moby-Dick*, explicitly thematize and therefore directly compel the reader to consider the ultimate grounds and purposes of human life, and through their images and figuration evoke a mysterious, indeterminate, and mythical horizon of sense and judgment. However, even those literary works with more limited or "this-worldly" concerns refer the reader to some source of sense and judgment that goes beyond convention—I would submit, again, that this belongs to what we mean by and treat as "literature."

Serious literature might, therefore, be defined as literature about those events, experiences, and perceptions that, to a greater or lesser degree, are not adequately encompassed within the everyday frameworks of sense, and one might characterize literature as exploring—pointing to—a background of sense that would more adequately accommodate the full(er) range of human experience and the realities of human life. Such a background would consist not only of the conventions that sustain the functioning of society, but would reach back into history, forward into the human future, and "upward" and "downward" into those aspects of human experience from the sublime to the primal that are ignored, distorted, or denied in the everyday social world—including the normative constraints and demands we feel which are not adequately explained by and may even contradict conventional notions of goodness, and realities such as death, catastrophe, unpredictable eros, and inevitable dispossession.

Literature, in proportion as it is demanding and demands to be understood, compels the reader to consult this deeper ground.

READING FROM/FOR TACIT KNOWLEDGE

One might ask how works of secular literature can be revelatory—can be an apocalypse—being creations of mere mortals like ourselves and not purported missives from God. Literary works, especially fiction but also the representational and interpretive choices of nonfiction, have only the authority that we grant them. The problem is a version of the paradox Meno poses in the Platonic dialogue bearing his name—how can we look for something when we don't know what it is we are looking for? In this case—how can art teach us something if, in order to recognize it as true, we must in some sense already know it? And even if we can answer Meno's challenge as Socrates did, mutatis mutandis—that art midwifes our anamnesis or "rememoration" of knowledge that had previously been unconscious—why should we trust this "knowledge"? How do we know that the work is not simply confirming us in our prejudices?[10] And indeed, why should we think there *is* some normative structure to be known that is not merely some culture's or individual's prejudice?

I have alluded several times to the role of tacit knowledge in our sense-making, an idea I owe to the philosopher Michael Polanyi, for whom "the tacit dimension" was central in escaping the circularity of Meno's paradox. Polanyi, who began his career as a chemist, making significant contributions in his field, thought that positivist philosophers of science misunderstood the nature of scientific discovery and that scientific progress could not be wholly accounted for by the accumulation of empirical data and the systematic testing of hypotheses against this data. Science, he argues, rests on procedures that cannot be fully formalized, that depend on the trained individual's intuition—an ability to sense the direction in which the answer lies, to intuit the direction of fruitful inquiry, without being able to explicitly state all the reasons for that intuition.

Taking scientific discovery as his paradigm, Polanyi argues for the relevance of this paradigm to all fields of knowledge, including art, politics, and morality, contending thereby that knowledge in these humanistic realms is just as much *knowledge* as scientific knowledge, although the methods and standards of verification (or, in the former case, what he calls "validation") are different. Polanyi proposes that we must conceive of "reality" not as a fixed object "out there" (the objective existence of which we might then deny) but as that which conditions and responds to our perception and inquiry into problems, not only scientific problems but human problems—problems of sense—as well. All our inquiries into that reality depend on tacit intimations of the direction in which reality or the resolution of a problem lies. An increasing grasp of reality is accompanied by an increasing sense of coherence.[11] The reality we come to know through reading and reflecting on literature is provisional, as all our knowledge must be assumed to be, but if Polanyi is right, we should not deny that literature can occasion knowledge of the conditions of sense—the conditions of our humanity—unless we want to deny the possibility of any kind of knowledge at all.

Reality, that is to say, is revealed in and through the trajectory of increasing coherence, no less in literary critical discussions than in science, even if it must be conceived very differently in the two instances.

The work of this book could then be conceived as a Polanyian practice of literary criticism aimed at articulating what we come to *know* in reading and reflecting on the work, that is, making the tacit explicit so that it might be more thoroughly integrated into our everyday consciousness. Such a practice begins with attending to those aspects of the work (in content and in form) which are surprising, unusual, disturbing, or otherwise depart from our expectations or conventional ways of making sense but which nonetheless seem *right*—and trying to make explicit our initially tacit sense of reasons for their rightness. This practice of reading surely focuses on the work, in all of its aspects and elements, but with the idea that that the ultimate object is not the meaning of the work but the conditions of our understanding and judging it: those human and historical realities, including the normative standards inherent in the human world, to which we are referred in our efforts to understand it. These realities are what are revealed to us in the effort to comprehend and articulate what we comprehend in reading.[12]

This conception of how we gain knowledge through the engagement with literature bears on my approach (not to say "method") in the following chapters. While I conform to a common, if not consensus, literary-theoretical belief that consultation of biographical and critical sources is vital to preserving the intentionality of the work and preventing one's own interpretations from merely reflecting what one already believes (on a shallower level than the deep tacit knowledge that figures in the conception of discovery just outlined), the Polanyian view implies that the personal encounter with the text is essential and in some sense fundamental; the realities one may come to know through reading are not simply there "in" the text but are a product of that encounter. They are what we come to know through the process of close reading, interpretation, critical reflection, etc., though not always explicitly and less as "interpreted meanings" than as intuited directions and—some-times—normative imperatives.

This also means that I do not assert my readings as the only and final way to read a particular text. My intention is to articulate the aspect of each text that has been brought to light by, and in turn illumines, a reading attentive to the problem(s) of apocalypse, and my hope is that my readings will bring out these aspects for my own readers—and possibly convey something of those imperatives. (I do not take this to be a particularly original stance; it may in fact be implicit in the majority of literary criticism, but the statement of it here seems important in light of my claims about literature itself as apocalyptic—revelatory.)

THE REVELATIONS OF TRAGEDY

Tragedy presents a special case of literary sensemaking. It is tragedy that most directly confronts us with those aspects of human experience which pose the greatest challenge to sensemaking—with what we might call "real-ity." As Northrop Frye claims, "Without tragedy, all literary fictions might be plausibly explained as expressions of emotional attachments, whether of wish-fulfillment or of repugnance: the tragic fiction guarantees, so to speak, a disinterested quality in literary experience"[13]—*disinterested* in the sense not of *detached* but *objective*. Tragedy and tragic literature point us to the ways in which conventional sense breaks down, and toward a different and more adequate background of sense, one that acknowledges the radical limits of human knowledge, power, and will.

In Aristotle's famous characterization, tragedy is "the imitation of an action . . . effecting through pity and fear the *catharsis* of such emotions."[14] It is worth noting that, for Aristotle, tragedy has its origins in the natural ten-dency of humans to imitate, specifically to imitate human action, and more specifically "noble (*spoudaios*) actions and noble persons."[15] More than that: for Aristotle, tragedy would seem to be the ideal realization of such imitation: tragedy *is* what we get when the imitation of serious human action is developed to an art. This seems to me essentially right. Imitation, as James Redfield writes, is not mere copying but "the discovery of form in things,"[16] and Aristotle suggests that the form of human action and human life is the pursuit of happiness, the end or telos of human life—defined in his *Ethics* as an "activity of the soul in accordance with virtue."[17] Thus tragedy— which one might expand to include all such works that imitate or represent "serious" human life, or human beings insofar as they are acting seriously—is the representation of what is most foundational to our humanity: the proper and desired end of a human life, and what conduces to it or stands in the way of it. That the ideal form of this imitation (representation) of serious human life should be reached in a plot that ends in catastrophe and evokes pity and fear and their catharsis (whatever precisely that means) would seem to indicate something essential—and disturbing—about the human condition.

It is of the essence of tragedy that it should be revelatory. Aristotle argues that poetry is more philosophical than history, telling not of the particular but of the universal, that is, not (only or necessarily) of what people did but of "the sort of thing that (in the circumstances) a certain kind of person will say or do either probably or necessarily." This difference comes out not in the subject matter—poetry may well depict historical events, and if its characters and plot are invented, those characters and their actions are just as "particular" as those of history. Rather, it is in its presentation that poetry reveals the "universal," the underlying laws or principles according to which human life unfolds. And those laws—or at least their particular manifestations or implications—are ordinarily obscured from us. Pity and fear are evoked most effectively, Aristotle says, when "incidents . . . come unexpectedly and yet occur in a causal sequence in which one thing leads to another,"[18] that is, when they are surprising—shocking—yet strike us as *right*.

These laws of probability and necessity might seem to be causal rather than normative—those rules according to which one thing results from another. But tragedy treats those incidents in which disaster has its source in human action—for Aristotle, in some *hamartia*, a "mistake" or "error" that is morally tinged—and the laws which bring down catastrophe on the protagonists are not just natural or causal laws but the moral laws that they have, often in ignorance, transgressed—and the "cause" of their outsize punishment is often their own horror, or the horror of others, at what they have done. For Hegel, tragedy emerges not so much from an error but from an irreconcilable conflict of duties. In either case, though, tragedy educates us both to the laws of the universe (some of which are the gods' laws, indifferent and at times even hostile to human welfare) and the possibility of transgressing against them despite one's will and intention.

That Greek tragedy was a popular art form need not conflict with the idea that the ground of sense to which it referred its viewers was other than the one they would tend to inhabit in everyday life. Revelations can, of course, be revelations of what we already, at some level, know but that needs to be made conscious, or made conscious again. Indeed, in some sense, the revelations of literature *must* reveal to us something we already know, since fiction and poetry do not (generally speaking, or primarily) provide us with new empirical information. It is we who judge the literary work to be plausible and compelling. Literature can nonetheless be revealing because, again, in making sense of it we must appeal to our *tacit* knowledge, our intimations of a way of construing things that would be more comprehensive and coherent.

The conditions of sense, we might say, merge into the conditions of human life generally—that is, how I make sense of what I and others do depends on our biological and psychological constitution and on social and cultural constraints. While some of these conditions may be universal and unchanging, most are historical, changing as the organization and character of human society changes. The demands made upon us are not identical to those made by the Greek gods (even if the notion of the gods may still speak to some of us). To discern the sense of our own modern lives and our catastrophe-ridden time, we have to look (also) at more recent works, and especially those which confront, in subject matter and form, the most pressing present challenges to making sense of our lives and of human life. This is the approach of this book.

TROUBLING THE TRAGIC FORM

Norman Maclean's *Young Men and Fire* explicitly poses the problem of modern tragedy. The book, a work of nonfiction, details the events that led to the deaths of thirteen Smokejumpers fighting a forest fire in Mann Gulch, Montana, in 1949. In it, Maclean, a neo-Aristotelian professor of English at University of Chicago, speaks of wanting to "transform catastrophe into tragedy."

The form Maclean finds for the story of the Smokejumpers is significantly different from the form of classical tragedy: *Young Men and Fire* is narrative rather than dramatic; it tells the story of an "outfit" rather than an individual, the destructive force is natural rather than divine or human, and it situates the story of the Smokejumpers in a frame story about Maclean's own investigations. It therefore provokes us to ask what Maclean means by "tragedy," whether Maclean has achieved his goal of transforming catastrophe into tragedy, and if so why a "modern tragedy" would have this form, which opens upon more general questions of what kind of tragedy is possible in modernity.[19]

In Chapter 1, I will follow Maclean into Mann Gulch and argue that his task, as he conceives it and as it is manifested in his work, *is* fundamentally one of making sense—that is, to find tragic form for the events of that August day in 1949 is to find their deeper significance, a significance which is not fabricated but which is implied by the shape of the events themselves and needs to be drawn out by the "storyteller." Maclean intuits that this significance is "tragic," which for him means that it pertains to the absolute defeats that human beings face, defeats that are not simply arbitrary or random but which reveal the underlying workings of "the universe" and even something worthy of awe—the magnitude both of the destructive forces and of the heroism of the human beings that confront them. Such confrontations and the catastrophes that follow from them demand sensemaking of a special kind.

Maclean's innovations suggest something not only about modern literature but about the modern historical situation that would demand a new tragic form (and perhaps something particularly, if not exclusively, American, especially if America is seen to represent one extremity of modernity—modern autonomy, individualism, freedom, self-determination, utilitarianism, rationalization, and "progress")—the absence of the kind of order that underpinned classical tragedy, and the need to contend with a radical uncertainty about the prospects for and conditions of making sense of human experience, and indeed about the very viability of a (truly) human life. This is suggested by Maclean's framing of the story as the *search* for a story, as well as by his explicit reflections on whether the story he wants to find is there to be found or whether, on the contrary, the reality is the grim fact of "bod[ies that] ran out of brains for lack of oxygen and rolled downhill into black death,"[20] with no further sense or meaningfulness.

Fire suggests that one can only make sense of the men's deaths against the background of an inhuman sublime, which in the book is manifested in powerful poetic descriptions of the geological setting of the events, vast both spatially and temporally, and in the awful but beautiful force of the fire itself. *Making sense* here means not only explaining what led to the catastrophe— filling in "the missing pieces"—but evoking and accounting for the compelling power of the events of Mann Gulch despite their devastating sadness. *Fire* shows the story of Mann Gulch to be not only the terrible tragedy (in the colloquial sense) of the deaths of thirteen young men but an encounter with the immense and inhuman forces of the universe, that is to say, with *reality*, with that which resists our wishes and will.

Fire remains classically tragic to the extent that it finds some positive resolution in the evocation and affirmation of an underlying order to what happened at Mann Gulch, and—by implication—to human existence generally; Maclean seeks and finds a catharsis the reader is meant to share—we have learned something about nature and can live in profounder accord with it as a consequence of that understanding—at least in profounder consciousness, if not in avoidance of all future disasters. We can at least affirm some reason, if not justice, in what has happened, and humanity endures to affirm the heroism of the Smokejumpers.

The penultimate pages of *Fire*, however, suggest the limits of the tragic. They consist of a phantasmagoric description of the final conflagration, which in its poetic wrenching of language and its invocation of the atom bomb and the end of the world suggests the uncertainty of this sense, and perhaps of any sense, in our current historical situation, in which humanity has become capable of—and perhaps inexorably compelled toward—self-destruction, and in which, therefore, all previous ways of conceiving the trajectory of human history are put into question.

FROM TRAGEDY TO APOCALYPSE

If literature, by definition, reveals a ground of sense and judgment radically different from, and in some measure opposed to, that which governs "business as usual," then every literary work is, in some (formal) way, an apocalypse in its etymological sense of "unveiling," "uncovering." Tragic literature like Maclean's is apocalyptic in the further sense that this revelation comes with and through catastrophe. But Maclean's work suggests a third sense according to which we might distinguish between the tragic and the apocalyptic, having to do with the conditions of sense to which modern works refer us. The modern apocalyptic work, as opposed to the tragic, confronts the end of humanity as the end of the conditions of sense that have hitherto prevailed, the undoing of sense that such a possibility threatens.

This apocalyptic thread is, for better or worse, subdued and perhaps even finally denied in Maclean's work. But I find it followed to its logical conclusion in several otherwise diverse twentieth-century American works. Chapters 2 and 3 consider works I read as fully, if figuratively, embodying the genre or mode of modern apocalyptic—namely, Cormac McCarthy's *Blood Meridian* and poems by Robert Lowell and Wallace Stevens—and explore the implications thereof for how we make sense of our contemporary situation. But first a look backward for a broader and deeper sense of the apocalyptic genre and sensibility which they take up and transform.

The best-known work declaring itself an apocalypse is the New Testament Book of Revelation (ἀποκάλυψις [*apokalypsis*]) or the Revelation of St. John, which epitomizes the original apocalyptic genre. This genre has been characterized as relating a vision of "eschatological salvation,"[21] vouchsafed to the author by a divine figure. The Book of Revelation is also the source of the modern usage of "apocalypse" to mean cataclysm, as the vision it recounts is that of the end of the world. Although the direct referent of the word is the vision per se, the end itself—the event envisioned—is a revelation as well, both in Revelation and in apocalyptic works generally—a revelation of the fragility and limitations of the old order and of the forces or powers that would sweep it away, a revelation of God's judgment against that order. There is both a destructive and a creative aspect to the Jewish and Christian apocalyptic vision—it is "God and heaven's in-breaking on earth"[22] which destroys the former order of things. Contemporary secular visions of the end share this quality of revelation; as Eva Horn puts it, "What is revealed by the apocalypse is the true value and the true power of everything and everyone. The end of the world is the *unmasking of all things*, the manifestation of their true essence."[23]

Apocalyptic visions are historically associated with crisis, a crisis which is beyond the power of the individual or the collective to rectify.[24] The apocalyptic vision emerges when it does not seem or no longer seems that reform is possible, that only some utter disruption of the current state of things could create the conditions for the restoration or establishment of right order. The imagining then of the end of the current world and the ushering in of a new one could be simply a matter of consoling fantasy, but it is also a matter of apprehending the current state of the world as unsustainable, incoherent, and evil.

The apocalyptic vision therefore also implies a wholly different ground of judgment and sense than that of the present world, a different standard of "good" and "bad" than that of the reigning powers on earth. And the recognition and inhabiting of this different ground may be the most important aspect of the apocalyptic vision. As Frank Kermode notes, from early on, with the first disappointment of the prediction of the coming of God's kingdom, believers had to adjust their understanding of the meaning of the revelations and expectation of the End. In his well-known formulation, Kermode writes that even Christians as early as John and Paul begin to conceive the End as "immanent" rather than "imminent."[25]

In Kermode's account, this immanentization of the apocalypse seems to have two aspects. First, the categories of the apocalyptic vision become something like archetypes—recurrent types embodied in different historical figures and events, categories according to which we make sense of history—as opposed to singular instances which are to occur only once at some point of the future. Kermode cites Josef Pieper's comment that "many have been called Antichrist because many have indeed been Antichrist, or types of him, so that Nazism is a 'milder preliminary form of the state of Antichrist,' and so is any other tyranny."[26] This is to see these regimes not just as bad human institutions responsible for earthly ills, but as instantiations of the battle between God and Satan, ultimate good and ultimate evil.

The other and corresponding implication of seeing the End as "immanent" is that the individual's life becomes a synecdoche for the eschatological arc of human history. Kermode quotes Rudolf Bultmann:

> *[T]he meaning of history lies always in the present,* and when the present is conceived as the eschatological present by Christian faith the meaning in history is realized. . . . Always in your present lies the meaning in history, and you cannot see it as a spectator, but only in your responsible decisions. In every

moment slumbers the possibility of being an eschatological moment. You must awaken it.[27]

In Bultmann's demythologized, existentialist view, one conceives every moment in history in light of salvation and the ultimate victory of God over evil, but this is not understood as some future event for which one passively waits; each individual is called upon to be instrument of the realization of this end which is a present moment of decision, and, just as any and many particular earthly evils may be understood as Antichrist, the possibility of victory over those evils, in the world and in oneself, is ever-present.

The works I will discuss are more obviously apocalyptic in the modern sense of alluding to catastrophic endings, but the original sense of revelation—and the religious origins of the apocalyptic—is relevant too to understanding what "modern apocalyptic literature," in the sense I mean it, would be. As has been widely observed, even modern apocalypticism is not new, nor is its appearance in "secular" literature, particularly in the United States. American literary critics since the mid-twentieth century have explored the apocalyptic mood in writers going back to Pilgrim times, corresponding to a more general apocalyptic sensibility animating American culture—from the Christian and Biblical apocalyptic worldview of the Puritans to twentieth- and twenty-first-century imaginings of nuclear, ecological, and other disaster. "The history of apocalypse in America," writes John Hay, is "a history of a highly variable yet remarkably common vision of the future"[28]—a vision of (perennial) world-ending violent cataclysm brought about upon humankind by its own sins, seen in light of the imagined standard of "God's kingdom on earth" which is revealed by the catastrophe and is either to be achieved through it or only to stand as the measurement of our dire failure. As Hay (and others) describe it, this "millenarian strain" is rooted in the Puritan expectation of "a purifying fire that will transfigure the decaying moral fabric of the nation and obliterate the material manifestations of our wicked desires"[29]; its secular offshoot emphasizes the destruction of humanity rather than the realization of the kingdom of God—apocalypse as comedy morphing into apocalypse as tragedy.

Even this secular apocalyptic sensibility—the expectation of a cataclysm brought about not by supernatural beings but by natural and human events—has its roots prior to those twentieth-century developments that would seem to make such a cataclysm realistic, such as atomic weaponry and climate change. The modern apocalyptic imaginary emerges in the nineteenth century with all its interdependent destabilizations—industrialization, colonialism, the troubling of traditional religious belief, and so on—and reflects not only the fear of a literally world- or species-ending event but some deeper and more diffused unease about the state of things. Mary Shelley's *The Last*

Man, published in 1826, is generally recognized as the "first major example of secular eschatology in literature," and, as Warren Wagar puts it, it marks a significant change in Western consciousness, the possibility of imagining "a purposeless end generated by the world-order itself" without any divine intervention or participation.[30]

As twentieth-century technologies have made it all the easier to envisage mechanisms whereby the world-order might reach its end, apocalyptic forms have proliferated into a pluralistic, contested, and contradictory disasterscape. Apprehension or expectation of catastrophe is widespread, but the dreamed-of shapes of that catastrophe and the attitudes toward it are manifold, as more recent analysis of modern apocalyptic literature, film, and television, as well as apocalyptic tropes in cultural and political discourse, has shown.[31] Apocalyptic and post-apocalyptic visions[32] range from conservative fantasies of the survival of the nuclear (so to speak) family to liberal or leftist critiques of the existing order, from tales of species-wide destruction to more limited disasters, from futuristic fiction to works that portray historical or contemporary events as apocalyptic. Of course, the category of "apocalypse" is itself not fixed; it is heuristic, and the expansion of its application—first, from the original genre of divine revelation to stories of secular catastrophe, and more recently from narratives of literal and total catastrophe to more local and sometimes figurative ends-of-worlds—is itself significant, suggesting a transformation and broadening of the conception of the apocalyptic in accord with the need to make sense of our current situation(s).

Among the most potent developments to emerge from the late-twentieth- and early twenty-first-century exploration of the apocalyptic imaginary is the elaboration of the "immanence" of apocalypse, the insight that apocalypse is most illuminatingly conceived not as a future event that may either occur or be avoided, but rather as a present reality. In the last decade of the twentieth century, theorists from socialist political and economic theorist Michael Harrington to the ecocritic Andrew McMurry introduced variants of the idea of "slow apocalypse": not the end that comes with a single bang but the creeping disaster that constitutes our daily lives.[33] This conception of apocalypse as ongoing condition rather than singular event has led in recent years to the corollary that apocalypse does not equally affect all of humanity but is and has been and will be unequally distributed, the most profound and widespread suffering and damage befalling the marginalized, the poor, and peoples of color—slavery and the colonization of the Americas already effecting the ending of worlds for countless Black and Indigenous people. Indeed, as Jessica Hurley notes, the insistence on a universal plight can hide such injustices, as the focus on the potential species-ending catastrophe of a nuclear holocaust has obscured the daily inequities wrought by the nuclear-industrial complex.[34]

As "imaginary" suggests, apocalypse is not an empirical object to be found in the world (indeed, how could it, being the world's end?) but a form, or class of forms—an imagistic and narrative structure—through which individuals and collectives have made sense and continue to make sense of their situations. It should be clear by now that this ought not mean, however, that we should dismiss apocalypse as *merely* imaginary, that is, unreal, but the relationship between apocalypse-as-form and apocalypse-as-reality is complex; it has been argued that apocalyptic visions, both literary and extraliterary, distort the reality of our situation rather describe it, either because our situation is in fact not apocalyptic or because the character of the "real" apocalypse is other than the stories would have it—and that the specter of looming disaster is used to foment fear and justify the abridgement of rights and freedoms,[35] or that it perniciously undercuts mitigating political action. Narratives of apocalypse, especially in mainstream cinema and fiction, have as often perpetuated (ideological) fantasies as they have revealed the true catastrophe(s)—or have only done the latter unconsciously, their tropes betraying fears and wishes that critics have shown to be implicated in the violence and instability of modern life, though the works themselves (mis)identify the threat as elsewhere, often in the guise of a racialized Other.[36]

In the recognition of the tendencies of apocalyptic fantasies to conceptually entrench an unjust status quo and to work against positive political transformation, literary critics have increasingly turned to a growing canon of alternative apocalyptic stories by voices from historically oppressed and marginalized groups and from the global South—James Baldwin, Leslie Marmon Silko, Nnedi Okorafor, Indra Sinha, and others who turn the apocalyptic form to liberatory ends or, at the least, dissect the threat to "humanity" and show in various ways how we cannot all suffer the end of the world together because we do not inhabit one and the same world.

Fully acknowledging that there are not-so-little apocalypses everywhere—for which the wealthy White world bears significant responsibility and against which it is unfairly shielded, at least in the short term—I want in this book to return to my own and others' persistent sense that there is *also*, still, a threat to humanity as a whole. I would argue that the foregoing critiques mean that there is all the greater urgency to reconceive "humanity" in light of this shared threat, and I will suggest that literature is critical to this reconception.

With this aim, the works that I will discuss may seem oddly, even perversely, parochial, written as they are by straight White American men. I did not choose these texts because of their provenance, but in retrospect I believe that there is a sense, if not indispensability, to the identity of their authors: while writing from within a world of relative safety and privilege, they recognize that this world, too, will not in the end be spared, and they furthermore see and articulate, from within that world, the internal sources of its disastrous trajectory. These authors recognize themselves as inheritors of one or more original sins, and their works evoke a nonconservative apocalypse, recognizing the endemic self- and other-destructiveness of modern Western civilization and the need to conceive our humanity differently.

It is this dire unsustainability—both material and moral or spiritual—of the modern (Western) human project that is brought to light in the works to be considered. As mentioned previously, none falls into the popular genre of apocalyptic and postapocalyptic fiction that imagines some literal, near-future end of the world as we know it. Yet in each there is a strong "sense of an ending"; they allude to the passing away of worlds and of humanity and make use of apocalyptic imagery—the bomb (Maclean), the "darkening of [man's] day" (McCarthy), the Flood (Lowell), and the aurora borealis (Stevens). I characterize these works as apocalyptic because they suggest that making sense of human experience and human history depends upon recognizing that the modern situation is radically untenable, governed by a logic and by forces whose direction is toward destruction. To return to the "imminent" and the "immanent," there is a sense both of an unveiling that will come in time, that this world will pass away, but also of another reality that is present even now—not literally another world, a supernatural sphere that is elsewhere in space, but a true order of meaning that is radically other than the one we typically inhabit. In each work treated here, this other order is conveyed in particular by ambiguous and evocative—and disturbing—poetic imagery, which seems to refer to some reality but cannot be made sense of with reference to our ordinary experience. And, as in the Judeo-Christian apocalyptic visions, these two dimensions are integrally related.

Our ordinary sensemaking depends tacitly on the assumption of a future that is continuous with the present. These works reflect the challenges to that sense posed by the anticipation of a radical break. Such a break implies that the conditions of human life are other than we took them to be, that we have failed to recognize the reality which will inevitably "break through" into the world as it (apparently) is. We engage in "business as usual" under the assumption that we can continue it indefinitely; if we anticipated catastrophe, we would be called upon to enter a state of emergency or to dramatically alter our ways in order to avert that catastrophe. Even if no action were possible, for whatever reason, going on doing what we are doing would still have a very different sense, or perhaps would cease to make sense entirely, knowing that it could not be sustained—or was actively contributing to bringing about the catastrophe.

The works treated here share this sense of radically unsustainable conditions. The fact that none predicts or imagines a concrete world-ending event is in fact significant, because they therefore imply that our apocalyptic situation is not "just" a matter of some possible or probably future catastrophe, but of a pervasive current crisis.

The most obvious difference between the Judeo-Christian apocalyptic visions and the modern visions is that in the former it is God—an intelligent and benevolent power—that "breaks in and breaks up the established order"[37] and establishes a new order. The end is not just an end but a beginning; there *is* a new order on the other side of cataclysm, and it is divine, ultimately good. Some modern, secular apocalyptic visions have had a positive moment—Marx's communist revolution; images of humanity living in harmony with nature after the breakdown of an industrial civilization radically at odds with ecological conditions. But the works in which I am interested raise the specter of an end that is really and only an end. They suggest in different ways that even if the species is not extinguished, whatever survives will be diminished and crippled, no longer capable of a fully human form of life or consciousness, of a fully flourishing human life. (If there is a God, he is either wholly removed from human affairs or else he is the bungler of the Gnostics, and I will explore the emergence of a modern Gnostic vision in my discussion of McCarthy.)

From Maclean's foray into the apocalyptic, I proceed in Chapter 2 to Cormac McCarthy's *Blood Meridian*, which wholly immerses us in the dark vision that only fitfully breaks through Maclean's generally humane and healthy-minded narrative voice.

McCarthy's vision is one in which the ultimate destructive forces of the universe are revealed as historical and inhuman forces even as they manifest themselves through human violence and human evil—and it confronts the trajectory toward destruction as intrinsic to humanity, if not inevitable. It is no longer nature but history that defies human aspiration and leads human beings on a trajectory toward destruction. *Blood Meridian* is infamous for its depiction of a world populated by characters barely human and for its uncompromising narrative in which violence apparently triumphs totally over justice, real or poetic. The dominating character, Judge Holden, articulates a philosophy of war and violence which proceeds from the apprehension that only power is real, that all moral constraints on human beings are illusory. McCarthy's novel thus raises the problem of how to conceive of the normative constraints and imperatives that bear upon us when it becomes apparent that goodness, at least as traditionally and historically conceived, is impotent against the overwhelming forces which are in fact driving human history, and driving it toward destruction—in particular the human proclivity for violence and domination, unleashed as it has been within Western civilization with its Faustian breaking-loose from traditional constraints.

It is not just the story of *Blood Meridian* that seems apocalyptic but its style. McCarthy employs arcane, elevated diction that is at times Biblical, evoking a world beyond, in light of which this one is mere shadow—but the world evoked through his strange and estranging descriptions and metaphors is alien, dark, and hostile, or else empty void. The world as we find it in the novel seems to confirm the judge's orientation within it, with any moral constraints or deeper meaning to human activity seeming mere rumor or impotent dream, and nothing to prevent history from barreling along according to its belligerent and destructive logic.

I suggested above that literature educates us by challenging our ordinary manner of making sense, and that in narrative, the problem of making sense largely concerns the action, the unfolding of the plot, while in poetry—at least in modern lyric poetry—making sense is more a matter of discerning what is suggested by figures that do not make literal sense, and this involves attending to a deeper ground of association—a ground which could be called *mythical*. Maclean and McCarthy's uses of poetic description already present this kind of challenge in addition to the demands of comprehending their plots, but in Chapter 3, I turn from narrative to lyric poetry, and more specifically elegy, to reflect more exclusively and directly on this aspect.

Both elegy and tragedy can be thought of as modes of coming to terms with those things that disappoint and deny human desire and needs—realities that resist conformity to our wishes. If tragedy allows for making sense of loss or catastrophe by showing it to be in conformity to some law, elegy affirms and articulates the significance of the lost object, and shows how its value—its spirit—still persists in the abiding world, if only in the elegiac poem itself. The elegies I discuss, however—Robert Lowell's "The Quaker Graveyard in Nantucket" and Wallace Stevens's "The Auroras of Autumn"—both written shortly after the end of World War II—mourn not only or primarily the loss of an individual within the world but the loss of a world entire. And the myth that makes sense of the loss or ending of a world is, by definition, an apocalyptic one.

There are two aspects to this loss of world. Like *Blood Meridian*, Robert Lowell's "The Quaker Graveyard in Nantucket" depicts human history as driven by violence and greed, a motor destined to impel human beings toward a cataclysmic end. The loss of world here is literal, and the only consolation is the kind of awful exhilaration of seeing the coming destruction from a distance—from a cosmic viewpoint—and grasping its terrible logic, seeing humanity's own deepest tendencies leading it (us) toward destruction. Lowell's poem allows us to inhabit such a perspective both through what it depicts and through its prophetic, oracular tone, which carries the reader along with thundering and inexorable force such that the final lines, which intimate a world after human beings—"The Lord survives the rainbow of His will"—feel like a dramatically fitting, if terrible, conclusion to the human career.

In Wallace Stevens's "The Auroras of Autumn," however, even this prospect of consummation through consciousness is called into question. Like much of Stevens's poetry, "Auroras" is concerned with the myths according to which we make sense of our experience, and it expresses a fear that these structures of sense are themselves illusory and evanescent and that the reality of our world is not a human reality but something inhuman—the distant and indifferent flaring of the northern lights.

THE END OF READING: TOWARD A RESPONSIBLE APOCALYPTIC CONSCIOUSNESS

Returning to the idea that literature educates us by referring us, in our attempts to understand it, to the deep conditions of our human and historical situation: what is it—or what *kind* of thing is it—that we come to know through reading these works and reflecting on the new apocalyptic genre they seem to create?

As my summary indicates, the particulars of this modern apocalyptic sensibility vary from work to work. But in general, the veil they rend is that of what one might call the liberal individualistic view of the world and of history—liberal in the popular rather than the technical political sense of the word: that human life is given satisfactory meaning and purpose through "the pursuit of happiness," primarily through love, family, helping others, meaningful work. Coinciding with this view is a sense that it is temporally sustainable—that because it ought to be appealing to everyone and to fuel capitalistic growth and prosperity, there is no need for war, ideological or economic—that we live at or after the end of history, in a sustainable cosmopolitan commercial society, with no dramatic upheavals to come, only the furthering of individual freedoms, tolerance, and material well-being.

The works I read suggest two fundamental challenges to this conception of the world that have emerged in the nineteenth and twentieth centuries and manifest themselves to one degree or another in the literature of the modern (American) apocalyptic sublime.

First, there is what one might call the ontological challenge: the inhumanity and incomprehensibility of the world shown to us by modern science, the fact that the natural world is out of all proportion with and utterly indifferent to human concerns. The roots of this vision can be traced back to Lucretius, and it emerges more widely in the nineteenth century after the Enlightenment and Darwin, as in *Moby-Dick*; it is a vision of the "naturalistic sublime." With the emergence of quantum physics in the twentieth century, "nature" becomes incapable even of being conceptualized; physical reality can be represented only by complex mathematical and statistical formulae. Rather than the reality of God's plan underlying (and to some degree belying) the reality of the perceptible and social world, it is the random and chaotic reality of atoms and void—or something even stranger.

The fact of a physical universe governed by purely physical laws, indifferent and even incomprehensible to human beings, does not automatically imply meaninglessness in human life. Various philosophers have argued, I believe persuasively, that the domain of human experience, action and judgments is sui generis and not reducible to the facts of biology or physics. But others continue to take the materialist view that human concepts such as "love," "goodness," or "justice" have no objective correlate because, put crudely, what is real are physical objects and forces—thus human experiences can be reduced to physical realities (love is "really" the reaction of dopamine molecules, agents of the laws of evolution) and ideal concepts cannot be correlated to or derived from any physical reality. And regardless of whether the fear is rigorously defensible, there remains something disturbing about the idea that all our experience rests upon a physical reality that is dumb, random, and perhaps ultimately beyond our reckoning.

This apprehension of the inhuman and unreasoning forces governing the physical universe—and even organic life—is one source of the crisis of nihilism in the late nineteenth century. This crisis seems to have largely abated after a few generations—after secularism became simply a way of life—but the perception of the meaninglessness of "nature," and the potential threat it poses to sense, continues to simmer beneath the surface, ready to reemerge when things go wrong and we must cast about for deeper sources of meaning. As the future becomes threatened, we must find absolute meaning in the present. This is true of the individual's death; many who are not religious find the sense of their lives in what they give to others and are reconciled to their deaths by the idea of bequeathing something to the future, or at least by the idea that humanity will survive them. When humanity itself becomes threatened, however, this source of sense becomes tenuous.

This leads to the other and in this way related challenge to the common sense of modern liberal individualism: the historical challenge. In 1945, it became realistically conceivable—and progressively more so thereafter—that human beings could annihilate themselves as a species. Even if nuclear weapons are not, as Hurley insists, the unprecedented threat to human life that they have often been conceived to be, they concretized for the White Western world the specter of the end of humanity and forced that world to come to terms with its own terminality, a terminality that slavery and colonialism had already imposed on Black and Indigenous people. While the threat of destruction of one people or culture by another (as for the ancient Jews) presents a challenge to sense, as does the threat to humanity from a major natural disaster (such as an asteroid or gigantic volcanic eruption), the idea that human beings might destroy themselves as a species presents a challenge to comprehending human history that is distinctive to the last seventy years, and I believe that the awareness of this threat suffuses the works that I read.

This is the apocalyptic sublime, which I would argue persists alongside the "apocalyptic mundane" Hurley and others bring to our attention—the vision of human history as driven by structural forces incommensurate with human ends, and driven not toward a human end (the realization of reason and freedom) but toward inhumanity and destruction.

The challenge to sense of living in an unsustainable world is not only the threat of no future. It is also a challenge to the way we make sense of the present. Actions make sense in relation to some end, and we cannot make sense of our collective actions if they are driving us toward an end that is radically other than what we would will—even if we might by luck (for instance, technological innovation) escape catastrophe.

The works discussed in what follows suggest that making sense of our present situation involves confronting both the inhuman immensity of the natural universe and the enormity of humanity's own inhumanity. In modernity, the traditional frameworks of sense with their imperatives and constraints are swept away, and lacking those, we need to conceive of a new objectivity—but this is severely challenged by the inhuman immensity underlying and relativizing all human knowledge, purposes and institutions.

Maclean, McCarthy, Lowell, and Stevens collectively refer us to a radically different ground of intelligibility. The efforts to make sense of these works involve a dispossession, the inhabiting of a human identity not bound up with the instrumentalizing possessiveness responsible for the destruction of human worlds. More fundamentally, they put us in the position of viewing humanity from the outside, from its end, a viewpoint which impresses upon us the need for what might be called an ethics of consciousness: a recognition that all the old certainties of judgment are gone, and a commitment to the ongoing task of discerning a new ground of judgment adequate to the modern situation in its enormous tenuousness.

NOTES

1. For instance, in Emily Temple's list of "The 50 Greatest Apocalyptic Novels" (including Shelley's *The Last Man* and Cold War classics such as Neils Shute's *On the Beach*), twenty-nine were published since 2000 ("The 50 Greatest Apocalypse Novels").

2. An exception is De Cristofaro, "'Time, No Arrow, No Boomerang, but a Concertina'"; De Cristofaro examines the temporal structure of David Mitchell's *Cloud Atlas* as paradigmatic of the ways in which contemporary postapocalyptic novels subvert traditional linear apocalyptic narrative.

3. I am far from the first to treat this figurative apocalyptic strain; indeed, in some recent criticism "apocalypse" has expanded to encompass any work that represents transformation through cataclysm—limited or all-encompassing, positive or negative. For Jessica Hurley and Dan Sinykin, for instance, apocalypse is a "form" which, in contemporary art and literature, "mediates the unevenly distributed risks of . . . cataclysmic violence" ("Apocalypse," 451).

4. As an example of "good apocalypticism," Maxine Levon Montgomery describes how Black American novelists used the myth of apocalypse in service of their "struggle for freedom from all forms of oppression and . . . the personal odyssey to realize the full potential of one's complex bicultural identity as an AfroAmerican" (*The Apocalypse in African-American Fiction*). Concern with "bad apocalypticism" is pervasive; as Hurley and Sinykin put it, "too often the diagnosis of an artwork as 'apocalyptic' is taken as the endpoint of critical inquiry, with 'apocalyptic' indexing nothing more than the exhaustion of hope and the failure of an artist's political project" ("Apocalypse," 452).

5. Berger and Luckmann, *The Social Construction of Reality*, 103.

6. Weil, *The Notebooks of Simone Weil*, 258.

7. Attributed to George Anastaplo.

8. Elder, *The Grammar of Humanity: The Sense and Sources of the Imperative to Consciousness*.

9. "Introduction," Melville and Kazin, *Moby-Dick*.

10. For an elaboration of this problem, see Potolsky, *Mimesis*, 4; Abbott, *The Cambridge Introduction to Narrative*, 154.

11. For a concise statement of this theory, see Chapter 1 of Polanyi and Sen, *The Tacit Dimension*; the theory is developed at length in Polanyi, *Personal Knowledge*.

12. For a fuller articulation of Polanyi's views and their bearing on the practice of criticism, see Atnip, "From 'Meaning' to Reality."

13. Frye, *Anatomy of Criticism*, 206.

14. Aristotle, *Aristotle's Poetics*, 50, 1449b.

15. As opposed to comedy, which originates in the imitations of the actions of base persons (1448b, in Aristotle, 48).

16. Redfield, *Nature and Culture in the Iliad*, 54.

17. Aristotle, *Nicomachean Ethics*, 12, 1098a.

18. Aristotle, *Aristotle's Poetics*, 55, 1452a.

19. For a sense of the recent debate on this issue see the first chapter of Terry Eagleton's *Sweet Violence*, in which Eagleton reviews dozens of accounts of the tragic and enumerates their contradictions and inadequacies; in her introduction to *Rethinking Tragedy*, Rita Felski marks out another broad set of current contentious issues on the subject, including the continuing question of whether a "modern tragedy" is possible.

20. Maclean, *Young Men and Fire*, 201.

21. Collins, *The Apocalyptic Imagination*, 5.

22. Duff, "Christian Apocalyptic," 7.

23. Horn, "The Last Man," 55.

24. As L. Michael White writes, the Judeo-Christian genre of apocalypse emerges from prophecy, which was originally not a prediction of the future but an indictment of present sin and a summons to God's people to do God's will. But after the destruction of Jerusalem and the Temple, oracles began "calling for people to hold fast, saying that there would be a restoration of the nation and that the enemies would eventually be punished by God. A future-looking sense of history was born . . . " (White, "Apocalyptic Literature in Judaism & Early Christianity.")

25. Kermode, *The Sense of an Ending*, 25.

26. Kermode, 26.

27. Bultmann, *History and Eschatology*, 155.

28. Hay, *Apocalypse in American Literature and Culture*, 14.

29 Hay, 7.

30 Wagar, *Terminal Visions*, 16.

31. For an excellent overview and more detailed discussion of many of the points that follow here, see Hurley and Sinykin, "Apocalypse."

32. For convenience, from here on I will simply use "apocalyptic" as the umbrella term for narratives of transformational and/or terminal catastrophe and (sometimes) its aftermath, acknowledging that it has often been productive to make finer generic distinctions.

33. See McMurry, "The Slow Apocalypse"; Harrington, *Socialism*, 278.

34. Hurley, *Infrastructures of Apocalypse*, 15; see also Peter Coviello, "Apocalypse From Now On," in Boone, *Queer Frontiers*, 61.

35. Such criticisms have been leveled at both ends of the political spectrum—from evangelicals' expectation of Biblical apocalypse and more secular conservative prophecies of the destruction of America by a tsunami of (illegal) immigrants to liberal and leftist narratives of ecological catastrophe.

36. For just one instance, the film of Cormac McCarthy's *The Road* has been characterized as "a journey from a dying liberal patriarchy to a reactionary and violent one" (Balthaser, "Horror Cities").

37. Paul Lehmann, quoted in Duff, "Christian Apocalyptic," 6.

Chapter One

From Tragedy to Apocalypse in Norman Maclean's *Young Men and Fire*

> Looking down on the world of the Mann Gulch fire for probably the last time, I said to myself, "Now we know, now we know." I kept repeating this line until I recognized that, in the wide world anywhere, "Now we know, now we know" is one of its most beautiful poems. For me, for this moment, anyway, my world was changed to this one-line poem. Finding it a poem, I hoped I could next complete it as a tragedy, more exactly as a story of a tragedy, more exactly still as a tragedy of this whole cockeyed world that probably always makes its own kind of sense and beauty but not always ours.
>
> Norman Maclean, *Young Men and Fire*

On August 5, 1949, fifteen men parachuted into Mann Gulch in Montana to contain an apparently controllable wildfire. Before the end of the day the fire had "blown up" into an inferno, and twelve of those men, along with another ranger fighting the fire, were dead or fatally burned.

The Mann Gulch incident is one we would colloquially refer to as tragic—shocking, horrific, seemingly senseless. But for native Montanan and long-time University of Chicago English professor Norman Maclean, the events had remained, in some sense, simply "catastrophic" and needed to be *transformed* into tragedy. Maclean devoted much of the last years of his life to doing just that—to investigating and writing the story of what had happened at Mann Gulch, which would be posthumously published as *Young Men and Fire*, a "nonfiction" account of the events of 1949 interwoven with the story of Maclean's own investigation decades later.

Maclean's aim of transforming this historical event into a story, a poem, a tragedy—an aim which he states and reflects upon explicitly throughout the book—raises the question of what such a transformation entails and why it might be necessary. This is neither a narrowly literary critical question nor one confined to Maclean's work; it is a question about the role of literary and narrative art in apprehending and accommodating ourselves to the realities of human life—realities which are often difficult and sometimes disastrous—and about the role of modern literature, in particular modern tragic literature, in making sense of these realities under the conditions of modernity.

What, then, does it mean for Maclean to be "transforming catastrophe into tragedy," and what is the significance of the fact that his efforts to do so take the form that they do—an odd hybrid of history and memoir, journalism and prose poem? I submit that Maclean's project is best understood as an attempt to make sense of the disastrous events according to a different and in some sense "higher" order of meaning than common sense, and representing those events such that this sense is manifest. This amounts not just to explaining why things went terribly wrong, but also seeing in the catastrophe an intimation of certain hidden or unacknowledged conditions of human life, not only material but ideal, so that the meaning of the events is to be found not merely horizontally, so to speak—in their outcomes, good or bad—but vertically, as manifestations of a background order encompassing both heroism and enormity. In other words, the events of Mann Gulch seem at once to radically disrupt the everyday order according to which we make sense of things, and to indicate the possibility, indeed the necessity, of a different ground of sense. What makes *Fire* tragic literature, then, is that it represents this disruption in a way that implies this different and more comprehensive kind of sense, one which sees human life as subject to hostile forces and conditions that can never be finally and fully comprehended but still affirms a normatively structured order. What makes it modern tragic literature is its recognition that that the sense that one finds cannot be other than fraught, tenuous, provisional—and perhaps radically threatened, if the work finally moves beyond the tragic to the apocalyptic.

In its generic innovation, then, *Young Men and Fire* is revealing of the relations between tragedy and its historical conditions, illuminating the conditions of sensemaking in the absence of a shared traditional or religious order and with the unfortunately topical and ever-increasing probability of global cataclysm.

The following passage gives a sense of the dimensions of the task as Maclean conceived it:

> Although young men died like squirrels in Mann Gulch, the Mann Gulch fire should not end there, smoke drifting away and leaving terror without consolation of explanation, and controversy without lasting settlement. Probably most catastrophes end this way without an ending, the dead not even knowing how

they died. . . . *This is a catastrophe that we hope will not end where it began; it might go on and become a story.* It will not have to be made up—that is all-important to us—but we do have to know in what odd places to look for missing parts of a story about a wildfire and of course have to know a story and a wildfire when we see one. *So this story is a test of its own belief—that in this cockeyed world there are shapes and designs,* if only we have some curiosity, training, and compassion and take care not to lie or be sentimental. It would be a start to a story if this catastrophe were found to have circled around out there somewhere until it could return to itself with explanations of its own mysteries and with the grief it left behind, not removed, because grief has its own place at or near the end of things, but altered somewhat by the addition of something like wonder—wonder, for example, because we can now say that the fire whirl which destroyed was caused by three winds on a river. If we could say something like this and be speaking both accurately and somewhat like Shelley when he spoke of clouds and winds, then *what we would be talking about would start to change from catastrophe without a filled-in story to what could be called the story of a tragedy, but tragedy would be only a part of it, as it is of life.*[1]

Thus Maclean sees a catastrophe in need of a form that must be created or discovered. This form includes or constitutes an explanation for why the catastrophe happened, and this explanation is a kind of consolation—the austere consolation of understanding. The catastrophe remains a catastrophe as long as it goes without explanation—but causal explanation is not all that is required, as Maclean implies with his reference to Shelley.[2] More foundationally, the form Maclean seeks is one that will make what has happened intelligible, that will show the events to conform to some "shape" or "design" which is not imposed but belongs to their reality.

Maclean alternately refers to this form as the form of tragedy and the form of a story of which tragedy is "only a part, as it is of life." This apparent discrepancy could easily be reconciled if we take him to be using the term unrigorously, at times meaning "tragedy" in the sense of the literary genre and at times in the colloquial sense of a terrible event, but it could also be that there is a real ambiguity in *Fire*'s relation to the genre of tragedy. Is the literary (or dramatic) form of tragedy indeed the form that Maclean is seeking, the form that will reflect or reveal the sense or meaning of the events of Mann Gulch—the reality of Mann Gulch? Or will he require some new form that deviates enough from previous tragedies that it constitutes some new genre? (Perhaps, to look forward, apocalyptic form.)

The form that Maclean finds is, of course, the book *Young Men and Fire*, and the question then is, what does the character of this form reflect about the kind of understanding he seeks—and, if we find it persuasive, the reality it reflects? Answering this question involves not only looking at how Maclean represents the events he depicts, but also judging the work with respect to its aims, both explicit and implicit.

THE STORY OF THE STRUGGLE TO TELL THE STORY

First: an overview of the form of the work and the specific questions raised by its peculiarity.

Maclean began what was to become *Young Men and Fire* (his working title was "The Great Blow-Up") at age seventy-three, after publishing his first and only other full-length literary work, *A River Runs Through It and Other Stories*. The original intention was both to memorialize the men who had died fighting the 1949 fire in Mann Gulch in Maclean's home state of Montana and to resolve certain long-unanswered and troubling questions about how and why they had died.

In particular, the investigation centers on the question of whether the men had been killed not by the fire they had been sent in to fight but rather by the "escape fire" set by foreman Wag Dodge. As the wildfire threatened to overtake the men, Dodge had lit another fire in the grass, burning away the fuel in his immediate vicinity; he tried to get the rest of the men to lie down with him in the ashes of his fire, a safe lee around which the inferno would burn, but they failed to understand or trust him and kept heading to the ridge, all but two eventually caught by the blaze. The father of one of the deceased charged that it had in fact been Dodge's fire that had overtaken the others, and the issue had never been satisfactorily resolved.

But the work is clearly not just about settling the facts, and it is not just about the Smokejumpers but about Maclean himself, which comes through in the work's dual structure: it tells the story not only of the events of Mann Gulch but of Maclean's investigation, beginning almost four decades later, into those events, and the work is permeated with Maclean's reflections on nearing the end of his life. So it is the story of an old man as well as of young men—an old man coming to terms with his own aging, the deaths of those he has lost, and his own lives not lived. And it is not just dual but multiple: tragedy and mystery story, history and memoir; it contains scientific graphs and nineteenth-century poetry, geological history and comic anecdote. This multidimensionality is at times bemusing, but it certainly contributes to the book's distinctiveness and arguably to its power, and it seems intrinsic to Maclean's endeavor, whether or not fully successful. *Fire* has the feel of groping toward something that cannot be cleanly and directly expressed.

Related to this genre ambiguity (not to say confusion) is the fact that Maclean was unable to finish the work before he died. The work was the driving passion of Maclean's final decade of life, and University of Chicago Press editor Alan Thomas, who was responsible for the book's final form, has suggested that one reason Maclean did not finish the book before he died was that the work itself was sustaining him, but Thomas and others have also suggested that something about the task itself resisted completion—that it was too big, too complex, too "protean."[3] Maclean originally meant *Fire* to be a lean, straightforward narrative,[4] but it kept expanding, and he could never finally circumscribe it, and certainly not contract it to the slim, tight work he originally envisioned.

Young Men and Fire is split into three parts. In Alan O. Weltzien's neat summary, "part 1 narrates the minute-by-minute story of the blowup, part 2 narrates the story of Maclean's research and eventual understanding of the fire, and part 3 serves as an imaginative funeral service and benediction, as the men meet their death."[5] The first part tells the story of the blowup according to the facts as pieced together immediately after the initial events. Yet this narrative is incomplete—first, with respect to the conditions of the disaster, and secondly with respect to its significance. These two gaps come together for Maclean (as they did for many trying to make sense of the catastrophe) in the question of Dodge's escape fire—whether it was this fire which burned the men. To know this is, for Maclean, essential not only to be able to give a complete account of what happened, but to know whether it had the necessity he saw as essential to tragedy. If the men were burned not by the main fire but by Dodge's fire, their deaths would, he seems to believe, no longer be inevitable but contingent, the product of a terrible mistake or accident: Dodge, in trying to save himself and his men, would have killed them unnecessarily.

The second part, then, is aimed at solving the mystery, in the form of a narrative of its own, a "quest story"; as Maclean says, "For a time, our story becomes the story of trying to find it" (164), and this story "end[s] happily" (285) with a proximal—negative—answer to the question of Dodge's guilt. Here Maclean describes his treks into Mann Gulch with Forest Serviceman Laird Robinson and the two remaining survivors, Robert Sallee and Walter Rumsey, searching out the exact locations of Dodge's fire and the crevice through which Sallee and Rumsey escaped. He then recounts grappling with fire science and mathematics to graphically plot out the course and speed of the fire versus the course and speed of the men to see whether it was "inevitable"—and therefore "tragic"—that the main fire, the fire they went to fight, should catch them. By the end of Part 2, Maclean has answered the major questions he felt to be essential to telling the story—why the rest of the men did not run straight up to the ridge like Rumsey and Sallee; how it was that Dodge's fire could burn at a right angle to the main fire (if it did)—the questions essential to understanding why the young men and the fire behaved as they did, so as to lead to their terrible convergence. He has "exonerated"

Dodge and his escape fire. He has to his own satisfaction shown the catastrophe to be "inevitable"—or, rather, located or accounted for its inevitability, the moment when the tragedy was inevitable.

The scientific investigation culminates in a graph showing the fire closing the distance to the men as they ran up the gulch.

Maclean characterizes the convergence of the lines as "the tragic conclusion of the Mann Gulch story; the two lines converging to this conclusion constitute the plot." He then suggestively says: "Along each line are numbers which are turning points in the race. . . . If they also have religious significance they are stations of the cross, and if they have literary significance they mark off acts of a drama" (269). One might say that the conclusion of Part 2 fills in the missing pieces of the drama—the action—so as to show its literary significance, and Part 3 redescribes the final conflagration to evoke some kind of "religious" significance—but it remains to be seen what each of these means.

Like *War and Peace* as characterized by Henry James, *Young Men and Fire* could be described as a "loose baggy monster,"[6] if not quite so large. But also like *War and Peace* (or, perhaps more relevantly, *Moby-Dick*), its bagginess is arguably appropriate (if not "perfect"), and the question then becomes: Why

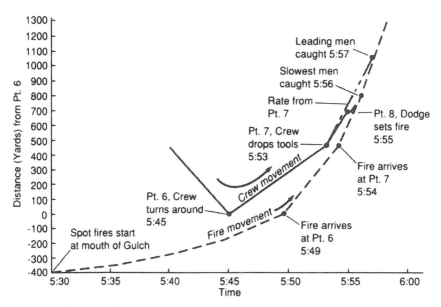

**Richard C. Rothermel's graph of the relative positions
of the fire and the men at Mann Gulch on August
5, 1949. From *Young Men and Fire*, p. 269.**

or in what way is it appropriate—what is it about the story or the reality that the work means to convey that it cannot be contained within a lean, linear narrative, or in the dramatic form of classical tragedy? Why must this tragedy take such a form?

FROM CATASTROPHE TO STORY: THE SEARCH FOR SENSE

Next, a closer analysis of what it means for Maclean to transform a catastrophe into a story before going on to consider what it means for him to transform it into a tragic story or tragedy.

Classical narratologists distinguished between the *sjužet*, the plot as it is conveyed through narrative discourse, and the *fabula*, the story or the events as they occurred (or, in fiction, are imagined to have occurred). In nonfiction such as *Fire*, the author's task is to take "what happened"—the *fabula*—and emplot it—transform it into *sjužet*—which is both a matter of ordering (how to reveal to the reader what occurred) and selection (of the infinite number of facts, what is relevant to the telling of the story). The question is, what is the principle of this transformation—what makes a plot a plot, that is to say a good plot? Or as we might say colloquially, what makes a story a story?

Commonsensically, we all know a story when we hear it, so that it is hard not to say, a story is, well, *a story*! Much of our common sense was originally and acutely articulated in Aristotle's *Poetics*: a story (or a plot, *mythos*) is an account of events with a beginning, a middle, and an end—that is, it starts from a state of affairs which needs no prior explanation to be intelligible, which "doesn't necessarily follow from anything else, but something naturally exists or occurs after it," then follows out the consequences of that beginning to their resolution, the state of affairs which "naturally follows from something else, either necessarily or in general, but there is nothing else after it."[7] In other words, a story is "an imitation of an action,"[8] a telling of a series of events that have a certain unity. For Aristotle, the unity is that of a chain of events linked, in his terms, by relations of necessity and probability. For instance, he praises Homer for not including in the *Odyssey* two events which, according to tradition, happened to Odysseus but neither of which "[made] the occurrence of the other necessary or probable."[9] Some initial event sets off a cascade of consequences, and the story consists in following out those consequences to the end, the point at which all the major consequences have played out. Or, some event disrupts an apparent stability, and the story is the account of the progression to a new stability.

We typically think of our interest in a story from the perspective of the beginning, from the "inciting event": the characters find themselves in some kind of predicament and we want to know how it turns out. But if we know how it turns out, as in the case of *Fire,* we can also think of our interest from the perspective of the ending. That is, we want to know how the ending came about, what led to it. A story, or, more broadly, narrative, has thus been characterized as a form of understanding or explanation because of its relation to causality—or, better, conditionality, since human action is not *caused* as events in the physical world are caused; rather, it is *conditioned* by various social, psychological, and other external and internal factors. Nothing *caused* Anna Karenina to commit suicide as my pushing this book off the table will cause it, with physical necessity, to fall, but numerous factors conditioned her action, and Tolstoy's novel could be said to perspicuously present those conditions. The historian and philosopher of history W. B. Gallie claims that the story is "a form of human understanding *sui generis* and . . . the basis of all historical thought and knowledge."[10] A story constitutes a kind of explanation—and this is especially pertinent to stories that relate historical events, as *Fire* does. It shows how things came about, why they turned out the way they did.

Thus first of all to turn the catastrophe of Mann Gulch, the death of thirteen men, into the story of Mann Gulch means to show how and why things came out the way they did, to answer the questions remaining after the Forest Service's investigation decades before. And this is how Maclean most consistently characterizes his task, as in the following passage:

> After the autumn rains changed into mud slides, the story seems to have been buried in incompleteness, pieces of it altogether missing. As a mystery story, it left unexplained what dramatic and devastating forces coincided to make the best of young men into bodies, how the bodies got to their crosses and what it was like on the way, and why this catastrophe has been allowed to pass without a search for the carefully measured grains of consolation needed to transform catastrophe into tragedy. (143)

But this passage itself points to the fact that the kind of "explanation" a storyteller must give is not merely a matter of giving a causal account of one thing leading to another. The questions Maclean wants to answer through his narrative are not identical with the questions the Forest Service attempted to answer (or not) in its investigation. Even if Maclean sometimes seems to treat his task as a kind of causal explanation, he is ultimately concerned with a broader kind of understanding: not just with explanation but with "consolation," not just how it happened but with "what it was like on the way." (I will deal later with the question of why this should be "consoling.")

This brings up another aspect which we implicitly feel to be a criterion of a story, or at least a good story, namely that it enables a kind of *experience*. A story worth the name is more than just a sequence of events, one causing or conditioning the next—it is structured in such a way as to engage our interest in the unfolding itself, not just to explain the final outcome, and I take this engagement not to be a statement just about our psychology (e.g., we like to be held in suspense) but about the kind of understanding a story represents, an understanding that is irreducibly temporal, that depends fundamentally on its unfolding in time. That is to say: in literature or literary nonfiction, somehow the experience of the narrative is integral to the kind of understanding (or "explanation") that the narrative represents or occasions.

To the extent that a story depicts the experience or situation of a character, the experience of reading can be thought of as vicarious experience—imitating an experience we (or someone) might have in the world. Rather than just reporting, works of fiction place us within a situation so that we may inhabit it, so that we may "feel" tensions and anticipate their resolution, anticipations which may be confirmed or thwarted, to our satisfaction or distress (emotional or cognitive), so that we have a context within which to imagine how someone in such a situation might respond. As Maclean characterizes his role:

> A storyteller . . . must follow compassion wherever it leads him. He must be able to accompany his characters, even into smoke and fire, and bear witness to what they thought and felt even when they themselves no longer knew. This story of the Mann Gulch fire will not end until it feels able to walk the final distance to the crosses with those who for the time being are blotted out by smoke. They were young and did not leave much behind them and need someone to remember them. (102)

Maclean attempts to capture and convey, as far as possible, the experience of the Smokejumpers, and in particular of those who perished. He recognizes that merely in putting their experience, or his imaginative reconstruction of it, into words, he will already be transforming it, since in the end their consciousness would have likely been reduced to the drive and desire for survival—as he puts it, "courage struggling for oxygen" (301). But this transformation will be true to their spirit and to their actions, and thus will help to redeem their deaths by memorializing them.

Much of the book, however, does not represent a character's experience. There are the tracts on fire science, Maclean's reflections on storytelling, the phantasmagoric descriptions of the final conflagration "from above." But the book could still be said to constitute an experience for the *reader*, based in an identification with the narrative consciousness—with Maclean as narrator, or with the perspective he is trying to achieve. Essential to this experience is some kind of catharsis, which for Maclean comes through the process of his inquiry and discovery, and the structure and substance of the book indeed seems intended not merely meant to convey information but to effect an analogous catharsis. That catharsis, we will see, is for Maclean (who uses the term "purgation") a dispossessing and searingly illuminating encounter with the structuring laws of the universe, laws indifferent and sometimes inimical to human happiness—a dramatically different order of sense than the everyday.

The experience of reading a narrative is essential to the narrative form of explanation because the temporal unfolding of narrative creates or implies a certain kind of sense—a background order of intelligibility that is revealed only *as* the background of a sequence of events and actions that we follow with identification and interest, with expectation and desire for a resolution that is both plausible and adequate. Roland Barthes claims that it is "*la passion du sens*" that compels us to read, and Peter Brooks glosses this as "both the passion *for* meaning and the passion *of* meaning: the active quest of the reader for those shaping ends that, terminating the dynamic process of reading, promise to bestow meaning and significance on the beginning and the middle."[11] Narrative is a form of meaning or a way of creating meaning—a particular kind of meaning that develops in time—and plot, for Brooks, is "the design and intention of narrative, a structure for those meanings that are developed through temporal succession, or perhaps better: a structuring operation elicited by, and made necessary by, those meanings that develop through succession and time."[12] The experience of reading, whatever else it may be, is thus an experience of the development of meaning.

To say that plot structures meanings that develop in time means first of all that the meaning of any one part of the narrative cannot be understood except in relation to the other parts. While we must have some understanding of a work's opening lines on our first reading, they only have their full significance *as* a beginning, as setting up what will be developed in what follows. Complementarily, the end of the work does not refer merely to whatever it directly recounts or describes but has its significance *as* an ending and in light of (as a resolution of) all that has preceded it.

The connections between any two parts of the narrative, which constitute some relation of meaning, can be of one of several kinds: the earlier part may provoke the question "what will happen?" (as when a character is in a precarious situation) or "what does that mean?" (as when something mysterious is described); the later part answers or casts some light on the question. Barthes observes that these are the two kinds of relation that fundamentally structure the forward drive of the narrative,[13] the desire that propels our reading. I would add the question of "how will it happen?" which is essential to the forward drive of *Fire*: as when in the first paragraph Maclean writes that the Smokejumpers "were still so young they hadn't learned to count the odds and to sense they might owe the universe a tragedy" (19). What is this tragedy and how will it come about? This may be a variant of "what does it mean?" but one distinctive and analytically separable from the kind of mystery that arises in a detective story, the clue or enigma (something in the diegetic world) whose significance only becomes clear later on.

In a narrative that strives to be more than just entertainment, and which also strives not just to be consoling but true, or truthful (not just in nonfiction like Maclean's but in serious fiction generally), there must be some connection between this desire and meaning, on the one hand, and truth or reality—in some sense of the word—on the other. As Frank Kermode claims, the *peripeteia* of a good story functions not just to prolong the action or create suspense but to reveal something along the way; peripeteia "is a disconfirmation followed by a consonance; the interest of having our expectations falsified is obviously related to our wish to reach the discovery or recognition by an unexpected and instructive route."[14] Instructive *because* unexpected, yet persuasive.

The connection between desire and reality can, I submit, be found at the level of the *conditions of sense*. A narrative will only satisfy our desire if in its unfolding it conforms to what we find plausible and right, not necessarily with respect to what we expect in "the real world"—we don't expect a story to proceed just as ordinary life proceeds (and would generally not be satisfied if it did)—but with respect to those conditions of the sense and significance of human life and experience which are often obscured, distorted, or denied in our everyday experience.

The conditions of sense of a story are not identical with those of everyday life—we recognize that stories are not just chunks of life presented for observation; they are crafted fictions that, moreover, conform to certain conventions which are part of what we appeal to in order to make sense of them. Nothing in "real life" would, for example, explain why characters in *King Lear* speak in iambic pentameter. But these "unnatural" aspects of artistic form still have reference to the conditions by which the audience or readers would properly make sense of their own lives, and by which we make sense of ours, to the extent that the work still resonates with us—to the extent that it refers to abiding and not merely historically particular conditions. Regular meter or rhyme in Shakespeare, for instance, might serve as an image of a kind of inevitability, rightness, or conformity to law.

To briefly restate from the Introduction: in general and on the whole we make sense of our everyday experience and orient our actions with reference to largely instrumental ends (ours and others' needs and wants) and largely conventional moral constraints and demands (to respect other persons, to fulfill our obligations, to act civilly and justly). And the background of our needs and wants and felt duties is a largely tacit and often confused and conflicting tapestry of notions of the way things are and the way they ought to be, images and ideas of goodness, happiness, responsibility, love and so on—all that we have internalized from our upbringing, experience, and popular culture. Serious literature challenges this background. It presents characters and situations which, through their very nature or the way in which they are presented, cannot be adequately made sense of with reference to this background and imply a more comprehensive and, in some measure, conflicting ground of sense—a ground which defies our wishes or ideology.

Thus to turn catastrophe into a story—the kind of story Maclean wants to tell—fundamentally means to represent events so that their unfolding seems surprising and yet right, in accord with conditions that we ordinarily fail to recognize.

We might finally ask how this is related to the "carefully measured grains of consolation" Maclean sees as essential to transforming catastrophe into a story, into tragedy. There seems to be a tension between the idea of consolation and the idea of truth—what if the truth is *not* consoling?

The idea of *mourning* illuminates the intrinsic connections between loss, narrative, consolation, and reality.

"THE SHAPE OF REMEMBERED TRAGEDY": MEMORY AND MOURNING

At the center of *Fire* are the young men of the title. For Maclean, an essential motivation for and meaning of "turning catastrophe into tragedy" is finding a way to memorialize these men—to show their lives to have been significant even though they died so young. We might also, therefore, think of *Fire* as an act of mourning, the story as consolation for loss, but also as an enactment of relinquishment—not only of the men but also of something more personal to Maclean, which he sees figured in them.

Mourning is the typical response to the loss of a beloved object—paradigmatically, the death of a loved one, but also potentially something ideal or abstract, anything to which one is deeply attached. In Freud's classic account, "reality-testing has shown that the loved object no longer exists, and it proceeds to demand that all libido shall be withdrawn from its attachments to that object"; after lengthy and difficult effort, the demand is fulfilled.[15] To the extent that it is not, the individual remains mired in melancholia, unable to relinquish the attachment and move forward with life.

For Freud, as Peter Homans argues, "mourning . . . was essentially conservative, only consolidating, repairing, and rescuing lost parts of the ego from the wreckage inflicted upon it by the commands of reality," but subsequent psychoanalytic theorists saw successful mourning as having a "progressive" character, culminating in "new values and new psychological structure."[16] In the case of the death of someone close, that structure may take the form of adopting certain characteristics, values, or interests of the person, or simply internalizing their memory. But often the loss is, as Freud notes, more "ideal." Such cases are perhaps more difficult to mourn, more prone to give rise to melancholia, given the additional challenge of coming to terms with a loss that is more abstract, as when "the object has not perhaps actually died, but has been lost as an object of love" or "the patient is aware of the loss which has given rise to his melancholia, but only in the sense that he knows *whom* he has lost but not *what* he has lost in him."[17] In the latter case—which I propose is the case with Maclean and the losses with which he deals in *Fire*—it is not just the individual who must be mourned but whatever it is that the individual embodied or represented for the mourner. *Fire* could be read as not only an act of mourning but of the preliminary process of coming to understand what has been lost and must be mourned.

The obvious loss is the deaths of the young men. But from the beginning, the men are clearly representative of further losses: Maclean's personal losses, including that of his own youth, the world of his youth, and finally his impending death. As he says of the stories of *A River Runs Through It*, which share his loving and at times nostalgic relation to the early-to-mid-twentieth century life in the American West, "I meant these stories in part to be a record of how certain things were done just before the world of most of history ended—most of history being a world of hand and horse and hand tools and horse tools. I meant to record not only how we did certain things well in that world now almost beyond recall, but how it felt to do those things well that are now slipping from our hands and memory."[18] The losses mourned in *Fire* will finally amount to the threatened disappearance of a human world altogether. These losses are universal or at least general, and the work makes this manifest. *Fire* does not just represent Maclean's mourning but can be seen as effecting mourning in the reader, first evoking the attachments before playing out the loss. Through the work the losses are shown as losses for the reader as well, and we come to feel and perceive them as such.

Loss is an encounter with reality, and mourning involves coming to terms with that reality: both accepting it *as* reality, and making sense of it. Gene Ray describes the process from trauma (sudden, violent, and destabilizing loss) to the beginnings of mourning in a way that suggests the centrality to this process of finding a *form*—a narrative form, perhaps an artistic form: "From the outside, something breaks through and in: an intervention into the stabilized form of psychic life. . . . Then, maybe, a reach, a throw. In a potlatch of words and images, something like an approach. Out of which, maybe, a capture, a first remembering-forgetting of representation, the work of emplotment . . . a passage back, from the disturbed body to the shared word."[19] The "shared word," though, must acknowledge the new reality—not just as a moral imperative (that we live in reality as opposed to fantasy) but in order to free ourselves. Ray states the alternatives: we can "refuse our traumas and thereby remain in their power. Or we succumb to their pathos and make a home in melancholy. Or we mourn them and learn to accept that we must now be different. Finally that's what mourning means: accepting the burden of change."[20] It is not just that we find some new and consoling structure of significance—coincident with a new way of being in the world—that happens to accord with the loss, a kind of compromise between what we would want (to have back what we lost) and what the reality principle demands (that we face up to the loss). It is the understanding of the reality *of* the loss, the reality underlying the loss, the reality responsible for the loss and that makes the loss the kind of loss (to us) that it is, that *is* what allows us to come to terms with it. Reality *is* the consolation for loss—the austere consolation of consciousness.

Reality in this sense is not just the facts, but the totality within which the facts make sense. Tragedy, then—or, more accurately, tragic narrative, the particular kind of tragic narrative that *Fire* is—is the form that mourning takes, its structures of significance as the "consolation" for the loss, at least when the loss results from the transgression of some law. (Elegy would be the other, perhaps more obvious, literary form of mourning, and *Fire* also has a strong elegiac element.[21]) The structures of sense and significance revealed by Maclean's representation of the loss—the "shapes and designs" of the universe—are the reality we come to know through that loss.

Making sense of the events of Mann Gulch, then, means first of all for Maclean determining how it happened, filling in the "missing pieces," showing all the decisions and contingencies that led to men's deaths. But it also means finding full expression for the significance of what has happened. The significance of a catastrophe like that of Mann Gulch is at first inchoate: it just makes us feel terrible. And perhaps it also elicits a strange and disturbing kind of awe—both of which we may just try to bury, the grief because it is unbearable, the awe because it seems inappropriate, even obscene. Making sense of it means giving form to those impressions, to which journalistic reports and conventional expressions of sorrow are inadequate.

Let us now look at the particular kind of sense Maclean seeks in *Fire* and the form he finds.

FROM CATASTROPHE TO TRAGEDY: SEEKING TRAGIC SENSE

The very first lines of *Fire* set up the story as one of tragic conflict and tragic inevitability:

In 1949 the Smokejumpers were not far from their origins as parachute jumpers turned stunt performers dropping from the wings of planes at county fairs just for the hell of it plus a few dollars, less hospital expenses. By this time they were also sure they were the best firefighters in the United States Forest Service, and although by now they were very good, especially against certain kinds of fires, they should have stopped to realize that they were newcomers in this ancient business of fighting forest fires. It was 1940 when the first parachute jump on a forest fire was made and a year later that the Smokejumpers were organized, so only for nine years had there been a profession with the aim of taking on at the same time three of the four elements of the universe—air, earth, and fire—and in a simple continuous act dropping out of the sky and landing in a treetop or on the face of a cliff in order to make good their boast of digging a trench around every fire they landed on by ten o'clock the next morning. In 1949 the Smokejumpers were still so young that they referred affectionately to all fires they jumped on as "ten o'clock fires." They were still so young they hadn't learned to count the odds and to sense they might owe the universe a tragedy. (19)

This opening paragraph and the development of its themes through the opening chapter raise the questions and the desire for resolution that will shape the narrative, stir the expectations which will be satisfied or thwarted in the progression toward the conclusion—including expectations, tacit or explicit, of what would constitute a (proper or adequate) conclusion.

The expectation that the opening provokes is that this story is headed toward "tragedy"—toward a collision with forces which would overwhelm all human skill, bravery, ingenuity, and technology—and the strong foreshadowing of the first paragraph is confirmed and concretized in the last line of the first section[22]: "It is hard to realize that these young men would be dead within two hours after they landed from parachutes no longer made of silk but of nylon, so they would not be eaten by grasshoppers" (31). With this revelation of the ending comes the question of how the narrative will arrive there, both in terms of the unfolding of events and in terms of the telling of the story.

Naming tragedy in the beginning lines already indicates something about the form of sense to which the narrative will conform, or which it will reveal. It tells us not only that things will end badly (which most readers, knowing the subject of the book, would anticipate in any case) but that its events are the proper subjects for dramatic or literary tragedy—that tragedy is the form that will allow Maclean to make sense of the events of Mann Gulch.

The traditional subject of tragedy (ancient and Shakespearean), traditionally understood (by the majority of theorists of tragedy from Aristotle through the mid-twentieth century), is the exceptional individual who transgresses some law or order—human or divine—and suffers retaliation for this transgression.[23] As Northrop Frye puts it: "The tragic hero is very great as compared with us, but there is something else . . . compared to which he is small," something which "may be called God, gods, fate, accident, fortune, necessity, circumstance, or any combination of these,"[24] and which seems finally to be the emanation of some law which the action of the tragedy reveals: "[W]e see the tragic hero as disturbing a balance in nature, nature being conceived as an order stretching over the two kingdoms of the visible and the invisible, a balance which sooner or later *must* right itself. The righting of the balance is what the Greeks called *nemesis* . . . "[25]

In Aristotle's terms, the violation of this balance would be the hero's flaw or error—*hamartia*—and the righting of the balance produce pity for the hero's suffering and terror that we, too, decent people as we are, could commit such a violation and suffer the consequences.

Modernity troubles and arguably undermines two conditions of tragedy thus understood—first, the great individual, and second, that of an order of the universe more and other than physical law. With democracy and the democratic sensibility, focus and value in serious art shifts from the extraordinary to the ordinary, from the ventures and trials of someone noble and elite to the everyday struggles of more average people.[26] And, as George Steiner writes in *The Death of Tragedy*, in Greek and Shakespearean tragedy "mortal actions are encompassed by forces which transcend man" but which are not simply random, which reflect an ordered universe; "the triumph of rationalism and secular metaphysics," which deny such forces, is the end of the tragic sensibility.[27]

Those twentieth-century works which, contra Steiner et al., have lain some claim to the name of tragedy could be classed roughly into two camps—on the one hand, social and psychological tragedies of everyday life, such as Ibsen's "Ghosts" or O'Neill's "Long Day's Journey into Night," in which individuals are crushed by the hostile or indifferent social world or by their own inner demons or some combination thereof. On the other, there are the absurdist plays such as Beckett's which suggest the tragedy *of* the lack of some ultimate sense to human activity.

Fire, I propose, presents itself as an alternative to either of these, and in certain ways more continuous with classical tragedy, though in others clearly not. His protagonists, the Smokejumpers, are extraordinary in their physical capacity and willingness to risk themselves, but they are a "democratic elite." And unlike Ibsen or Beckett, Maclean still seems to refer to an order of meaning beyond the social and even beyond the ethical—to what seems to fall into Frye's category of "something beyond." As I will develop, this is not so much named or invoked explicitly as implied, and, I would argue, implied mainly by the poetry of Maclean's work.

Fire seeks to show events as conforming to a kind of order, but it confronts this search for order as a *problem*. One of Maclean's few published scholarly essays is on King Lear and tragedy, and in it he suggests that the "most tragic region" of the play (which in turn is "the most tragic of Shakespeare's tragedies") is "the region where suffering takes on such dimension that even Shakespeare could find no better word that 'madness' to contain it." Lear's madness is, as Maclean characterizes it, the product of the loss of the belief in "a universe controlled by divine authority, harmoniously ordered and subordinated in its parts"; Lear comes instead to see a world "in which man is leveled to a beast," but a beast possessed of a "sadistic ingenuity by which he sanctifies his own sins."[28] For Maclean, then, terrible suffering raises the question of order, and Maclean claims that "the question of whether the universe is something like what Lear hoped it was or very close to what he feared it was is still, tragically, the current question."[29] If writing events as a story is a kind of explanation that makes the events intelligible according to a certain narrative logic, then writing events as a tragic story shows them not to make sense according to the logic of everyday life—of our pursuit of our own happiness or the calculation of instrumental ends—but sees in them a different kind of sense and attempts to make this sense manifest.

But what kind of sense could that be? If Steiner's claims about "the death of tragedy" and its causes have merit, then the success of Maclean's project would depend on finding some alternative to the kinds of mythological, religious, and metaphysical order underpinning classical and Shakespearean tragedy. I have suggested above that his poetic language especially often gestures toward such an order; a few critics suggest that this background order of meaning is theological.[30] Along those lines, I propose that the work seeks to point (and to orient the reader) to something that transcends the everyday, not to the God of Maclean's Presbyterian father, or any doctrinal religion, but to certain ultimate conditions of sense, which cannot be stated directly but can only be suggested or evoked through poetic imagery and narrative form.

This accords with what we see in the first paragraph of *Fire*. First: the deaths of the men at Mann Gulch are not sheer, senseless accident. They can be explained. They conform to some order. And this order, the opening suggests, is not just that of nature but of human action, and it is normative if not quite "moral": the men at Mann Gulch died (the story will show us) because of what one might call hubris—the overconfident and mistaken belief that they could triumph over the forces of nature, that they could indefinitely win against the odds.

At the same time, this is no mere cautionary or morality tale. The young men are beautiful and compelling in their youth and their recklessness, and they are not simply foolish to think that this is a fight they might win. They have in them a touch of the divine; they are large enough to confront the elements, and it is this largeness that brings down the wrath of the universe upon them. Again, this is classically tragic. As Frye puts it, "The tragic hero is typically on top of the wheel of fortune, halfway between human society on the ground and the something greater in the sky. . . . Tragic heroes are so much the highest points in their human landscape that they seem the inevitable conductors of power about them, great trees more likely to be struck by lightning than a clump of grass. Conductors may of course be instruments as well as victims of the divine lightning."[31]

It is essential that these two sides of tragedy are in an irreconcilable tension. As Frye goes on to develop, there are two "reductive" ways in which the fatedness of tragedy can be understood: either "that all tragedy exhibits the omnipotence of an external fate," that the hero's destruction is the carrying out of some preordained malevolent plan in which the hero has no agency, or contrarily that "the act which sets the tragic process going must be primarily a violation of *moral* law"[32] and thus that the hero *deserves* their fate. Neither of these, Frye argues, adequately describes what happens in great tragedies. On the one hand, what destroys the tragic hero does not emerge *ex nihilo* but in response to something that the hero has done. On the other, the destruction and suffering are out of all proportion to the hero's actions, which may not even be moral transgressions; furthermore, the hero is compelling in the extremity that has brought them up against the destructive force.

In these dimensions Maclean clearly finds, or wants to find, the significance of classical and Shakespearean tragedy in the events of Mann Gulch. Yet it quickly emerges that not only does Maclean (for reasons to be discussed) require a narrative rather than dramatic form for his tragedy but that he must depart from classical tragedy in other ways—due to the difficulty, and perhaps the impossibility, of finding a *meaningful* inevitability in the events of Mann Gulch.

TRAGIC INEVITABILITY

If Maclean wants to memorialize the fallen as tragic heroes, his approach may seem odd on the face of it. We get hardly any sense of the individual personalities of the Smokejumpers, the substance of their lives, except for a few poignant facts—for instance, that Eldon Diettert was a "fine research student who was called from his [19th] birthday dinner to make this flight and told some of the crew that he almost said no" (29). Only foreman Wag Dodge appears as a notably distinct personality (taciturn, solitary) set off from the general character of the rest of the men, who are young and unformed—each remembered, Maclean notes, as simply a "great guy" or a "wonderful boy"— "which," he adds, "is undoubtedly true" (29), but not much to go on for character development.

One can easily imagine a work that aimed to memorialize the men by bringing them vividly to life as individuals. The Smokejumpers were hardly without distinction; David Navon, for instance, "was . . . something of a four dimensional adventurer; he had been first lieutenant in the 101st Airborne Division and had parachuted into Bastogne" (29). But Maclean singles them out only in brief, if piercing, snapshots: Hellman "was handsome and important and only a month before had made a parachute landing on the Ellipse between the White House and the Washington Monument. At the end he wished he had been a better Catholic, and men wept when they saw him still alive" (29).

As the latter passage demonstrates, Maclean portrays his subjects from the beginning as defined by their end—by their premature deaths, which Maclean sees and wants to show as being their fate, their tragic destiny. It is in the events leading up to their deaths that they become something more than their finite lives, that their lives attain a form that can become a story and therefore a memory. As Maclean writes in "USFS 1919," a fictionalized account of an episode from his own childhood:

> I had no notion yet that life every now and then becomes literature—not long, of course, but long enough to be what we best remember, and often enough so that what we eventually come to mean by life are those moments when life, instead of going sideways, backwards, forward, or nowhere at all, lines out straight, tense, and inevitable, with a complication, climax, and, given some luck, a purgation, as if life had been made and not happened.[33]

For the adolescent narrator of that story, its form turns out more comic than tragic, though not without its poignant losses. But for the young men who died in Mann Gulch, the form is the form of tragedy, and what counts within the form of tragedy is not the full and complex personality *per se* but only those aspects of character which lead to the protagonist's tragic fate: a fate which is not just his destruction but a kind of realization, if not the realization one would wish for. Tragedy makes catastrophe intelligible not just by showing how it came about but by showing it to be in accord with some deeper sense or mythological basis. The protagonist's fate is not the realization of a personal desire nor of mere unfortunate contingency but of "law"—the nature of this law as yet to be examined. There is something, therefore, fundamentally *impersonal* about tragedy[34]—at least classical tragedy, which is the tradition of tragedy which Maclean seems to be trying to claim.

In *Fire*, what makes the men extraordinary, and therefore is the condition of their being tragic heroes—and in turn the condition for properly mourning them, recognizing the fullness of what their loss represents—is something they all share; it is their "collective character." As Maclean says, "this tragedy is not a classical tragedy of a monumental individual crossing the sword of his will with the sword of destiny. It is a tragedy of a crew, its flaws and grandeurs largely those of Smokejumpers near the beginning of their history" (28–29).

As a crew, the Smokejumpers share with classical tragic heroes their extremity and exceptionality; they quite literally embody Frye's description of the tragic hero as "halfway between human society on the ground and the something greater in the sky" (207), and this is a reflection of their character as well: "Most people," writes Maclean, "have a touch of the Icarus complex and, like Smokejumpers wish to appear on earth from the sky. . . . From the start, Smokejumpers had to have a lot of what we have a little of, and one way all men are born equal is in being born at least a little bit crazy, some being more equal than others" (21). It is not just craziness that drives them, but the desire to confront themselves and "the universe." For the Smokejumpers, smokejumping is a way "to make unmistakably clear to themselves and to the universe that they love the universe but are not intimidated by it and will not be shaken by it, no matter what it has in store" (28), and this need "could be within a lot of us" (28).

The references to "all men" and "a lot of us" illuminates part of what makes *Young Men and Fire* a modern tragedy—the Smokejumpers are special but in a way that many people might be special, and so *Fire* could be called a democratic tragedy. But it is not a story of an everyman ground down by everyday injustice (as, for example, Miller's *Death of a Salesman*) or destroyed by baseness and contingency (as in the Coen brothers' *Fargo*), at the mercy of which any of us might, if unlucky, find ourselves. It is the story of an "elite," a word Maclean uses several times throughout the book to describe the men, who only encounter disaster *because* they are elite. It might better be called a meritocratic tragedy, and in this aspect Maclean departs from the general trajectory of Western tragic drama and seeks to recover the mythical or larger-than-life character of classical tragedy.

Perhaps the greatest challenge for Maclean in transforming catastrophe into a modern tragedy that is nonetheless large is to make convincing, after the departure of the gods and the Protestant sublimation of God to the harsh light of interior conscience, the idea of "something greater." For the men to be tragic heroes, for catastrophe to be tragedy, Maclean must also show what destroyed them to have been a worthy foe, and a foe of mythical proportion.

"The universe" is Maclean's term for that "something greater," his equivalent of or substitute for fate and divine law. "The universe" is the cosmos as active agent, encompassing not only natural force—the Smokejumpers' task was to put out a fire "before suddenly the universe tried to reduce its own frame of things to ashes and charred grouse" (33)—but also spiritual condition—as in "the need to settle some things with the universe" (28), "they might owe the universe a tragedy." Its character becomes clearer as Maclean moves from the historical background of the Mann Gulch fire to the scientific and geological, though as we will see, fire and earth are mythical images and not merely material conditions.

FROM MAGNITUDE TO MYTH

Maclean devotes the first few sections of *Fire* to conveying the conditions of the tragedy—the historical, characterological, and scientific background that will allow the reader to understand what transpires. After sketching the character of the Smokejumpers, Maclean highlights the "few apparent weaknesses" that he sees as leading to the disaster—noting in particular that "one danger of making almost a sole specialty of dropping on fires as soon as possible is that nearly all such fires will be small fires, and a tragic corollary is that not much about fighting big fires can be learned by fighting small ones" (31–32). This is continuous with what we would expect from classical tragedy, in which, as traditionally understood, the unfolding of the plot is the realization of character and the working out of unresolved tensions.

What follows, though, is a novel kind of background that begins to reveal the nature of "the universe" as it operates in Maclean's modern tragedy.

Having dropped various firefighting terms—"ground fire," "crowned," "spot fires"—Maclean says "we had better be sure of the meaning of these key words" (33), explaining that "to know one fire is to see how what was dropping live ashes from a dead tree at the end of one afternoon by next afternoon had become one kind of fire after another kind of fire until it had become a monster in flames from which there was no escape" (34). From this evocation of a "monster in flames" he immediately shifts back to a straightforward exposition of the different kinds of fires, their behavior, and methods used to control them. At the same time, he is describing what will unfold in the story of Mann Gulch: what starts out as a ground fire (which "most often . . . is just a lot of hard work to get under control" [34]) gets into the branches of the trees (it "crowns"), and can then throw spot fires out ahead of it. "The separate spot fires soon burn together, and life is trapped between the main fire coming from behind and the new line of fire now burning back toward it. Then something terrible can happen": a "blow-up," where "the convection effect or a change in the wind blows fresh oxygen between the two fires, suddenly replenishing the burned-out air," which has become hotter than the point of ignition, so that the air itself ignites (35). Maclean concludes the passage by quoting fire scientist Harry T. Gisborne's description of the burnt body of a grouse that had been trapped and caught in such a blowup, "still alertly erect in fear and wonder" (36).

This kind of "mixed discourse"—here, shifting back and forth between a more or less literal and "flat" description and a figurative or poetic and intense "literary" mode—is characteristic and I think illuminating of the difficulties of Maclean's task and of his achievement, of the special character of modern tragedy, deriving from the special character of "modern reality." One can no longer separate the divine from the mundane, the scientific from the theological—the universe within which human beings live is a *uni*verse, a unity; there are no "supernatural" forces that stand apart from nature and intervene in it, but neither is "nature" simply "nature"—the matrix of human life is human history, biology, psychology; physical force; the laws of morality, beauty, and narrative. Thus to understand what happened at Mann Gulch we need history, science, poetry, image, story.

There is something hierarchical about this mixture: the poetic and imagistic seem to encompass the other modes of explanation—not to supersede them, but to provide some ultimate ground of understanding—as becomes clearer in a subsequent section in which Maclean describes the setting of the catastrophe, the gulch characterized by its geology and contextualized within geological history:

> The Smokejumpers were on their way to a blowup, a catastrophic collision of fire, clouds, and winds. With almost dramatic fitness, the collision was to occur where vast geological confrontations had occurred millions and millions of years ago—where old ocean beds, the bottoms of inland seas, were hoisted vertically by causes too long ago to be now identified and were then thrust forward by gravity into and over other ocean beds, cracking and crumbling them and creasing them into folds and creating a geological area called in the subdued language of scientists the "Disturbed Belt," a belt that includes in its geological history much of not only northwestern Montana but western Alberta and eastern British Columbia. (44)

Maclean goes on to describe how the "Disturbed Belt" is itself part of an "overthrust formation" that stretches from Alaska to Mexico. I am tempted to reproduce the whole passage, for its effect is dizzying and not captured by paraphrase, as Maclean progressively expands both the geographical and the temporal context. It culminates: "As the western continent was raised, squeezed, and compressed, great slabs of sedimentary layers slid over each other inland or eastward for a distance varying from a few miles to a hundred miles or more" (45). It is as if we were backing up to progressively approximate a God's-eye view of time and space, to witness the spasms of the planet itself.

Beyond the basic description of the lay of the land that the firefighters and their would-be rescuers had to navigate, this geographical excursus is unnecessary to explain "how [the Smokejumpers] got to their crosses, and what it was like on the way"—and yet it is somehow essential to the sense of the events' significance, of their magnitude. The Smokejumpers' encounter with the Mann Gulch fire occurs against a backdrop of almost incomprehensible temporal and spatial immensity and violence.

Maclean furthermore links the mystery of what happened to the Smokejumpers to the mystery of what shaped the landscape, noting two cliffs that seem once to have been connected by an arch:

> There are also missing parts to the story of the lonely crosses ahead of us, almost invisible in deep grass near the top of the mountain. What if, by searching the earth and even the sky for these missing parts, we should find enough of them to see catastrophe change into the shape of remembered tragedy? Unless we are willing to escape into sentimentality or fantasy, often the best we can do with catastrophes, even our own, is to find out exactly what happened and restore some of the missing parts—hopefully, even the arch to the sky. (46–47)

While I find this particular analogy somewhat contrived, on the whole Maclean's description of the geological background of the tragedy is evocative and compelling—but what, if anything, does it reveal about the actual character of the events of Mann Gulch?

Maclean's use of natural landscape and natural history as spiritual backdrop is continuous with that of the nineteenth-century Romantics, and he would therefore seem susceptible to the criticisms of Romanticism as ungrounded, sentimental, confused, indulging in the pathetic fallacy; as Robert Hughes describes it, the Romantics "learn[ed] to see nature as the fingerprint of God's creation and thus as a direct clue to his intentions. . . . It became a medium of endless wonder, edification, and joy. And of muddle, too: for extreme nature lovers passed from trying to find God in Nature to conflating Nature with God."[35]

Parts of *Fire* such as the missing keystone may be subject to such criticism, but what saves Maclean from falling into a hopeless "muddle" is that he does not go so far as to claim a specific or explicit "meaning" of the grandeur of the setting of his story or its resonance with the events. He allows the image to remain image, and, furthermore, he retains a degree of irony, puncturing high-flown description with the mundane and the factual.

Still, the power of the images speaks for itself, and that power and its resonance implies some awful reality (in the original sense of "awful," eliciting awe) dimly apprehended. This reality is "the universe"—the matrix within human beings live—and it is, therefore, what Maclean needs, and what we need, to make sense of after the challenge to sense presented by the Mann Gulch fire:

Do not be deceived . . . by the scenic beauty of the Gates of the Mountains into believing that the confrontations and terrors of nature are obsolescences frozen in stone, like the battles of satyrs in Greek bas-relief, remnants of mythology and witnessed if ever by dinosaurs and now only by seismographs. It is easy for us to assume that as the result of modern science "we have conquered nature," that nature is now confined to beaches for children and to national parks where the few remaining grizzly bears have been shot with tranquilizers and removed to above the timberline, supposedly for their safety and our own. But we should be prepared for the possibility . . . that the terror of the universe has not yet fossilized and the universe has not run out of blowups.

Yet we should also go on wondering if there is not some shape, form, design as of artistry in this universe we are entertaining that is composed of catastrophes and missing parts. (46)

If the explicit intent of the work is to explain how the catastrophe happened and to memorialize the fallen, the underlying intent is to grapple with and convey something of the character of "the universe" as it comes into view in the Smokejumpers' confrontation with it in Mann Gulch. The quote above suggests that terrible as the loss of the young men is, it would be a terrible loss of a different order—about which we must admittedly be ambivalent—if "the terror of the universe" *had* fossilized, if "modern science" (and we might add, rationalization) had confined or domesticated or banished all the forces that might threaten human welfare. In such a universe, there would be no catastrophe, but therefore no tragic heroes either—and nothing resistant to subordination to the calculations of the human ego. (One thinks of the Crystal Palace of Dostoevsky's Underground Man.)

The attraction of the story of Mann Gulch—for terrible as it is, it compelled Maclean and, as he tells it, compels the reader—is, I think, that in its basic facts it appears as such a confrontation with "the universe"—with "nature" as that whole of reality beyond human institutions and not subject to human control, a reality that includes not only physical laws but the ground of sense and significance—what one might call *myth* insofar as it refers to those ultimate and normative foundations of judgment and action which are inextricably bound up with images and narrative structures, if not necessarily specific stories of divine or supernatural beings. Our grasp of these basic conditions of making sense of human action—good, evil, heroism, justice, love, and so on—cannot be extricated from images and stories of good and evil, of heroism and villainy, of love and vengeance; the stories themselves are not "myth" as I use it here, but myth is at once what we come to know through them and the condition of our comprehension of them.

Thus in *Fire* Maclean seeks, with arguable success, not to impose tragic or mythical sense on a catastrophe in order to give it consoling meaning, but rather to convey the sense that the events seem properly to have—a sense which cannot be grasped, represented, or evoked except indirectly, though narrative and image, because it is the foundation and condition of this knowledge rather than a fact to be known: myth—as the ground of sense and judgment, the ground of our knowledge, the whole within which the various aspects of our experience have their meaning—always and necessarily remains (in some degree) tacit.

Fundamental to the ground of sense as Maclean finds and conveys it in *Fire* is what has been called the *sublime*: that which exceeds human comprehension and may be inimical to human strivings, yet which demands that we reconcile ourselves to it.

ON THE SUBLIME

While the word "sublime" does not appear in *Fire,* Maclean wrote about it in his essay on eighteenth-century poetry and criticism, noting that the sublime has been conceived in three intersecting ways: as a creation of God, an effect of the natural world, and a characteristic of language.[36] These three aspects merge in eighteenth-century lyric poetry, conceived by its creators as "an expression in *language* 'elevated from common Language the most that is possible,' reflecting a *soul* transported by the most magnificent of natural *objects*, such a soul and such natural objects being, in turn, creative expressions of the Divine Creator."[37] So Maclean's conception of the sublime is that of a spiritual quality belonging to the objective world (that is, not merely human fancy) but generally only accessible through representation in language.

The idea of the sublime as linguistic is perhaps the oldest, going back to Longinus's seminal essay "On the Sublime" (*Peri hypsous*), which focuses on style—on the features of writing or oratory that are characteristic of greatness, features that do not merely persuade the audience but carry them away. For Longinus, "the Sublime, wherever it occurs, consists in a certain loftiness and excellence of language" which overcomes our rational judgment. "To believe or not is usually in our own power; but the Sublime, acting with an imperious and irresistible force, sways every reader whether he will or no."[38] This is what has come to be called the "rhetorical sublime," as opposed to what one might call the "objective sublime," the sublime as a characteristic of those objects or aspects of the world that awe and astonish.

The sublime in writing is not, however, *purely* rhetorical for Longinus, but rooted in "greatness of soul."[39] This is to say that the rhetorical sublime, to be truly sublime, must be rooted in the objective sublime: it must express something beyond language, in "lofty ideas" and images of what is truly great—for Longinus, the noble and the divine and most paradigmatically "divine nature in its true light, as something spotless, great, and pure," which he sees represented, for instance, in Homer's description of the mortals and mortal world shaking with the passage of striding Poseidon, or in the opening of Genesis: "God said let there be light, and there was."[40] Longinus's five sources of the sublime (great thoughts, strong emotion, figuration, noble diction, and dignified composition or structure) jumble together the linguistic and nonlinguistic—respectively, the sublimity created or conveyed by the manner of representation and the sublimity of what is represented—and Longinus does not make a point of distinguishing "form" and "content." His account implies that the two cannot be sharply differentiated. What we know of the gods is conveyed through those literary works or passages that strike us as adequate to them, which is to say, adequately sublime.

Later critics, beginning in the eighteenth century, focused not on sublime language but on its source or its object, on the nonlinguistic correlate which accounted for the sublimity of sublime language. This source, generally speaking, could be categorized as grandeur in nature (the vast starry sky, craggy mountains, the endless ocean) as an expression or manifestation of divine grandeur.

Subjectively, then, the sublime is what moves me, what elicits my awe, admiration, eros; objectively, it is what is supremely "great," and definitions of the sublime have tended to characterize this greatness in terms of its divine provenance or of its ungraspable or unrepresentable character. These two qualities can be seen as correlate—God is that which is beyond human grasp. For the eighteenth-century critics, the question is: why do we take pleasure in the terrifying? Or: why are we moved and compelled by sensible impressions in ways other than we might expect, based on utilitarian rationality? And the answer is, for British theorists of the sublime including Edmund Burke, that what so moves us is a manifestation of the divine.[41] The apprehension of the sublime for these Enlightenment-era theorists is therefore ultimately affirmative of a normatively ordered universe, a universe whose order accords with the human need for significance, even if it does not always respond to our desire for happiness.

But the reality, the ontological status, of this order beyond what we can grasp, is a matter for skepticism—a skepticism which Philip Shaw argues is present from (at least) Burke's *A Philosophical Enquiry into the Origins of Our Ideas of the Sublime and the Beautiful*, which indirectly exposed the "fault line in the history of the sublime," the tension between conceiving the sublime as a quality of the world and as a quality of language. If "it is language . . . that brings about the transformation of the world, enabling us to hymn the vastness of the cathedral or the depths of the ravine,"[42] then we might wonder whether the sublime in fact has some objective correlate or is merely a rhetorical creation.

Furthermore, to the extent that rationalization marginalizes religion from everyday life and the world is interpreted in secular rather than religious terms, the sublime becomes decoupled from the divine, and the emphasis shifts from sublimity as the manifestation of God's power to sublimity as the experience of what is simply beyond our grasp. Accompanying this decoupling is growing skepticism regarding the existence or objectivity of any transcendent meaning or ground of human life and suspicion regarding any pretense to knowledge of such a ground. The trajectory culminates in the "postmodern sublime," the representation or apprehension of the sheer fact or existence of the nonrepresentable, the unlimited.[43] As Jean-Luc Nancy puts it, "The sublime is: *that* there is an image, hence a limit, along whose edge unlimitation makes itself felt."[44] Whatever is beyond that edge *may* underwrite a humanly meaningful order, or—more probably, according to the current temper—it may not, as in the vision of the universe governed by sheerly physical forces, or a world determined by vast humanly created economic or technological systems become terrifyingly independent of human purposes.

In *Fire*, then, Maclean seems to be looking for a sublime that is neither merely formal—that is, simply what is beyond our ken—nor divine in the traditional sense—that is, the manifestation of a supernatural being or beings, of a creator concerned with human welfare. Through image and figuration, he evokes a sense of the awesome power of nature as more than natural. Natural immensities become an image of the pervasive power of the universe as it governs human life and therefore demands to be faced up to—confronted, respected, and comprehended to the limits of our power. The work may be conceived as an attempt to demonstrate that just because the sublime is something we summon in language doesn't make it unreal. Maclean can't *prove* this; he can only show it to be more compelling than the alternative, which would be to deny any validity to the sense that the Smokejumpers' confrontation with the Mann Gulch fire reveals something transcending the full grasp of human reason—that our awe and terror are, or at least may be, a response to the apprehension of something truly awesome or terrible,[45] and something, therefore, an encounter with which cannot be senseless or meaningless, cannot but be significant—and therefore not just catastrophic but tragic. Maclean wants to show the fire as representative of something ultimate that demands confrontation: for the men, in the form of the catastrophe they could not escape; for Maclean, in the form of the catastrophic event that demands understanding.

SUBLIMITY AND CATHARSIS

Terror and pity are, per Aristotle, the central emotions of the catharsis or "purgation" occasioned by tragedy; if the sublime is that which terrifies, it should then be essential to that catharsis. Near the end of Part 2, Maclean gives an explicit account of his conception of "purgation":

> Near the end of many tragedies it seems right that there should be moments when the story stops and looks back for something it left behind and finds it because of things it learned, as it were, by having lived through the story. . . . Usually they are announced by minor characters, and generally they are about nature. We are so often wrong about nature that it comes as a relief of some kind to be right about it, especially after there has been some great disruption in it. Such moments of relief near the end of tragedy must be important parts of what from classical times has been called the purgation of tragedy. At times it seems as if tragedy tries at the end to take away some of its own tragedy, and if some tragedies never restore our stability, at least most of them allow some success in struggling to attain some stability on our own. (281–82)

If what follows is, as Maclean forecasts, the tragedy's "purgation"—which is to say, the revelation or attainment of some knowledge of "nature"—then there are two or perhaps three successive moments to this purgation—first the purgation of explanation, and then the purgation of terror and pity.

The first of these is a tour de force explication of one of the final remaining mysteries—how Dodge's escape fire could burn straight up toward the top of the ridge (so Sallee and Rumsey, the other two survivors, could more or less run alongside it up to the ridge and to safety), while the main fire could burn in a perpendicular direction, toward the head of the gulch (forcing the rest of the men to run up the gulch and eventually overtaking them). The explanation is essentially that the heat of the main fire created a sucking wind pulling in the opposite direction of the wind blowing the fire up the gulch; when Dodge lit his match the two winds momentarily neutralized each other such that Dodge's fire simply burned upslope, as fire will do absent other forces.

For Maclean, therefore, purgation is a kind of knowledge. The consolation of tragedy, the release from pity and fear, comes with and through understanding—in this case, understanding the (material and efficient) causes of things.

But knowledge of nature (in this case, literally knowledge of the natural world) is not sufficient. Certainly its utilitarian consequences are not adequate consolation. Maclean does include an excursus on what fire science and fire safety have gained from study of the Mann Gulch fire, but follows it with: "After saying what I had been building up to about the influence the Mann Gulch fire had on future firefighting, I went back to work. I felt better, though, for the interlude" (223). This kind of knowledge can only be a marginal and temporary consolation. Nor does "pure knowledge," the sheer fact of understanding the *how* and the *why*, seem to be enough. It is, first, unattainable in its entirety, at least in this case. At the very end of Part 2, after the account of how the two fires could have behaved as they did, Maclean considers the final question of what kept the other Smokejumpers from following Rumsey and Sallee straight up the ridge—why they headed up the gulch, eventually to be overtaken by the fire. He recounts that he, Laird Robinson, and the two survivors had come up with three possibilities after their investigative return to Mann Gulch—that it was a branch of the main fire or Dodge's fire or a combination of the two—and recalls that "we split our four votes among these three alternatives, with each of us willing to admit he might be wrong and could never be sure that he was right" (289).

Dodge's fire may, then, have been responsible for the men's deaths after all, if it had prevented them from going up to the ridge. The exact truth will never be known. Though understated, this is, to say the least, surprising coming after the pages of detailed account, reflecting years of painstaking work, of investigation aimed at determining precisely what had happened and in particular at exonerating Dodge's fire from any part in the Smokejumpers' deaths.

In Aristotle's theory of tragedy, catharsis is of course something undergone not by the characters but by the audience as they see events unfold. The final uncertainty of what happened at Mann Gulch indicates one reason for Maclean's use of narrative rather than dramatic form in *Fire*—a traditional dramatic presentation would indicate a definiteness that the 1949 events cannot have. The true story that can be told is Maclean's story.

If purgation is a matter of knowledge, the impossibility of knowing with certainty what had happened would seem to be fatal to the task of finding tragic form for the Mann Gulch catastrophe. The conclusion of *Fire*, however, indicates that "the facts," while vital, are not the ultimate determinant of sense Maclean is seeking. It is not only because of this final indeterminacy that Maclean turns to a different kind of sensemaking beyond "explanation" in the final pages of the work; rather, the second moment of purgation brings to the forefront what has been the backdrop of the whole work: some inhuman magnitude, on the one hand, and on the other hand some consummation of Maclean's own personal struggle with his identity and acceptance of his own approaching death.

TOTAL CONFLAGRATION (THE
ELEVATION OF RETROSPECT)

By the end of Part 2 Maclean has reached the limits of what can be gleaned
from the testimony of the survivors, the evidence left behind, and scientific
and mathematical modeling about what happened in Mann Gulch from
5:55 to 5:57 p.m. on August 5, 1949—from when the men passed Dodge and
his fire, from when they disappeared from the view of Rumsey and Sallee,
who had reached the ridge, until the fire caught them.

> The last Sallee can recall seeing them, "They were angling up the slope in the
> unburned grass and fairly close to the edge of the fire Dodge had set." Then the
> smoke and the Great Ambiguity settle in. But I expect to see more. I have long
> expected to catch glimpses of them as far as they went. Could you expect less
> from a boy who grew up in the woods and grew old as a schoolteacher and so
> spent most of his life staying close to the young who are elite and select and, by
> definition, often in trouble? I came to Mann Gulch expecting to catch glimpses
> of them as far as they go. That's why I came. (277)

There is something terribly evocative about the image of the young men
disappearing into the smoke, never to be seen again alive, as if they have left
this world for another. What that image evokes is, I think, the ultimate object
of *Fire*, the object Maclean sought in Mann Gulch and seeks to represent in
the work: he identifies with these young men who lived the life he once lived,
but lived it to the extreme limit, and beyond. He pities them for the terror they
faced, for their untimely end, but he also finds in their story the image of an
encounter with something absolute—awful but compelling in its very abso-
luteness. This is what he tries to convey in the final descriptions.[46]

Maclean describes the blowup in three different ways. He begins: "We
would not have started to follow the course of wildfire if we had not assumed
that all of us, when called upon, could view an earthly scene from imaginative perspectives," invoking the Sky Spirits from Hardy's *The Dynasts*, "who
comment upon tragedies of man from distant horizons" (279). At the most
basic level, Maclean is saying that the storyteller needs to be able to imagine
all that is essential to the story, even (in a true story) what he has no record
of. The allusion to the Sky Spirits, however, implies that he means something
more: the possibility of and need for an objective perspective which only
the storyteller, not the characters, can provide. Maclean then evokes Hardy's
poem "The Convergence of the Twain," on the sinking of the *Titanic,* excerpt-
ing from the poem:

Alien they seemed to be:

> No mortal eye could see
> The intimate welding of their later history,
>   Or sign that they were bent
>   By paths coincident
> On being anon twin halves of one august event,
>   Till the Spinner of the Years
> Said "Now!"

Maclean summarizes the analogy between the collision of ship and iceberg and the convergence of men and fire: "Hardy's convergence is between the elite, brightly lit, and fastest ship of its time, the *Titanic*, with an iceberg moving inexorably out of 'a solitude of the sea / Deep from human vanity'" (279).

The poem describes the disaster of the *Titanic* as fated—foreseen and decreed by some consciousness and power outside and beyond the human actors involved—and through the allusion and the analogy—ship and men, iceberg and fire—Maclean invites us to see the Mann Gulch fire similarly. But what does this mean? Not, surely, that either disaster was the product of some sort of supernatural intervention; the actions of human beings and the forces of nature are perfectly sufficient to explain each "convergence." And it is notable that Hardy refers not to God or gods but to "[the] Immanent Will that stirs and urges everything" and "the Spinner of the Years"—not a personal deity interested in human affairs, but some impersonal force.

What the poem seems to dramatize, rather, is the event from a distant perspective, in both time and space: a perspective that, looking backward, traces the history of ship and iceberg to see them as *destined* for collision—a perspective "from a distant horizon" that can therefore make sense of what, from "the view from the ground" (279), must seem to come out of nowhere.

To describe the events as Hardy's poem does is to see them as necessary, as the product of an order which is not just that of physical laws. The poem does not simply assert the facts as foreordained; it suggests that the *Titanic*'s fate was seeded in the hubris of its creation. It begins with references to vanity and pride and proceeds by picturing the ship's powerful engine and its luxurious features now dark and silent and sludge-covered at the bottom of the ocean ("Steel chambers, late the pyres / Of her salamandrine fires, / Cold currents thrid, and turn to rhythmic tidal lyres")—an Ecclesiastical vision, redeemed only by the strange beauty of Hardy's mannered and baroque language. The poem arguably conveys a sense of all human life and striving as a kind of hubris, beautiful but doomed. The sunk ship becomes a *memento mori*, a universal image of death, the Immanent Will and the Spinner of the Years images of the implacable force that thwarts human reachings and overreachings.

Hardy's vision is bleaker than Maclean's, devoid of the humanity of *Fire* (literally devoid of any reference to *people*), but through the allusion Maclean suggests that, like the sinking of the *Titanic* in the poem, the catastrophe of Mann Gulch must be made sense of from some hovering perspective that can see the events as unfolding according to some order beyond human intentionality but not mere random chance. Maclean pictures this order here as "Geometry":

> From the ground, our approaching tragedy, like the *Titanic*'s, had been linear, arithmetic, and two-dimensional. From the ground, it had occurred on one line as Behind caught up to Ahead, but the Spinner of the Years, viewing wildfire and young men from an even more distant horizon than our own, would see Geometry as well as Arithmetic in what was occurring at lower elevations. Not just Geometry but Solid Geometry—lines becoming curves and curves closing into circles and circles blowing up into spherical monsters whirling burning branches into the sky. . . .
>
> In between these geometries for something like four minutes was a painfully moving line with pieces of it dropping out until there came an end to biology. Then it was pure geometry, and later still the solid geometry of concrete crosses. (280–81)

Literally, of course, Maclean is just referring to the fact that after the blowup, the fire would be burning at the men from all sides, until it overcomes them. But the nominalization and abstraction—"Behind," "Ahead," "Geometry," and, later, "biology"—makes the Smokejumpers' lost race for their lives into a clash between human life and something enormous and inhuman. The capitalization of "Geometry" suggests a divine being, but this divinity is wholly impersonal: mathematical, even if monstrous.

It is notable that Maclean identifies himself—or the storyteller—with Hardy's Sky Spirits, and even with the Spinner of the Years, who is the one who sees what Maclean describes. Obviously the storyteller is not the one who determines ahead of time what happens. For Maclean and Hardy, there is no intelligent being determining events according to some divine plan. In Maclean's account, even the Spinner of the Years is described not as causing or decreeing events but as *seeing* what happens according to the determining forces of Geometry and Arithmetic. But the storyteller occupies the position of the hovering spirit who sees, though only retrospectively, the sense and significance of things.

This passage suggests an order of significance that is not precisely a moral order, meting out "poetic justice," nor a divine one, proceeding according to some providential plan, nor merely a scientific one, reflecting nothing but the blind laws of physics, chemistry, biology. This is the order of myth as defined earlier; the events seem to reflect the foundational and finally unknowable determinants of the significance of human action that encompass the moral and the scientific but ultimately transcend them. This is the consolation of tragedy—to find the events as reflective of a larger meaning or order, imagining the death of the Smokejumpers as an encounter with what, in the final section, will appear as the ultimate destructive force of the universe, with the end of the world. There is something heroic in that very confrontation.

Again the question arises of what all this has to do with reality. One can say that it is entirely fantastical—there aren't "really" Sky Spirits; the fire is just fire, physical process. But if the account *works*, if it is compelling and plausible—if it seems not merely invented but to refer to something "really there"—it is because the events themselves seem images of deeper structures of meaning, which demand to be represented, inhabited, and, to the extent possible, understood.

The effort to see the catastrophe not just as a senseless accident but as having tragic form illuminates the conditions of sense of a human life. That sense must transcend the individual life and not end with it, for what premature death makes devastatingly clear is that if the sense of my life depends on my own enjoyment or fulfillment, the universe will often make nonsense of my life. The figures of the Sky Spirits and of Geometry suggest such a sense, one that is not simply consoling but demands a kind of dispossession, an identification with a perspective outside oneself, a decentering of consciousness, seeing one's own life as "a thin line moving among these expanding solids" of an order that encompasses and will outlast it.

We are socialized and instinctually disposed to inhabit the world from the perspective of our own egos—to make sense of things with reference to how they impact us, how they further or hinder our own needs and desires. One might say that tragedy reflects and educates us to a perspective that is decentered, displaced from that of our own egos—that is, a perspective outside of oneself, even if one cannot precisely locate that "outside" except as a kind of relative objectivity—and dispossesses us of the sense that our lives are ours to freely determine in accordance with our wishes.

For Marie Borroff, the Geometry passage is the proper end of the book as Maclean left it. She argues that none of what follows, "neither the analogy of the atomic bombs, nor the analogy of Christ on the cross, nor the final analogy, much as I am moved by it, of the lonely suffering of his wife in terminal cancer, really works."[47] I would suggest that this "not really working" may be intrinsic to the task Maclean has set for himself, and that in his final attempts we see the movement from a tragic sense to one I would call "apocalyptic." To see this we need to proceed to the final moments of Maclean's "purgation."

THE END OF TRAGEDY: "JUST CONFLAGRATION"

In a modern and secular world, not only can the sublime background of sense not be directly represented, we must continually confront our uncertainty that there really is such a ground. Maclean ends his book with such a confrontation. Part 2 concludes with the chilling observation that "in the conflagration that was about to occur, no component any longer had any individual responsibility for the simple reason that in a moment there were no individual components. Just conflagration." With this dissolution of individual actions and events into "a world where human values and seemingly natural laws no longer apply. . . . The Mann Gulch fire was passing beyond issues and settlements into a world of pictures—perhaps more exactly into thoughts that pictorialize and feel and cannot reduce themselves to numbers" (289). After the work of explanation—everything that goes into the graph that shows the tragedy to have been inescapable—some further sensemaking is necessary. That this further sensemaking can finally be achieved only through images perhaps already indicates something about the character of the ground of sense—that it cannot be finally proven or definitively articulated but only compellingly evoked.

Part 3 attempts this "pictorialization," which Maclean connects to the kind of objectivity alluded to in his invocation of Hardy. "It would be natural near the end," he writes "to try to divest the fire of any personal liability to those who died in it and to become for a moment a distant and detached spectator. It might be possible then, if ever, to see fire in something like total perspective as it became total conflagration" (293). This attempt first represents the fire as a grotesque and confusing—perhaps inassimilable—multiplicity:

> Pictures, then, of a big fire are pictures of many realities, designed so they change into each other and fit ultimately into a single picture of one monster becoming another monster. The pictures and the monsters are untroubled by mathematics. The monster becomes one as it extends itself simultaneously as a monster and a real animal or more likely just as part of a real animal—after it disgorges itself, all that can be seen of it from afar are its fried gray intestines. Oddly, as destruction comes close to being total, destruction erects for brief moments into the sexual and quickly sinks back again into destruction. The two don't look much different, and they aren't and they are. (294)

What the images at the end collectively convey is a nightmarish quality—the point, it seems, is horror, and the *breakdown* of sense. The wildfire "procreat[es] its meanings" and because of this proliferation "some of what even a seasoned firefighter sees never seems real" (294). The phantasmagoria resembles the Book of Revelation; the fire has become an image of the end of the world, an apocalyptic vision. The old order is passing away, and what is to come we can scarcely imagine.

To this point we are arguably still in the realm of the tragic—the tragic sublime, the limit or horizon of sense, but a horizon that still allows for the possibility of sense even if it is a terrible kind of sense, the sense of "this whole cockeyed world that probably always makes its own kind of sense and beauty but not always ours" (208). The fire is monstrous, but the men therefore perish heroically in a battle with a monster. There is, however, something beyond the theological, and that is "the nuclear," which seems at the end to threaten even this tragic sense. In his last image of the fire, Maclean finally compares the smoke rising from Mann Gulch to the mushroom cloud, "the outer symbol of the inner fear of the explosive power of the universe" (295).

> When last seen, the tri-visual figure had stretched out and was on its way, far, far, far away, looking like death and looking back at its dead and looking forward to its dead yet to come. Perhaps it could see all of us.
>
> No one could know the power of it. It stretched until it became particles on the horizon, where it may have joined the company of the Sky Sprits as particles, knowing what we do not know, probably something nuclear. (295)

This is a grim vision—what abides, beyond human life and human striving, is the power of destruction; history is figured as a procession of death, the dead of the past and the dead yet to come, which will include "all of us," Maclean and me and you, gentle reader. In the end, the atomic metaphor suggests, it may include all of humanity, phylogeny recapitulating ontogeny. The grimness is softened by Maclean's humane irony, but that is for the moment the only consolation offered—the consolation of consciousness, of the possibility of putting ourselves into the position of Thomas Hardy's Sky Spirits, imagining and comprehending the destruction and the end.

Maclean does not end here but goes on to reaffirm the final heroism of the Smokejumpers in confronting their deaths. Then, from the elevated if not soaring language of his benediction ("By this final act . . . ") there is in the final paragraphs a marked deflation from the poetic to the soberingly prosaic. A short few sentences about the time of death as recorded on the men's watches. A promise from "the Office of Air Operations and Fire Management of Region One of the United States Forest Service" to care for the crosses marking the location where each man fell. And finally a short and personal note from Maclean—"I, an old man, have written this fire report" (301)—that reads more as a postscript than a conclusion, musing finally: "Perhaps it is not odd, at the end of this tragedy where nothing much was left of the elite who came from the sky but courage struggling for oxygen, that I have often found myself thinking of my wife on her brave and lonely way to death" (301).

The ending of *Fire* is anticlimactic, and may seem inadequate.[48] Poignant as it is, the allusion to Maclean's wife initially seems (or seemed to me) out of place, certainly at odds with the emphasis throughout the book on the exceptionality of the men in their youngness and their eliteness, and with the evocation of the terrible and sublime terrain—literal and figurative—in which they struggled and fell.

But I would argue that the ending is integral to the form of the work, even if it is in some sense a failure—much as Wayne Booth came to see the unwieldy form of the whole as succeeding in the poignancy of its unrealized attempt.[49] The ending brings the story back to Maclean, and it is a sad image, even with all he has achieved—in his life, in the work we have just finished reading—he is left thinking of his wife dying, now dead, and himself an "old man" who has also lost many others and is bound soon to follow them. Perhaps in itself death does not present a problem of sense, but Maclean has raised the specter of the atom bomb and the end of the world, and with these associations the final word of the book again suggests a discontinuity with future generations.

For Booth, Maclean was bound to fail because the story he wanted to tell was "too complicated,"[50] but the real difficulty of the task Maclean took on goes beyond the particularity of *this* story and to the problem of telling a modern tragedy, which is perhaps (in one of its forms) the very problem of modernity.

Had he lived longer, Maclean might have found a more powerful and "rounded" ending to *Fire*, and it may even have been a "better" book, but the form as it is reflects something essential about the late-modern condition, the necessarily provisional character of any conviction we might achieve about the deeper significance of our lives. Yet at the same time it is as compelling a testament as there could be that there is such significance to be glimpsed if never fully comprehended, and to the necessity of seeking it, with all our power, to the very end.

THE LIMITS OF TRAGIC FORM

In trying to grasp the form of *Fire*—to make sense of Maclean's own efforts to make sense, and our experience of their success and failure—we must, I have argued, reference something like the sublime—that which is ultimately beyond human comprehension or control, which impresses itself upon human experience, which is at once inimical to human welfare, as destructive power, but also a fundamental and perhaps essential source of the meaning of our humanity, the extreme limits in relation to which human beings define themselves.

Maclean briefly alludes to the possibility that the destructive power will ultimately be totally destructive—acknowledging that the overarching narrative of humanity has an end, the end of the world. The idea of a true end to humanity undermines the sense of human life; the continuation of humanity has always been the condition of the sense of human life—the individual life ends, but the race goes on; even if the world ends, the saved live on in God. If, in modernity, a true end becomes a possibility, we do not know how to think it. One might say that to be able to think it we would need the secular analogue to everlasting life—the idea that it matters absolutely what we do, the need to be "good for nothing"—really nothing. This predicament is what the apocalyptic literature of the twentieth century demands that we confront and with which it brings us into contact with in our attempt to understand and judge it.

In the end, Maclean retreats—as all of us must, to the extent that we must continue to live in the human world—from the abyss of the end of the world back to limited if still terrible ends: the deaths of the Smokejumpers, his wife's death, his own coming death. The terror in *Fire* is the terror of nature, and while coming to terms with the reality of this terror—with "the explosive power of the universe"—demands a kind of dispossession, it doesn't yet call into question the viability of the very conditions of our humanity. In the next chapter, I turn to Cormac McCarthy's *Blood Meridian*, in which the terror of the universe is actually the terror of the bivalent nature of human beings, of that in human beings which would undermine the conditions of our own humanity. This is the ultimate threat to the intelligibility of the human world, and therefore the ultimate challenge for contemporary literary form.

NOTES

1. Maclean, *Young Men and Fire*, 207–8, my emphasis. References from here forward will be to this text unless otherwise noted.

2. Marie Borroff notes that "when Maclean spoke of Shelley's poems 'The Cloud' and 'Ode to the West Wind' in an earlier version of one part of the Mann Gulch fire story, he said that they were 'mixtures of the poetic and the scientific imaginations'" ("The Achievement of Norman Maclean," 127).

3. In the Publisher's Note to *Fire* and in a personal interview. Thomas later argued that Maclean was also was stymied by the mathematics and the need to find an adequate representation of "inevitability" (Thomas, "The Achievement of 'Young Men and Fire'").

4. Conversation with John Maclean, July 10, 2015.

5. Weltzien, *The Norman Maclean Reader*, xxii.

6. James, *The Tragic Muse*, 4.

7. Aristotle, *Poetics*, 13.

8. Aristotle, 12.

9. Aristotle, 15.

10. Gallie, *Philosophy and the Historical Understanding*, 1.

11. Brooks, *Reading for the Plot*, 19.

12. Brooks, 12.

13. Barthes, *S/Z*, 17 ff. Barthes designates these, respectively, the proairetic and hermeneutic codes; discussed in Brooks, *Reading for the Plot*, 18.

14. Kermode, *The Sense of an Ending*, 18.

15. Freud, "Mourning and Melancholia," 243.

16. Homans, *The Ability to Mourn*, 26.

17. Freud, "Mourning and Melancholia," 245.

18. McFarland, Nichols, and Maclean, "Montana Memories," 81.

19. Ray, *Terror and the Sublime in Art and Critical Theory*, 1.

20. Ray, 2.

21. Thanks to David Wellbery for this observation. I consider elegy in Chapter 3.

22. The manuscript was broken into short "chapters" (as Maclean referred to them) which in the published work are not numbered but marked by tree icons; I will refer to these as "sections."

23. Eagleton calls this (in a version articulated by Dorothea Krook) the "popular-academic" conception—though he contests that "hardly a word of this definition generally holds true" unless one restricts tragedy to a very limited number of works (*Sweet Violence*, 7).

24. *The Anatomy of Criticism*, 207.

25. *Ibid.*, 209.

26. See Felski, *Rethinking Tragedy*, 8–9.

27. Steiner, *The Death of Tragedy*, 193.

28. Maclean, "Episode, Scene, Speech, and Word: The Madness of Lear," 599–600.

29. Maclean, 601.

30. See in particular the discussion of Maclean in Toole, *Waiting For Godot in Sarajevo*.

31. Frye, *Anatomy of Criticism*, 207.

32. Frye, 210.

33. "USFS 1919: The Ranger, The Cook, and a Hole in the Sky," in Maclean, *A River Runs Through It, and Other Stories*, 127.

34. This is not to deny that characters in tragedies may be strong personalities and that these personalities may be well developed in their presentation, especially when the tragic conflict is essentially a conflict of character or moral decision, as in *Hamlet*.

35. Hughes, *American Visions*, 138.

36. He associates each of these aspects with a particular critic or theorist: "the sublime as an effect of the Divine Creator (Addison), the sublime as an effect of natural objects upon the natural mechanism of man (Burke), and the sublime as an effect of

language (Lowth)" ("From Action to Image: Theories of the Lyric in the Eighteenth Century," 418).

37. Maclean, 418; the internal quotation is from Joseph Trapp, *Lectures on Poetry* (London, 1742), 204.

38. Longinus, *On the Sublime*, I.3–4.

39. Longinus, *On the Sublime*, XI.2.

40. Longinus, IX. 8–9; Maclean makes this point: "Even though Longinus is interested primarily in analyzing literary qualities, he makes clear…that sublimity is a quality reflected by certain natural objects and that, in turn, sublime objects reflect the presence of a Divine Creator and his intentions in respect to man" ("From Action to Image: Theories of the Lyric in the Eighteenth Century," 415).

41. The Kantian answer—that through the apprehension of the limits of reason, reason affirms its own powers—may be compatible with the British answer, but it deemphasizes and effectively denies any significant status to the object of awe.

42. Shaw, *The Sublime*, 6.

43. "The canonical definition of the sublime: the sublime is the presentation of the nonpresentable or, more rigorously, to take up the formula of Lyotard, the presentation (of this): that there is the nonpresentable." Philip Lacoue-Labarth, "The Sublime Truth," in Librett, *Of the Sublime: Presence in Question*, 27.

44. Jean-Luc Nancy, "The Sublime Offering," in Librett, 38.

45. One might say that Maclean wants to show that not only our ordinary passions, defined by Dennis as those "whose cause is clearly comprehended by him who feels it," but our "enthusiasms," passions whose "cause is not clearly comprehended by him who feels them" (*The Grounds of Criticism*, 1704, cited in Shaw, 31), have reference.

46. The first passage I discuss in what follows is actually in Part 2, *before* the final reckoning about the escape fire. But I would make the editorial argument that it might well have been moved to Part 3 and at least is of a kind with the passages in Part 3, in working through "image" rather than scientific explanation.

47. Borroff, "The Achievement of Norman Maclean," 131.

48. As it did to Marie Borroff, who gently relates a similar sense that the ending fails: "If his creative energies had lasted, he would surely have been able to contrive an ending equal in power to the memorable final paragraphs of 'A River Runs Through It.'" (131).

49. "The plot of the book is the plot of the struggle to tell it: the narrator says, in effect, 'I tried, and tried, and tried again, and just like life itself, the material overpowered me, but I kept on trying, and failed.' And thus he succeeded." (Booth, "The Struggle to Tell the Story of the Struggle to Get the Story Told," 51).

50. Booth, 51.

Chapter Two

Beyond Morality, Beyond Nihilism

McCarthy's Blood Meridian *and the Ethics of Apocalypse*

Where force is sovereign, justice is absolutely unreal.

Simone Weil, *The Need for Roots*

Cormac McCarthy's *Blood Meridian* may stand alone in American literature in its seeming insistence on depravity and inhumanity as the defining features of human beings. Not only uncompromisingly unromanticizing but gleefully deromanticizing of the American West, the work could be called the apotheosis of the American apocalyptic sublime as it emerges at the end of *Young Men and Fire*: an image of the end of humanity as we know it, or as we have dreamed it to be.

The idea of America has always been bound up with the sense of a historical trajectory toward something new, a new condition of humanity, the departure from the old world, old ways, old institutions—the utopian dream of the Puritans, America as the "city on the hill," as close as humanly possible to God's kingdom on earth, giving way to the secular eschatology of the individual's liberation from oppressive hierarchies and traditional mores, and of (hu)mankind liberated from nature through technological progress. America could thus be seen as the ultimate test of whether this liberation will lead to a significant freedom, or meaninglessness, or the end of civilization or the end of the world—whether, that is, there is or is not some other ground outside of traditional society and hierarchical institutions on which the humanity of *homo sapiens* might be grounded.

This could be considered the theme of *Blood Meridian*, as stated in the first chapter, after the book's nameless protagonist, the kid, has run away from home, drifted from one tersely narrated, short-lived, and violent residency to

another, and eventually ended up in Texas (America writ large): "His origins
are become remote as is his destiny and not again in all the world's turning
will there be terrains so wild and barbarous to try whether the stuff of creation
may be shaped to man's will or whether his own heart is not another kind of
clay."[1] From the epigraph of the book, which traces a proclivity for violence
back to humankind's distant origins, to its enigmatic conclusion which seems
to envision some post-catastrophic future, *Blood Meridian* conveys the sense
that its young protagonist's destiny has implications reaching far beyond the
nineteenth-century Mexican-American borderlands.

Blood Meridian follows the peripeteia of the kid, who eventually joins
up with a group of outlaws and mercenaries, led by John Joel Glanton, con-
tracted by the Mexican government to kill Apaches. The bulk of the book
relates the gang's travels (the refrain "They rode on" recurs dozens of times)
and their increasingly violent and unlawful activity—they are to be paid by
the scalp and become less and less discriminating as to where they get those
scalps—interspersed with tales of violence told by and of other characters.

The spiritual leader of the gang is an erudite monster of a man called Judge
Holden (though there is no evidence he holds any actual legal credentials),
and from their initial encounter the judge seems to want something from the
kid which the kid instinctually resists. Arguably what the judge wants is for
the kid to relinquish his minimal but nonnegligible moral scruples and to
join the judge on the dark side—or the dark*er* side, since the kid is, after all,
already an active member of a merciless band of scalphunters. But the kid
commits the occasional random act of kindness, whereas the judge wantonly
drowns puppies and sodomizes and murders children.

The gang's exploits culminate with their massacre at the hands of the
Yuma, from which only a handful escape, including the kid and the judge.
The kid evades the judge's attempts to kill him but also refrains from killing
the judge when he has the opportunity. Years later, the kid, having become
"the man," encounters the judge again at a saloon, tells the judge he "aint
nothin," and is murdered by the judge in the outhouse. The book proper ends
with the judge dancing in the saloon in a sudden present tense that implies
immortality, a persistence through history to our own time and whatever
beyond there may be: "He never sleeps, the judge. He is dancing, dancing.
He says that he will never die" (335). A short and obscure epilogue follows
in which "wanderers" move across a plain following a man who seems to be
digging postholes.

Such a summary of the plot gives the sense of the book's narrative arc
but little of the spectacular density of its language and imagery, which is at
least as essential to its distinctiveness. There is on the one hand a pervasive
sense of the grossness and decrepitude of this world—"Dry old crone, half
naked, her paps like wrinkled aubergines hanging from under the shawl she

wore" (97), urine and feces and pustulating wounds—and yet pulsing through it is a recurrently emerging current of strangeness and mystery. Describing a family of jugglers temporarily fallen in with the gang, McCarthy writes characteristically:

> [T]hese four yet crouched at the edge of the firelight among their strange chattels and watched how the ragged flames fled down the wind as if sucked by some maelstrom out there in the void, some vortex in that waste apposite to which man's transit and his reckonings alike lay abrogate. As if beyond will or fate he and his beasts and his trappings moved both in card and in substance under consignment to some third and other destiny. (96)

The passage, like countless others in the novel, combines a striking image which seems an undeciphered symbol—here, the circle of firelight giving way to the blackness beyond, the wind pulling the flames into the dark—with a possible interpretation, an "as if," that evokes a dark spirit world.

Like *Young Men and Fire*, *Blood Meridian* is also based on historical events. Glanton was a historical figure who did indeed lead a gang of mercenaries hired by the Mexican government to kill Apaches. Many of the incidents in McCarthy's book are based on a previous account of the scalp-hunters' exploits, the memoir of an adventurer named Samuel Chamberlain who purports to have traveled with the gang for a time. Chamberlain describes Judge Holden with many of the attributes taken up by McCarthy, including his size, his erudition, and his appalling proclivities for rape and murder. "Who or what he was no one knew but a cooler blooded villain never went unhung,"[2] Chamberlain writes.

Chamberlain's account is lively; at times it is moving, as when he describes the killing of some members of the gang, who are too wounded to travel, so they are not captured and tortured by the Apaches—"As we cleared the grove, Glanton fired his pistol, when we all heard the dull crashing sound that told us the deed was done. All felt sad and guilty" (Chamberlain, 281)—an episode repeated in McCarthy. Other passages disturb simply by recounting the facts of the violence: "There was in [Glanton's] camp drying thirty-seven of those disgusting articles of trade, Apache scalps, cut with the *right ear* on, to prevent fraud, as some Indians have two circles to their hair" (Chamberlain, 270). But as these brief quotes should indicate, Chamberlain's account is on the whole a straightforward, conventional narrative, and the events and characters he describes undergo a profound transformation in McCarthy's novel. The violence is described in visceral detail, the Judge expands into a grotesque and superhuman character, the roguish humanity of Chamberlain's narration is replaced by an impersonal voice, and McCarthy offers much less than Chamberlain of the normal human interaction between the members of the gang. This underscores the problem posed by *Blood Meridian*: what is the aim of McCarthy's representation and elaboration of this story? If Maclean sought to transform catastrophe into tragedy, into what does McCarthy seek to transform historical atrocity? And what does or might that transformation indicate about how we make sense of the atrocities of our own time and those to come?

THE NIHILISTIC AND ETHICAL READINGS

Critics seem to agree that *Blood Meridian* reveals something essential but are divided on the question of what. As Barclay Owens notes, interpretations of the book fall roughly into two camps (or perhaps more accurately on a spectrum between two poles): the nihilistic—i.e., that McCarthy intends to show us that the world is without sense or meaning—and the moralistic—that the work in fact conveys ethical principles, however subtly or indirectly—i.e., that it conveys what Edwin Arnold calls "a profound belief in the need for moral order, a conviction that is essentially religious."[3]

In the nihilistic camp, the idea is that, as Owens puts it, *Blood Meridian* proves the "thesis" that "mindless, atavistic violence is the true nature of mankind, a genetic heritage in common with apes and wolves."[4] There are two parts to the nihilistic reading: first, that this *is* the "nature of mankind," and second, that there is (according to the perspective of the book) no position from which we can condemn the violence. In the words of Vereen Bell, whom Owens identifies as the progenitor of the nihilistic tendency of interpretation: "'War is God,' [the judge] proclaims (249), and this odd shibboleth is supported . . . by a genuine metaphysic that piece by piece the judge articulates. It is enacted everywhere in the novel by his dimmer protégés. It is put into words, with a Jacobean grandeur and cogency, only by the judge."[5] More on the judge's view later, but briefly, the judge acts as if there are no moral or normative constraints and argues that in fact there are not—that human life is in reality determined sheerly by force ("war") and that there is no other standard by which to judge actions or events. The nihilistic interpretation, then, argues that the book demonstrates what the judge explicitly articulates.

On the other side, there is the ethical interpretation which finds in *Blood Meridian* the affirmation of (a more or less conventional, liberal) morality despite the prevalence and ascendancy of violence and amorality in the plot and the lack of editorializing from the narrator. Harold Bloom sees the novel as a *bildungsroman* in which the nameless protagonist undergoes a moral development from a kid with a "mindless taste for violence" to a man capable of confronting the judge, an act of courage and a moral victory despite its practical failure and the kid's demise at the judge's hands. And although Lydia Cooper does *not* find the kid or anyone else in the novel to be a moral exemplar—her book on McCarthy is called *No More Heroes*—she argues that the book does have a moral intent, that precisely by representing characters entirely lacking in empathy and internal awareness, the work allows us to see "that the act of empathy is the key to ethical engagement with the world."[6] (The work is what might be called a "negative image of the good.")

Both readings begin from the recognition that amorality and immorality dominate the world depicted in *Blood Meridian*. The characters act, by and large, with stunning disregard for any moral precept, and the most willfully evil character—Judge Holden—gets away without punishment. The question is, as Owens puts it, "Why?"[7] What is the intention in, or effect of, depicting such violence, and depicting it in such a way that leaves unclear how the book means us to judge it?

Before continuing, it is worth reflecting on what it is about *Blood Meridian* that forces this question upon its readers in a way that few novels do, and what kind of answer would satisfy.

To the first issue: it is not enough to point to *Blood Meridian*'s pervasive and graphic violence. Consider the *Iliad*, which also overwhelms with its multitudes of detailed injuries and deaths, but does not leave us bemused, asking what the point of all that was; nor do critics suggest that Homer is trying to convey a nihilistic view. To most readers of the *Iliad*, Homer's piling up of bodies effectively conveys the violence of war and the shocking fragility of human life, which is the background against which Achilles's struggle has its meaning—the need to come to terms with and embrace his mortality and to find and affirm something more valuable than long life. Merely to depict violence and evil is hardly nihilistic; the confrontation with evil is, of course, a central theme of stories and literature throughout history.

Much rarer are stories in which evil seems to win in the end—villains may do considerable damage but are usually themselves brought to some sort of justice in the end—as is *Othello*'s Iago, to whom the judge is sometimes compared. But even a work such as Orwell's *1984*, in which totalitarian power triumphs over the hero not only in body but in soul, may still be seen as affirming a moral order in its narrative perspective, by telling the story in a way that makes it clear that certain actions are to be lamented or condemned—in this case, through presenting the story such that we thoroughly identify with Winston in his resistance to Big Brother and are appalled by the destruction of that resistance, by what is effectively the moral death of the character for whom we had been rooting.

In contrast, part of what disturbs about *Blood Meridian* and leads to the interpretation of the book as nihilistic is that not only is there no "poetic justice"—good rewarded, bad punished—but the book itself seems not to pass judgment on the characters' actions, either through the inclusion of a character who can act as moral conscience or through some external narrative perspective. Even if the kid is less bad than the rest—even if, as the judge charges, the kid "alone reserved in [his] soul some corner of clemency for the heathen" and insisted on sitting in judgment on himself (299)—he is hardly a moral exemplar. If he is not explicitly described as participating in, say, the gang's rape of dying native women, neither does he pass judgment. More importantly, the kid is hardly present as a *consciousness*. Like the rest of the scalphunters, excepting the "expriest" Tobin and the judge, the kid is laconic, inarticulate. This works against our identification with him, not only because the elevated literariness of the book ensures that most of its readers will be relatively intelligent and educated, but because we are given little sense of the kid's internal life, little with which *to* identify. It also means that he cannot refute or offer an alternative to the majestic and imposing, if appalling and perhaps not quite coherent, vision that the judge elaborately and eloquently articulates—nor can anyone else, including Tobin. No one can answer the judge's question: "For even if you should have stood your ground . . . yet what ground was it?" (307) Nor does the impersonal and omniscient narrator provide an alternative perspective, at least not in any obvious or explicit way. There is no moral commentary on events "from above" as in Fielding, George Eliot, Tolstoy.

This leaves the reader, the argument goes, with the impression that the heavens are empty, that there *is* no objective basis for judging between good and evil or good and bad, that there is no "what ought to be" but only "what is." And this in turn makes the question of the sense of the book particularly acute. To feel that a narrative has sense, we must not only judge it plausible (within the terms of the storyworld) but feel that there is some *point* to the story—not necessarily that it "teaches" us something or has a moral, but that it reflects and in some way affirms some fundamental justice or order to the universe. This affirmation must not be simplistic; a sophisticated reader will tend to be dissatisfied with a too rosily happy ending, in which all the good characters get what they want and all the bad characters are justly punished, because such a story appears as mere fantasy, its "justice" unconsoling because so thoroughly unbelievable. But we expect stories to reflect some normative order, an order which may well be violated but not without impunity, even if the punishment is only the judgment of God or its secular analogue—some affirmation from the narrative perspective that judgment, the comprehension of human action in light of normative standards, is possible and necessary, even if the good does not reign on earth.

The nihilistic and ethical readings characterize *Blood Meridian*'s relationship to such a normative order as, respectively, negative—that is, that what the work reveals is that there is no such order—or as positive—that it does in fact affirm a normative order in an indirect or subtle way. Both are persuasive at points, but, I will argue, neither the assumption of a meaningless universe nor of a conventional moral background allows us to make sense of the work or the world we feel we see through it.

The ethical reading is not so much wrong as it simply fails as a holistic interpretation of the novel. To say that *Blood Meridian* is a morality tale about the scalphunters' lack of empathy and self-knowledge is like reducing *Moby-Dick* to an admonition to be easygoing like Ishmael rather than mono-maniacal like Ahab.[8] This fails to account for the compelling power of the book, for what Harold Bloom calls the book's "three glories"—"the judge, the landscape, and (dreadful to say this) the slaughters"[9]—and for the sense that even if *Blood Meridian* does not undermine the possibility of moral judg-ment, it does disturb our conventional moral viewpoint and force us to inhabit a perspective from which moral choice and individual agency are superseded by deeper, darker, and vaster forces.

The nihilist reading seems initially more persuasive, but it finally breaks down because *Blood Meridian* does *not* subvert the possibility of moral judg-ment, even if it asserts that violence and lawlessness may triumph on earth. The egregious violence it depicts is horrifying and is, it seems, meant to be so. The "glory" of the slaughters (as well as of the judge) is importantly ambiva-lent. We may revel in some, such as Glanton's death at the hands of a Yuma warrior—"Hack away you mean red n*****, he said, and the old man raised the axe and split the head of John Joel Glanton to the thrapple" (275)—which evokes a certain satisfaction at the harsh justice of a violent man coming to his fated end, told with thrilling succinctness. But when it is the innocent slaughtered—when Glanton shoots an old woman, when an Apache boy the judge briefly "adopts" is found dead—these are not glories but horrors and we have no trouble in judging them, nor does the book subvert our belief in the objectivity of that judgment. Even when it is the Comanche slaughtering the filibusters, who have come into Mexico with their own violent purposes, the description is stomach-churning, the Comanches "passing their blades about the skulls of the living and the dead alike and snatching aloft the bloody wigs and hacking had chopping at the naked bodies, ripping off limbs, heads, gutting the strange white torsos and holding up great handfuls of viscera, genitals" (54). The reader may feel an exhilaration at the sheer extremity and the confrontation with a terrible reality, but this is to say that the glory *derives* in part from our recognition of the horror.[10]

The narration could even be said to confirm our judgment against the violence through the recurrent characterizations of the men as demonic or atavistic, inhuman or prehuman—"like beings provoked out of the absolute rock and set nameless and at no remove from their own loomings to wander ravenous and doomed and mute as gorgons shambling the brutal wastes of

Gondwanaland in a time before nomenclature was and each was all" (172). Again and again the men are described as embodying or carrying some awful darkness:

> Under the hooves of the horses the alabaster sand shaped itself in whorls strangely symmetric like iron filings in a field and these shapes flared and drew back again, resonating upon that harmonic ground and then turning to swirl away over the playa. As if the very sediment of things contained yet some residue of sentience. As if in the transit of those riders were a thing so profoundly terrible as to register even to the uttermost granulation of reality. (247)

The status of these perceptions is ambiguous—it is only "as if," only as the riders "appeared," and it seems unlikely we are meant to think that the landscape *is* sentient and expressing some supernatural judgment against the scalphunters—but they are at least compelling as images of depravity, counterposed in the latter quote to something pure, uncontaminated by human evil, strangely and mysteriously beautiful. There is, therefore, both a sense of judgment and also of meaning or at least meaningfulness, to which I will return.

Nor at the level of the plot is the novel without a sense of justice or normative order. What happens in the book is not random but proceeds according to a kind of law—one that is almost classically tragic. The scalphunters are not heroic, but they are extreme; they transgress all the boundaries within which human community is possible and thereby bring their fate crashing down on them. In the end they "reap what they sow": "those who live by the sword, die by the sword," crime does not pay. The judge lives on at the end, but he is not so much a human character as representative of some force (evil, Satan, humanity's violent nature). So the view that *Blood Meridian* seems to put forth is not that the violent triumph, that the criminal is rewarded, but rather that there is a deep and persistent tendency in human beings toward inhumanity and that this tendency will reliably erupt to wreak destruction on the violent and the peaceful alike. The dominance of this inhumanism in turn suggests the need for a reconceived ethics that is, if not "beyond good and evil," at least cognizant of its severe challenge to notions of human agency.

If *Blood Meridian* neither affirms conventional morality nor insists on complete meaninglessness, what kind of sense does it make, and what kind of sense does it enable or even compel us to make of the world it depicts?

I propose that *Blood Meridian*'s perspective is that of an utter objectivity which is nonetheless a judging consciousness, which recognizes that human history is driven not by and toward reason and freedom but rather by forces irrational and violent and toward recurrent catastrophe and perhaps annihilation, forces enormous and finally beyond comprehension: a perspective that sees against the background of what one might call "the apocalyptic sublime." This, I submit, is the reality to which *Blood Meridian* educates the reader, the ground to which we must refer to in order to "explain"—that is, to make sense of—the plausibility and compellingness of the language and the plot, as well as the disturbing ambivalence of the figure of the judge.

To see this, and unfold its implications, we must look at, and through, the most striking features of the work.

THE JUDGE'S CHALLENGE TO THE MORAL LAW

Let me give due to the claim that the novel illustrates Holden's philosophy, and acknowledge the limited truth in the so-called nihilistic readings of *Blood Meridian*.

What is the judge's view? One statement of it, perhaps the most explicit and simplest, is given by the judge in the course of an impromptu symposium with the other scalphunters on war:

> Might does not make right, said Irving. The man that wins in some combat is not vindicated morally.
>
> Moral law [said the judge] is an invention of mankind for the disenfranchisement of the powerful in favor of the weak. Historical law subverts it at every turn. A moral view can never be proven right or wrong by any ultimate test. A man falling dead in a duel is not thought thereby to be proven in error as to his views. His very involvement in such a trial gives evidence of a new and broader view. The willingness of the principals to forgo further argument as the triviality which it in fact is and to petition directly the chambers of the historical absolute clearly indicates of how little moment are the opinions and of what great moment the divergences thereof. For the argument is indeed trivial, but not so the separate wills thereby made manifest. (250)

On the first point Irving and the judge agree—that "might does not make right," nor does defeat imply wrongness. But whereas Irving unreflectively assumes a different but no less solid basis upon which one might in fact "be proven in error as to his views" (perhaps the judgments of a Christian God; the scalphunters make a few references to "the good book"), the judge proposes that there is no other such basis—that the one and only thing that gives to anything its value is a man's[11] willingness to stake his life on it, that humankind is determined not by its ideals but by its conflicts, not by the values over which men fight wars but by the wars themselves, by the willingness to fight and die—social (or antisocial) Darwinism raised to axiological significance.

There is also an epistemological component to the judge's view—man *cannot* know the moral law; there is no certainty to be found about what is right but only about what is efficacious in the struggle for power and for survival. "Man's vanity," he pontificates,

> may well approach the infinite in capacity but his knowledge remains imperfect and howevermuch he comes to value his judgements ultimately he must submit them before a higher court. . . . Decisions of life and death, of what shall be and what shall not, beggar all question of right. In elections of these magnitudes are all lesser ones subsumed, moral, spiritual, natural. (250)

All that human beings can know for sure is the verdict of the "historical absolute."

The view is darkly Nietzschean, as has been widely recognized.[12] As Nietzsche characterizes it, nihilism arises when the values that sustain human life seem revealed as contradictory to the facts of human life. For him, this insight was "a torture"[13]; it seems not to trouble the judge, which perhaps implies that his position is too facile, but he does recognize and articulate the fact that the way of the world is at odds with the human good or goods as traditionally conceived, the two major candidates being moral good and happiness. (In the final scene, the judge asks the kid what brought these people to this seedy tavern, and the kid says of some dour-looking man that he "come here to have a good time." The judge looks around askance and questions whether any of the patrons are there "to have a good time" (328). The implication is that while we may seek enjoyment or happiness, or to do good within some limited sphere, it is not those desires or conscious intentions that shape the broader contours and limits of our lives; we are, rather, determined by forces—historical, social, natural—outside our ken.)

The judge's argument raises or ought to raise a real question about the relation between *what is* and *what ought to be*, troubling the long-standing philosophical conceit, perhaps first articulated by Socrates, that "a good man cannot be harmed"—meaning, of course, not that good men cannot suffer bodily harm but that it is the soul that matters, and only *doing* wrong can harm the soul, not suffering it. From this perspective the fact that good men are in fact frequently harmed ought not undermine our belief in the reality of and absolute imperative toward goodness. The judge does not explicitly contest this belief but troubles it by arguing, with the backing of historical evidence, that force and violence are the *ultimate* law of the land. This ought to be disturbing. It is one thing to recognize that injustice sometimes triumphs over justice. It is another to see force, human or natural, as the very motor of historical change—with the implication, Holden suggests, that the trajectory of history is toward destruction—again, and again, and perhaps finally.

There is an implicit challenge here to two deeply influential stances in Western thought, the paradigmatic formulations of which one might attribute, respectively, to Kant and to Hegel. The first is the separation of the *is* and the *ought*: from the perspective of Kant, the rightness of an action is independent of its consequences, as the ideal of the good is independent of whatever happens in human history. That a good man cannot be harmed is a grammatical or logical assertion; it belongs to what we mean by "soul" that only evil actions and not physical harm can hurt the soul; likewise, duty is independent of consequences because of what "duty" means. From this perspective, it doesn't matter that the kid dies in the end and the judge dances on; we the readers, standing in for the watchful gaze of God or reading by the light of the Good, can damn the judge with our own judgment and grant the kid whatever redemption he deserves for his gestures of resistance to total inhumanity. Nor does it matter that human ancestors were scalping each other 300,000 years ago, as one of McCarthy's epigraphs informs us, and were still doing so a hundred years after the Enlightenment and are committing equivalent and perhaps worse barbarities yet today; this just means that God's kingdom or its secular analogue is not to be realized on earth but only to exist as an ideal reality, a standard of judgment by which we recognize our fallenness.

But both the judge and the novel as a whole—though with different implications—suggest that if goodness, justice, and humanity as we conceive them are truly impotent in the world then it may in fact be necessary to alter our conceptions of these ideals. I do not mean ceasing to believe that there is a difference between good and evil, but recognizing that there is some deep and perhaps irreconcilable tension between our moral ideals and the real conditions of human life.

The judge and other characters both articulate the idea that the idea that justice is senseless if it is wholly impotent. Early on the kid encounters a hermit who raises this problem:

God made this world, but he didn't make it to suit everbody, did he?

I dont believe he much had me in mind.

Aye, said the old man. But where does a man come by his notions? What world's he seen that he liked better?

I can think of better places and better ways.

Can ye make it be?

No.

No. It's a mystery. (19)

The hermit is a former slaver and perhaps a pedophile, and his "wisdom" is suspect. But I believe we are meant to think that he has a point, however crudely made: it would be difficult to sustain conviction in the ideal of the good or of justice as the proper telos of human life if the actual telos of humanity were shown to be wholly and irremediably other—not *contingently*, because good happened to lose to evil in this or that case, but *essentially*, because the real determinants of human life on the collective scale are not only independent of but contrary to moral law.

The second challenge is to the idea of progress, to the view of history as moving toward the realization of some good (or at least some "better"). As Hegel suggested, in order for us to make sense of history—in order for there to *be* history and not merely chronology—we must see events in light of some telos, some goal or end toward which they are moving. For Hegel, that end is reason and freedom; these are the inner essence of human spirit, of *Geist*, and therefore the story of humanity must be the story of the realization of that essence. Not everything that happens may tend toward that realization, but the standard of rational freedom is what allows one to judge whether an event or movement is "progressive" or "regressive"—and on the whole, Hegel seems to have believed this goal would inevitably be realized.[14] Though few today would subscribe to Hegel's particular formulation of the progress of human history, with its spooky metaphysical entity (whether or not this is a proper interpretation of *Geist*), and many would not share his optimism about the trajectory of Western civilization, the commonplace if largely unconscious assumption at least among liberals is still, I believe, that the "natural" movement of history is toward the Western ideals of individual freedom and rights, cosmopolitanism, and rational and peaceful self-government, and that if human life or civilization ends instead in collapse or annihilation, it will not be because of anything inherently problematic with those ideals but only because certain bad or inadequately enlightened people or peoples clung to stupid and mean beliefs and habits or reacted violently out of ignorance and fear. It will be contingent, not logical or necessary.[15]

If, by contrast, there is an irremediable divergence between the ideal telos of human life or human history, on the one hand, and actual human life and human history on the other, a different way of making sense is needed. The problem is not just that human beings are sinful and recurrently fail to live up to their ideals (or even, in McCarthy's vision, to have or to embrace such ideals), but that the trajectory toward destruction or inhumanity arises out of or as a *consequence* of values or qualities essential to Western civilization such as the insistence on truth (as Nietzsche famously and seminally argued), mastery over nature, and individual freedom and self-determination.

As the judge reflects when the scalphunters are camped one night among the ruined dwellings of the Anasazi—obliquely explicating the title of the book:

> If God meant to interfere in the degeneracy of mankind would he not have done
> so by now? Wolves cull themselves, man. What other creature could? And is

the race of man not more predacious yet? The way of the world is to bloom and to flower and die but in the affairs of men there is no waning and the noon of his expression signals the onset of night. His spirit is exhausted at the peak of its achievement. His meridian is at once his darkening and the evening of his day. He loves games? Let him play for stakes. This you see here, these ruins wondered at by tribes of savages, do you not think that this will be again? Aye. And again. With other people, with other sons. (146–47)

The passage describes a radically different view of history and the telos of human life in which history proceeds not linearly, toward some progressive realization of our humanity, but cyclically, in bursts of "achievement" (the judge has admired the stonework of the Anasazi) followed by inevitable "exhaustion" or destruction. And this cyclical character of history is, according to Holden, not accidental but intrinsic to the fulfillment, such as it is, of humanity's real telos, because what stirs the human blood is the game, and the ultimate game is war, where the stakes are the highest. (I'll return to this.)

Blood Meridian cannot, of course, *prove* that the trajectory of civilization in general or Western or American civilization in particular is essentially toward destruction. It is fiction, and highly selective and exaggerated in what it depicts, and one could argue that the world isn't, on the whole, like what McCarthy shows us. Many readers would not see the brutes that populate the pages of *Blood Meridian* as representative of contemporary Western society, and some would argue that while the contemporary Western world bears its share—or more—of crime and corruption, that at least culturally it asserts certain ideals of goodness and justice, which, though deeply contested, are contested (sometimes) on grounds of principle and not just power.

But the question is one of foundations and of direction—of what humanity is at bottom, of where history is headed in the long run. Like *Heart of Darkness*, *Blood Meridian* could be conceived as showing something about the conditions of human being by examining what happens at the extremes, outside the thick of civilization. (McCarthy's *The Road* imagines what happens to human beings when civilization collapses entirely. It suggests that, in general, they become cannibals.)

TOWARD A MODERN APOCALYPTIC GNOSTICISM

If the forces that fundamentally drive human action and human history are not reasons but causes, moving humanity toward chaos and destruction—the fulfillment of humanity's "empirical" nature rather than its ideal—then this, *Blood Meridian* suggests, entails making a different kind of sense of human action and human history.

The alternative to a "worldly" conception of the human good, one to be realized within the world or within history, is some utterly unworldly conception of the good: a view of human life which might be called *gnostic*.

Gnosticism is the modern name given to various religious sects that arose and flourished early in the first millennium, characterized by the belief that the world was not created good by a good and omnipotent God, but rather created evil or essentially corrupt by an incompetent or malevolent demiurge, and that human salvation is only to be achieved through a mystical knowledge, *gnosis*, of our true otherworldly spiritual home—knowledge of the true God, the true good, which is wholly alien to this world. As Hans Jonas writes, in gnostic belief "knowledge and the attainment of the known by the soul are claimed to coincide—the claim of all true mysticism"[16]—it is not that one seeks knowledge of how to gain salvation; rather, the possession of the knowledge *is* the salvation.

The judge's views suggest a modern and secular variant of the gnostic vision.[17] Holden argues, somewhat persuasively, that history is determined neither by man's conscious intention nor by providence but by the struggle for power on the one hand and sheer random chance on the other. The world was not created by an evil or incompetent supernatural power, but an indifferent natural power, which could be seen as having the same effect—a world whose laws are orthogonal if not hostile to human needs, purposes, and ideals. "The truth about the world," says the judge, "is that anything is possible. Had you not seen it all from birth and thereby bled it of its strangeness it would appear to you for what it is, a hat trick in a medicine show, a fevered dream, a trance bepopulate with chimeras having neither analogue nor precedent, an itinerant carnival, a migratory tentshow whose ultimate destination after many a pitch in many a mudded field is unspeakable and calamitous beyond reckoning" (245). The judge, then, makes *this* world his home. He lives as if this is the only world that there is. He could be seen as the embodiment of an Enlightenment thinking that is perverted by carrying its rational scientific strand to a totalizing conclusion—an absolute empiricist.

Holden is a citizen scientist; as the gang travels along, the judge collects specimens and makes notes on the ruins of ancient tribes and on natural phenomena, and "educates" the gang about the nature of the world. He insists on mastery of his circumstances and of the unknown, and denies that there is any power beyond the human: "Your heart's desire is to be told some mystery," he says to his dumbfounded traveling companions after discovering "a great femur from some beast long extinct" (251). "The mystery is that there is no mystery" (252). The thread of order as the judge sees it is a purely natural one, and there is no other standard of judgment, no objective moral law, only a Darwinian law of power. As Dana Phillips characterizes it, history in *Blood Meridian* is presented not as salvation history but as natural history—not moving toward a telos but driven by laws independent of and indifferent or inimical to human ends and welfare.[18]

This can be seen as a secular and historicized version of the gnostic view, and the judge believes that he is in possession of the truth, of *gnosis*, and this truth he takes to be that there is no truth, at least no moral truth. The judge's view is, finally, not a coherent system but a mishmash of multiple "philosophies of suspicion," philosophies that in one way or another would have us question the order of things as it ordinarily appears—Heraclitus, Nietzsche, Hegel, etc. Holden represents not so much a specific view but an attack from all angles on the idea of the moral law, tearing away at the fabric of our unreflective conviction in it. He acts as a caustic in the novel, scouring away any merely conventional or ungrounded ideas of the good, giving the sense that any idea of normative order which persists must do so in full and clear consciousness—if indeed any order *can* survive all the reductive critiques which might be applied to it.

What, then, are the implications?

Hans Jonas notes that one can derive two diametrically opposed moral stances from the gnostic vision, asceticism or libertinism: "The former deduces from the possession of gnosis the obligation to avoid further contamination by the world and therefore to reduce contact with it to a minimum; the latter derives from the same possession the privilege of absolute freedom."[19]

The judge's vision leads him to libertinism—or beyond. One might say he is not really a seeker of *gnosis* at all. Leo Daugherty, in his gnostic reading of *Blood Meridian*, interprets the judge as an "archon," one of the evil demons who created this corrupted world,[20] and this could imply that the judge is not seeking escape from this corrupted world but rather identifies with it. The knowledge that he has is not *gnosis*, knowledge of the true good, but only knowledge of the wholly fallen or corrupt character of the world as it is. For the judge, this vision of the world justifies the wanton violation of any moral law.

In light of what he takes to be the true "creator" of the human world, violence and the institution of war, and the consequent lack of authority of the various moral codes which are mere artifacts of the will to power (a phrase the judge does not use but which would be appropriate), Holden makes the argument in both word and deed for aligning oneself with the force that truly governs the world—that is, with *force*, which truly governs the world—not only because it is expedient but because in such an alignment man's own powers are released, his spirit strengthened and expanded. The judge's view is not just that power is the determining force of history to which we must acquiesce, that war is proof of our investment; we also love war. It is a sign of passion—it *is* passion, and Holden argues not just from expedience but from passion—war "endures because young men love it and old men love it in them" (249).

This is continuous with the judge's advocacy of "the dance" at the end. If the pattern of history is not moral, it can be appreciated as aesthetic—an aesthetics of force. The judge is looking for the thing that gives human life meaning despite its obvious violence, contingency, injustice. "If war is not holy, man is nothing more than antic clay," the judge tells the kid near the end (307). The judge's position is thus not nihilistic—at least not in the sense that everything is meaningless, that nothing has value—but rather an extreme and fatalistic aestheticism: what is valuable, what confers value, is passion, the willingness to die for something—war is "holy" both because it manifests that passion and because it is beautiful in itself. War is aesthetic, war is the dance.

JUDGING THE JUDGE

The judge, then, is not a nihilist but rather has found a *solution* to nihilism, or so he would have us believe: to identify himself, oneself, with the forces of history, which he equates with force per se, with violence and power, and to take joy, aesthetic joy, in the sheer exercise of power and skill, be it his *tour de force* orchestration of the gang to create gunpowder from urine and bat guano to save them from an Apache attack, or his amateur scientific studies which culminate in his destruction of the studied objects, or his exquisite dancing. Or his rape and murder of children.[21]

The question is whether the judge's view *is* "the view of the novel"—the reality or truth to which the novel educates us (which may or may not be equivalent to McCarthy's conscious intention)—or whether the novel embodies and enables a consciousness that encompasses Holden's, a perspective from which we may judge the judge.

There is a certain intuitive sense to the idea that the novel as a whole illustrates what the judge proclaims. He is the towering figure of the book, literally and figuratively, not just the most articulate but nearly the only one to speak at length; he dominates the plot as well, and of all the main characters, he is the last man standing—dancing.

There is even something admirable about the judge in his insistence on what seems to be the awful truth. He is more conscious by an order of magnitude than any other character in the book except perhaps Tobin, and he is the only character wholly consistent in his professed beliefs and his actions. The other scalphunters' vague references to the morality of "the good book" are laughable, and the "civilized" powers generally act by the judge's law under the thin cover of good manners.

History beyond the world of *Blood Meridian* provides additional and ample evidence supporting the judge's characterization of it—filled with slaughter, written by those with the power to win wars, time and again culminating in upheavals that crush the powerless and in the collapse of societies and civilizations. Even if power is not wholly independent from justice—if the demands of equal rights, freedom, and tolerance have political and sometimes revolutionary force because of their appeal to the otherwise unempowered—it is clear that these ideals, once institutionalized, are fragile and highly susceptible to distortion and corruption by vested interests and to disenthronement by reactionary movements. Given all of this, arguably the judge's aesthetics of violence is the only standard from which human life on earth could be considered generally "good."

Yet there are suggestions that the judge's is not the final word.

Bell claims that the judge contradicts himself when, after asserting "there is no mystery," he characterizes the world as "a migratory tentshow whose ultimate destination . . . is unspeakable and calamitous beyond reckoning" (245). Bell attributes this contradiction to the judge's "fear that there is indeed a mystery and that its being would deny his own. The very coherence of his argument and the cold passion of his commitment to it intimate a psychic rigidity born of dread."[22] I am not convinced that the judge is indeed in contradiction; it seems to me there is a difference between "mystery" and the simple chaotic unknown and unknowable. *Mystery* derives etymologically from ancient mystery religions whose initiates were *mystai*, and thus the word implies not just the unknown but something coherent and divine to be known, which gives meaning and purpose to human life. But there does seem to be a note of repressed desperation in the judge's insistence on order and control— the idea that "the freedom of birds is an insult to [him]" (199), the erasure of artifacts after he puts them into his book, and finally the obsession with the kid who continues to resist him. Poised and in control as the judge may be, his equanimity wavers when he is confronted by what evades or might evade his knowledge or control, particularly the kid's resistance of his influence. This indicates something of which the judge, with all his sophistication and iconoclastic knowingness, is in denial.

Ultimately the narrative perspective, I would argue, encompasses and exceeds that of the judge and reflects the "mystery" that the judge denies.

How does it do this?

One distinctive characteristic of the descriptive style of *Blood Meridian* is its extreme precision, the fine articulation of every detail of the environment—"Saddletrees eaten bare of their rawhide coverings and weathered white as bone, a light chamfering of miceteeth along the edges of the wood"

(246), or "regions of particolored stone upthrust in ragged kerfs and shelves of traprock reared in faults and anticlines curved back upon themselves and broken off like stumps of great stone treeboles and stones the lightning had clove open, seeps exploding in steam in some old storm" (50). Ordinarily we inhabit a human environment structured by our needs and interests—we see those things that are pertinent to our concerns; irrelevant detail fades into the background. The world as described in *Blood Meridian*, by contrast, is a world in which our attention is recurrently directed to the myriad and strange particularities of the visible—a world of "optical democracy" (247), as some critics have claimed, borrowing McCarthy's own phrase.

In fact, the attention to visible detail is not entirely "democratic" or indiscriminate—the overwhelming preponderance of description in the book is of the natural world and the world of objects; the human characters are described no less deftly but more sketched than painted. For instance: "The man was sitting in the grass with his legs crossed. He was dressed in buckskin and he wore a plug hat of dusty black silk and he had a small Mexican cigar in the corner of his teeth" (29). There are exceptions, such as the vivid descriptions of the judge, but the latter is practically a force of nature himself, and on the whole the description of human characters is precise but simple and colloquial, lacking the arcane vocabulary that McCarthy uses to render the landscape vivid and mystical. The people in *Blood Meridian* are, by and large, dark ciphers, shadowy types clothed and surrounded by material that seems more real than they. We get virtually no access to their inner thoughts or feelings and often they are described as if they are internally vacant, wholly determined by their environments. (If the narrator is "omniscient" either he is uninterested in the characters' interior lives or, as seems likely, they don't have much in the way of interiority.) Thus the work lacks a certain human presence, normal human consciousness; filled with people though it may be, it seems an inhuman world, seen inhumanly.

At the same time the very precision of the language, as well as a certain "baroque" or "literary" quality, brings the language to our attention, and therefore implies the work of *some* conscious narrator. The description is at once intensely visual—cinematic—and untranslatably literary. *Chamfering of miceteeth* is perfect; we see through it, see what it describes, but also notice it *as* perfect because of its unusualness. We see what is described, but we see— or read—it *as* described for us by some intelligence.[23] McCarthy's prose is, moreover, often incantatory—"stone upthrust in ragged kerfs and shelves of traprock"—here the repetition of plosives and fricatives, the trochaic meter, conveys the sense of an order that is not just that of the natural world—the sense of mystery.

Continuous with the poetic sonic effects is the recurrent figuration in the descriptions of events and setting. The world as seen in *Blood Meridian* is not just a world of acutely perceived things; the visible is constantly figured as the manifestation of some astonishing and threatening invisible through McCarthy's hallucinogenic similes.

> Crossing those barren gravel reefs in the night they seemed remote and without substance. Like a patrol condemned to ride out some ancient curse. A thing surmised from the blackness by the creak of leather and the chink of metal. (151)

> That night they were visited with a plague of hail out of a faultless sky and the horses shied and moaned and the men dismounted and sat upon the ground with their saddles over their heads while the hail leaped in the sand like small lucent eggs concocted alchemically out of the desert darkness. When they resaddled and rode on they went for miles through cobbled ice while a polar moon rose like a blind cat's eye up over the rim of the world. (152)

The similes are obviously not just intended to enable a more striking visualization of the phenomenon described (like Tolstoy's observation that "a baby's arms are so fat it they seem as if tied by string"[24]) or to give concreteness to the abstract ("my love is like a red, red rose"). The vehicle of the simile is generally abstract, if not practically speaking inconceivable ("a land . . . whose true geology was not stone but fear"), while the tenor is something concrete, material, visible, if uncanny (lightning, "gravel reefs," etc.). The effect of the similes is thus not to clarify or make vivid what is this-worldly but to evoke the otherworldly.

All of these qualities of the narrative—the detailing of the material world and the neglect or absence of interiority; the figuration evoking "some other order" which is uncanny, nightmarish, obscure—imply a radically impersonal narrative perspective, perhaps an inhuman one. In the typical novelistic third-person narrative perspective, the narrator seems to be someone like us (or like the author) except invested with some more or less limited power to see across time and space and into their characters' heads. The narrator's interests and judgments are those of a person watching the doings of other people. In *Blood Meridian*, by contrast, the perspective is detached, distant—not wholly indifferent to the fates of the characters, but as if having recognized the fundamental ill-fatedness and degradation of the human condition and continually looking through the individual characters and their interests, such as they are, to some transcendent ground.

The similes reveal this ground as an inhuman sublime which dwarfs human beings and surpasses their understanding. In *Blood Meridian*, it is a dark sublime, a supernatural or demonic world, dark to human understanding, a gnostic world in which some substantive principle of evil predominates and in which the good is alien and distant. The descriptions are not all dark and terrifying; the landscape has a stark and inhospitable beauty, and it often seems portentous. The portents, however, seem not to be aimed at human beings for them to guide their actions, but only intimations of some wholly different order of things.

FROM THE NATURALISTIC TO THE APOCALYPTIC SUBLIME, BY WAY OF *MOBY-DICK*

This sense of an inhuman enormity in the world, indifferent to human concerns, traces back to one of the essential literary ancestors of *Blood Meridian*, Herman Melville's *Moby-Dick*, and it is worth briefly returning to the nineteenth century to illuminate the distinctiveness of the sublime that emerges in McCarthy's novel.

The modern concept of the sublime emerged in the eighteenth century. Its seminal Enlightenment theorists, Kant and Burke, gave thoroughly rational accounts of the sublime and our pleasure in it—for Kant it affirmed the capacities of the rational mind; for Burke it gave us the thrill of danger from a position of safety. But in the nineteenth-century Romantic development of the concept of the sublime and its expression in painting and poetry, it is the overwhelmingness itself that is valued: when I stand awed beneath the vast starry sky, I am exhilarated not because it indirectly reminds me of my own cognitive powers, but because it suggests a power beyond me, a physical vastness or force which then seems symbolic of a spiritual power. The Romantics and their American counterparts, the Transcendentalists, invite God, domesticated by Descartes and Kant to a rational idea of perfection, back in in all his transcendent mystery—and sometimes terrible awesomeness—through the back door of Nature. As Emerson wrote in his essay "Nature," "Every natural fact is a symbol of some spiritual fact." The spiritual facts that Emerson, a Unitarian minister, found symbolized by the facts of nature were the facts of a universe ordered by God. The sublime was the greatness of God, and the individual who relied on his own perception could tap into the divine. "Revelation . . . attended by the emotion of the sublime . . . is an influx of the Divine mind into our mind."[25]

But contemporaneous with Emerson and to some degree in reaction against the optimism of his brand of Transcendentalism, a darker vision of the sublime was also emerging in America. In nineteenth-century American literature, the old suspicions of Epicurus and the ancient materialists as well as the Gnostics—that whatever ordered the universe, it was no loving and caring God—found new form, perhaps most fully embodied at that time in Melville's tale of the hunt for the White Whale.

In the "natural fact" of the enormous albino whale that took off his leg, Captain Ahab finds a concrete symbol—or manifested reality—not of a benevolent deity or divine Platonic Good but of some malicious power. In response to his first mate Starbuck, who objects to his revenge quest by protesting that the whale is just a "dumb brute," Ahab famously rejoins: "All visible objects, man, are but as pasteboard masks. But in each event—in the living act, the undoubted deed—there, some unknown but still reasoning thing puts forth the mouldings of its features from behind the unreasoning mask. If man will strike, strike through the mask!"[26] Ahab takes his own disfigurement as symbol and instance of all human suffering that defies human sense, and the whale as symbol and embodiment of those forces in the universe that bring such suffering. He admits even that "sometimes I think there's naught beyond" the mask of the visible. But it is only by construing the world as it impinges upon human beings as the manifestation of some intelligence—some "inscrutable malice" as it would seem, judging from the world's thwarting of human need and desire—that human beings can assert agency, can maintain spiritual integrity when the body is dismembered.

Ishmael, the narrator of *Moby-Dick*, also finds the eponymous whale as symbolic of something inimical to human happiness, not as a bringer of death and destruction but as an image of the universe's indifference, the absence of any "reasoning thing" whatsoever at work in the workings of the universe. Ishmael's fear is the one that Ahab ostensibly dismisses, that "there's naught beyond" the "pasteboard mask" of the visible world. This is most powerfully expressed in Ishmael's discourse on "The Whiteness of the Whale." The terror of whiteness is the terror of the void, the horrible idea that beneath and beyond or beneath everything humanly sensible and meaningful is a blanketing nothing.

In a sense, this is a vision yet more disturbing than Ahab's. For the latter, the universe is hostile to humankind; for the narrator (be he Ishmael or Melville) it is totally indifferent. Later in the novel, the cabin boy Pip is abandoned on the ocean and in his terror has a vision continuous with Ishmael's, of "the unwarped primal world" beneath the surface, "the multitudinous, God omnipresent, coral insects that out of the firmament of the waters heaped the colossal orbs," "God's foot upon the treadle of the loom" in the alien deeps.[27] God's laws are conflated with the laws of nature. This was a pleasing thought to the earlier Enlightenment scientists and philosophers; the laws of nature were a delightful order, and modern science thus now allowed man to grasp the mind of God. As Newton put it in the *Principia*: "This most beautiful system of the sun, planets, and comets, could only proceed from the counsel and dominion of an intelligent and powerful Being. . . . This Being governs all things, not as the soul of the world, but as Lord over all . . . "[28] But in Melville's vision, Nature in its deepest, darkest, and vastest being—the unfathomable depths of the ocean being both symbol and reality—is terrifying in its strangeness and beyond the grasp of human reason.

Robert Frost's 1922 poem "Design" reflects this vision as well. In it, the poet watches a white spider devour a white moth (on a white flower)—with unmistakable allusion to Melville—and asks himself what kind of "design" is manifest in the gruesome chance that brought the moth to the spider's grasp. The final lines of the poem suggest the two awful possibilities: "What but design of darkness to appall?—/ If design govern in a thing so small." Either the world's designer is cruel or indifferent, or there is no design of things at all, at least in the world beneath the level of ordinary human perception, the world of nature which is the very substrate of things. And in some sense these possibilities are indistinguishable, all of them issuing forth in an order of the world that is contrary to human reason, will, desire, and flourishing—a thoroughly inhuman world, and one that threatens meaninglessness. This is what one might call the naturalistic sublime (and it is what is figured in Maclean's fire and confronted in his book).

But in *Blood Meridian* is not just nature that is "red in tooth and claw," but humanity; it is not just the chaos and heartlessness of nature that is terrifying but the trajectory of human history. And this raises the specter of the apocalyptic sublime, which might be understood as this awesome and terrifying naturalism extended to human history.

THE APOCALYPTIC CONSCIOUSNESS

Human beings have been violent from the beginning, as McCarthy emphasizes with his epigraph describing the discovery of the prehistoric scalped skull. But the unprecedented eruptions of the twentieth century—the explosion of modern "enlightened" Europe into mechanized warfare; the Holocaust and other genocidal atrocities; the detonation of the atomic bomb and the proliferation of nuclear weapons—have made present and palpable a new possibility, namely that our dark and destructive tendencies are not just an unfortunate abiding fact of human life to be "muddled through" but might be determinative for our trajectory. The danger is not (just) meaninglessness, as threatened by a naturalistic and indifferent cosmos, but annihilation, at least the loss of civilization or of anything deserving the name "human."

The vision of nuclear holocaust or other civilizational collapse presses its way to the fore in McCarthy's later novels—in the postapocalyptic wasteland of *The Road* and, in *The Passenger*, in descriptions of Hiroshima and imaginings by various characters of the darkness to come. *Blood Meridian* does not explicitly treat the catastrophic developments of the last century or describe concretely the dire future, but it evokes both in its allusions to the ending of human worlds: in its thematization of the extinction of past cultures (the Anasazi) and present cultures (the annihilation of the buffalo) and in the final triumph of the judge over all moderating forces it conveys the possibility or probability of our own annihilation, physically or spiritually, especially as we read it in light of the enormities of the twentieth century and the Doomsday Clock ticking closer to midnight. This grim(mer) future still lies in the future in *Blood Meridian*, but the long shadow of the judge "dancing, dancing" at its conclusion seems to fall upon our own day and beyond, and in drawing its tale from the past it sounds the sources of crises to come.[29]

This, I would argue, is the background of *Blood Meridian*—it is not just a revisionist Western meant to confront us with the realities of historical violence, but a reflection upon what Hannah Arendt called the "subterranean stream"[30] of the trajectory of the global West.

But as the etymology implies, apocalypse is not only end but revelation—revelation that the laws of the world are not what we thought. The consciousness of *Blood Meridian* is, finally, outside the action; it is not the consciousness of the characters—even of the pontificating judge—but an observing consciousness. It is not indifferent to suffering and injustice, but it sees suffering and injustice, the actions and passions of individuals, in the context of historical enormity, comprised by the actions of individuals but moving independent of individual intention and agency. Individuals, their motives and beliefs, appear as tiny particles comprising the dark wave of prehistory and history and future, against a yet deeper background of mythical significance.

One could think of this consciousness as the Gnostic's divine spark that is imprisoned in fallen matter—including, perhaps, ourselves—and seeks to free itself—by way, perhaps, of our reading of the novel. Leo Daugherty equates the divine spark to the kid's weak moral impulses,[31] and I will demur, but I should say a word here about the kid, who is, after all, the protagonist, and whose progress determines the narrative, such as it is, of the book. *Blood Meridian* could from one perspective be characterized as the kid's tragedy; he is led by his own character and circumstances to an inevitable clash with a force that must overwhelm him. The kid shows himself as exceptional in a muted way. In his recalcitrant decency he is exceptional among the company he keeps, as well as in his dogged determination to survive. His heroism, if it can be called that, is not that of the classical tragic hero, halfway between men and gods, but an everyman's heroism, the heroism of a tough, basic humanity. He is similar in this respect to the Smokejumpers of *Young Men and Fire*, distinguished not primarily by his distinctive character or deeds—except for an extreme competency—but by the situation in which he finds himself.

What I am calling the consciousness of the novel encompasses the consciousness of the protagonists in both cases. *Fire* is as much about the observing consciousness—in that case, Maclean—as it is about the heroes of the "action" story. In *Blood Meridian* the balance is shifted yet further, such that primary focus is not the kid but the world he moves through, the forces he encounters (particularly the judge and what he represents). This could be seen as part of the distinction I would draw between the tragic and the apocalyptic, or classical tragedy and modern apocalyptic tragedy. In the former the hero or heroes are defined and elevated by the immense opposing forces that they encounter, even if they are finally crushed by those forces. In the latter the hero, if he is a hero, is dwarfed by those forces and virtually disappears against their immensity.

I would say that what Daugherty calls the kid's "divine spark" is, rather, the kid's natural humanity, his social nature. What we empathize with in the kid are his moments of humaneness, most poignantly near the end of the book when he tells his story to an old woman he finds huddled alone in the desert, and promises to help her to find her people, only to discover that the woman is long-dead, a dried husk of a corpse. Such gestures are surely good and hardly to be despised in a world so inimical to them.

They are, however, no match—either practically[32] or aesthetically—for the equally natural violent and sadistic tendencies the judge brings to conscious perfection. The fact that the judge is far (far) more erudite and articulate than the kid is, of course, hardly a reason to discount the kid's moral impulses. A number of contemporary moral philosophers argue that morality is fundamentally built upon sympathy or empathy, prior to any moral reasoning,[33] and there is even a contemporary suspicion of reason as potentially warping our moral sentiments.[34] But the very attractiveness of the judge, whose reasoning is not mere casuistry but an articulation of certain truths about the world and history, suggests that moral feelings are not sufficient to combat the forces he represents and the vision he conveys. What is needed is a vision that includes but supersedes that of the judge. And the only consciousness in the novel that encompasses the judge's is the consciousness of the novel itself, the narrative consciousness—and perhaps the reader's, but only after having confronted the judge, having worked through (by way of reading) the challenge that he presents, not just having reacted against him out of our conventional pieties.

In a sense this idea is Hegelian—that the development of humanity is the process of human spirit coming to know itself, coming to consciousness, in a way that sublates—enfolds and transcends—previous and inadequate modes of understanding. But contra Hegel, *Blood Meridian* suggests a tragic division in *Geist*: the divorce between the progress of consciousness and the trajectory of humankind. In reading the work we feel the incommensurability of any proximally livable and meaningful human world, on the one hand, and the utterly indifferent natural world and vast inhumanity and violence of history on the other. And it is unclear whether a reconciliation is possible—whether it is possible to live a human life in recognition of such inhuman conditions.

But the evocation of the sublime—the "mystery"—is why the novel is not nihilistic. The language continually summons images of some other and "unreckoned" dimension of existence. As Bell claims:

> *Blood Meridian* is haunted by the mystery that its own language challenges the very nihilistic logic that it gives representation to. The language itself is a presence, and the world as it enters into language is a presence; and whatever it is that this presence may be said to be is precisely what the judge and his cerebral violence have declared war upon. The richness generated out of such morally impoverished material seems intended to appear miraculous and in some sense transcendent and beyond the reach of the mind, which is finally merely a fact among others. (Bell, 128)

The language is thrilling, compelling—despite being (when it comes to the scalphunters) dark and disturbing—because of the sense of *depth* it conveys, a depth which seems not just fantasy but in accord with our experience and our sense of the world—not our everyday experience but those moments when for one reason or another things are thrown out of kilter, defamiliarized. The evocative ambiguity and strangeness of McCarthy's descriptions suggest a vast but only dimly glimpsed whole. This whole includes the reality of evil, but also, by implication, the reality of good, since evil can only be recognized as evil by the light of something that stands in opposition to it. Not ordinary goodness, though this has its place, but a searing light of some absolute ideal, dispossessed of self and objective.

This evocation of a transcendent ground of judgment is what transforms what might otherwise be apocalyptic horror into the apocalyptic sublime. The novel suggests, and embodies, a consciousness beyond the judge's because we are able to judge the judge, and not just by our preexisting and largely conventional morality but in light of the depths implied by the novel's poetry—depths which the judge shrilly defies in his insistence that "There is no mystery," no order that goes beyond what he wills.

The judge identifies himself with the forces of history, with the forces of violence, domination, and erasure, and so maintains a fiction of his own agency. The consciousness of the novel, on the other hand, is an ironic or double consciousness: it recognizes its impotence in determining the trajectory of history, but sees and judges that trajectory in light of some intimated and truly human (ideal) destiny. It could be characterized as a kind of ascetic— rather than libertine—gnosticism, the need for a detached and dispossessed consciousness, decentered from humanity, recognizing its conditionedness and dependency on some "mystery," as well as the ineradicability of certain moral demands, even if they are impotent in determining the structure of the world or the trajectory of history.

Blood Meridian suggests a distinction between human *fate* and human *destiny*. The novel is not nihilistic because while it sees the prospects for the human fate as grim, it implies that there is such thing as a human destiny, that there are ideals of humanity that are the light by which we understand and judge. (Perhaps a truly nihilistic novel is an impossibility, if the very depiction of degradation as degradation necessarily implies a standard of judgment.) But the novel suggests that the human destiny is far from assured, and just as soberingly, that perhaps the ends of happiness or flourishing must be ultimately subordinated to the imperative of consciousness.

Blood Meridian is not a morality tale because it recognizes that "being good" (empathetic, social, liberal) has proven insufficient, at least empirically—insufficient to stem the blood-dimmed tide—and perhaps ideally as well—insufficient to the ideal of a fully realized humanity, which includes not just the pursuit of individual happiness but also of excellence, struggle, mastery, truth, extremity. (Hence the ambivalence of the figure of the judge as both Enlightenment and Nietzschean figure—the compelling power of his awful consistency, competence, and iconoclasm.) The work is not nihilistic, on the other hand, because it does not deny the possibility of judgment in light of the good or the truly human, even if the standard is elusive and can only be suggested. It may be a modern tragedy, an apocalyptic tragedy, suggesting that there is a normative order but that it is inevitable that we should come into violation of it, maybe as an entire civilization and maybe catastrophically.

This is the apocalyptic sublime: the inconceivable immensity and enormity of a human past, present, and uncertain future proceeding according to a logic beyond our full comprehension and far beyond our control—an immensity and enormity which calls into question all our norms and standards, because of their seeming failure to secure a human future and because of the incommensurability of such norms and standards with the inhuman laws of necessity and chance that order the universe. At the same time this vision implies the austere light of some good that would be adequate to judge and to comprehend it.

I am reminded of Simone Weil's writings on the contradiction at the heart of the human condition:

> The essential contradiction in human life is that man, with a straining after the good constituting his very being, is at the same time subject in his entire being, both in mind and flesh, to a blind force, to a necessity completely indifferent to the good. So it is; and that is why no human thinking can escape from contradiction. Contradiction itself, far from always being a criterion of error, is sometimes a sign of truth.[35]

Weil's point is different, of course; she is speaking of a timeless contradiction in the human condition: the fact that human beings are matter and therefore subject to causal laws, and at the same time spirit subject to the laws of justice and desire for the good. One might say that *Blood Meridian* points toward a particular historical, modern form of this contradiction—the way in which force shows itself potentially and fatally determinative not just for individual human lives but for human history. The power and genius of the work is that it allows us to feel and to inhabit this particular tension between the necessary and the good and, potentially, to bring it to consciousness.

The judge figures, finally, as a perverted or inverted model of a consciousness we cannot fully or finally conceptualize and that McCarthy can only suggest through the form of the novel as a whole. All the mysteries of the work, including the baffling epilogue, figure above all this encompassing consciousness, a light by which—maybe—human destiny could govern human fate, or at least a light by which we would see the end clearly.

NOTES

1. McCarthy, *Blood Meridian, Or the Evening Redness in the West*, 4–5. Page numbers in this chapter will refer to this text unless otherwise noted.

2. Chamberlain, *My Confession*, 271.

3. Arnold, "Naming, Knowing and Nothingness: McCarthy's Moral Parables," 44; quoted in Owens, *Cormac McCarthy's Western Novels*, 10–11.

4. Owens, *Cormac McCarthy's Western Novels*, 4.

5. Bell, *The Achievement of Cormac McCarthy*, 120.

6. Cooper, *No More Heroes*, 75.

7. Owens, *Cormac McCarthy's Western Novels*, 9.

8. Hubert Dreyfus and Sean Dorrance Kelly offer such an interpretation (Dreyfus and Kelly, *All Things Shining*).

9. Bloom, *How to Read and Why*, 257.

10. Contrast for instance the admittedly thrilling scene in *The Matrix* where Neo and Trinity stylishly shoot up a whole passel of enemy security guards. (Relatively) bloodless and slick, this is a fantasy of violence that gives no intimation of its horror or cost.

11. I follow the judge here in speaking of "man" rather than "human beings" or "men and women" because war seems to me to be a traditionally and archetypally masculine mode of determination, which is not to say that women follow the moral law, but they have historically sought power through negotiation, beneficial liaisons, and manipulation rather than outright violence—though, to be sure, sustaining the conditions of their societies' wars.

12. See for instance Crews, *Books Are Made Out of Books*.

13. "Until now I have endured a torture: all of the laws by which life unfolds appeared to me to be in opposition to the values for the sake of which we endure life.

This does not appear to me to be a condition from which many consciously suffer; nonetheless I intend to gather together the signs from which I take it to be the fundamental character and the really tragic problem of our modern world, and as concealed necessity, the cause or interpretation of all of its needs. This problem has become conscious in me." *Saemtliche Werke*, 12:7 [8] quoted in Carr, *The Banalization of Nihilism*, 25.

14. The implications of Hegel's own view for individual ethics are unclear because the direction of history is for him relatively independent of individuals' conscious intentions. But in general if we see the direction of history as in accord with the realization of human good as we conceive it, this would be affirmative of that conception.

15. For instance, in his 2018 book *Enlightenment Now*, Steven Pinker acknowledges the recurrence and persistence of counter-Enlightenment sentiments and movements, but the argument of the book is that the core principles of the Enlightenment are the singular and solid foundation for human flourishing and that objections to them are essentially mistakes born of ignorance, self-delusion, or wishful thinking.

16. *The Gnostic Religion*, 35.

17. The gnostic themes and images in Blood Meridian have been widely recognized and scrupulously discussed by several commentators; see for instance Mundik, "Striking the Fire Out of the Rock"; Daugherty, "Gravers False and True."

18. Phillips, "History and the Ugly Facts of Cormac McCarthy's *Blood Meridian*."

19. Jonas, *The Gnostic Religion*, 46.

20. Daugherty, "Gravers False and True," 161.

21. Nietzsche, too, of course, proposed a solution to nihilism, and Crews and others think that the judge's solution is Nietzsche's solution, or the logical extension of Nietzsche's ideas. This strikes me as unjust to Nietzsche and the relative subtlety and complexity of his thought, but certainly his ideas have historically shown themselves susceptible to appalling political use. See Crews, *Books Are Made Out of Books*, 201–3.

22. Bell, *The Achievement of Cormac McCarthy*, 125.

23. Lydia Cooper uses this as evidence for the "ethical" perspective of the work, in a convoluted way—the narrative style has a formal literariness that implies a teller, but it does not judge; thus, she argues, the style emphasizes the amoral lack of moral conscience and empathy that characterizes Chamberlain and the other scalphunters. (*No More Heroes*, 69 ff).

24. From Anna Karenina, cited in Wood, *How Fiction Works*, 65.

25. "The Over-Soul," in Emerson, *Emerson*, 394; quoted in Novak, *Nature and Culture*, 34.

26. Melville, *Moby-Dick*, 133.

27. Melville, 308.

28. Newton, *The Principia*, 501.

29. Barcley Owens locates the impetus for the novel's reassessment of the American myth of progress specifically in the violence and upheavals of the Vietnam War era (*Cormac McCarthy's Western Novels*, 20ff).

30. Arendt is referring to what is revealed in the rise of Nazism and Stalinism: "The subterranean stream of Western history has finally come to the surface and usurped the dignity of our tradition" (*The Origins of Totalitarianism*, ix).

31. Cited in Owens, 11.

32. The so-called Parable of the Tribes is relevant here—violence will triumph over nonviolence because if you have an aggressive group and a nonaggressive one, the aggressive one will either dominate the nonaggressive or the nonaggressive will have to become aggressive to defend itself.

33. For example, Martha Nussbaum's claim for the importance of literature to our moral lives is based on the idea that literature expands our capacity for empathy, enabling us to identify with people unlike ourselves. See Nussbaum, *Love's Knowledge*.

34. This emerges in recent interpretations of *Moby-Dick* which see Ahab's sin as the elevation of reason over feeling, as in Hubert Dreyfus and Sean Kelley's *All Things Shining*.

35. Weil, *Oppression and Liberty*, 173.

Chapter Three

Mourning Our Myths

The Apocalyptic Elegies of Robert Lowell and Wallace Stevens

"Pitch this portent" troubles me now; portent was the corpse, why portent?
Maybe a sign of death and the end of the world.

Robert Lowell, letter to Shozo Tokunaga, January 10, 1969

If Maclean transforms catastrophe into tragedy by finding tragic form for the events of Mann Gulch, one could say that McCarthy transforms historical catastrophe into apocalyptic form, finding the events he describes as images of an end of humanity seeded within human nature and human history. McCarthy's work at the same time suggests the possibility of a consciousness that would stand outside and be able to comprehend this enormity, allowing us at least to comprehend and to judge it, and possibly to find a radically different way of being human.

In this chapter, I continue to develop the idea of the apocalyptic as both modern reality and emergent literary form, turning to Robert Lowell and Wallace Stevens, who elegize humanity as we have known it, and considering what is revealed by the kinds of elegy that they write.

Tragedy and elegy could both be thought of as modes of making sense of loss, or, in the case of tragedy, defeat, failure and destruction—"catastrophe"—more generally. Tragedy, the dramatic or narrative mode, makes sense of catastrophe by showing it to be in accord with law; classically, it shows the greatness of the protagonist to be inextricably tied to his or her downfall. Though tragedy does not typically deal with a particular real-world loss (*Young Men and Fire* being an exception), the genre could be said to model a way of making sense of loss generally, or at least a certain category of loss which is neither totally arbitrary or contingent (a "freak accident") nor simply universal and inevitable (aging, dying) but which is the consequence of some action with its roots deep in the protagonist's character or situation and ultimately in human nature or the human situation. It is for this reason that tragedy can be educative. This kind of intelligibility takes the form of a story because it is about understanding human action and its consequences—the seeming laws of the universe are what we come to know, what we are referred to, in making sense of the unfolding of the narrative.

Elegy, on the other hand, is the lyric mode of making sense of or coming to terms with loss.[1] Traditionally it laments the death of a person; it is distinguished from "other forms of pure lament or memorial" in that it "frequently includes a movement from expressed sorrow toward consolation."[2] The concern in the elegy is generally not, as in tragedy, to explain or show what led to the death of the departed, but rather to memorialize them—and through this memorialization to affirm that the good they represented persists in some ideal form, that the human world is and remains meaningful and ordered despite the loss of one of its members, even an extraordinary one. The elegiac poem could be said not only to assert this meaning and order but to constitute it—the poem *is* the form in which the good of what is gone or past not merely persists but takes on or is shown to have a meaning that transcends the lost object.

The elegy has thus been characterized as the literary form of mourning, as performing the "work of mourning" in Freud's sense.[3] As Peter Sacks puts it, the elegiac poem effects a "movement from loss to consolation" through the "deflection of desire, with the creation of a trope both for the lost object and for the original character of the desire itself"[4]: the elegy finds a figurative form for the lost object and for the poet's attachment to that object—which, if the poem is of any general interest, is an attachment with which the reader can identify. So, for instance, in the sixteenth century Ben Jonson reconciles himself to his son's death by recognizing that his son always belonged to God and not to him:

Seven yeeres thou'wert lent to me, and I thee pay,

Exacted by thy fate, on the just day.

Here, as is common in traditional elegies, the loss is understood as part of the order of things, and that order is divinely underwritten and thus ultimately to be affirmed.

The poem doesn't simply serve as a substitution for the object (as if it could), but transforms the object into something enduring—at one level, through the way it is described and figured in the poem, associating it to persistent images and themes; at another level, through the very writing of the poem. For instance, Jahan Ramazani notes that the structure of Milton's "Lycidas," one of the classic elegies in the English language, follows a characteristic pattern of mourning as described by Freud: "Each single one of the memories and expectations in which the libido is bound to the object is brought up and hypercathected, and detachment of the libido is accomplished in respect of it" enabling the "withdrawal of the libido from this object and the displacement of it onto a new one."[5]

In Milton's poem, the drowned Edward King becomes the shepherd Lycidas, who as Northrop Frye notes "is equivalent to Adonis, and is associated with the cyclical rhythms of nature"[6]—King's death becomes only a phase in the cycle of death and rebirth seen in nature and mirrored in myth; "Lycidas" is transformed through the course of the poem from the physical body ("For Lycidas is dead," in the first stanza) to immortal spirit ("For Lycidas . . . is not dead," in the penultimate stanza), the soul that lives on with God and the spirit that lives on in poetry—King's poetry and, more pertinently, Milton's. Milton's poem not only asserts that transformation but performs it; the poem constitutes the abiding order to which it refers, but this is persuasive insofar as the order to which it refers, or which it evokes, seems *real*.

This is not to say that to "believe" in "Lycidas" we must believe in fauns, satyrs, or even in St. Peter as represented in the poem, sporting "mitred locks" and carting his "massy keys." I think we need not even believe in the personal afterlife as Milton depicts it, the spirit of Lycidas attended by singing saints.[7] What must compel conviction is the *basis* of Milton's figuration, the implicit relation between the drowned Edward King or the dead generally and the imagery and narrative of the poem—the *myth* of the poem, as Frye characterizes it: "Within the total literary order certain structural and generic principles, certain configurations of narrative and imagery, certain conventions and devices and *topoi*, occur over and over again. . . . The short, simple, and accurate name for this principle is myth."[8]

Frye shows the Adonis myth to serve as this "recurring structural principle" in "Lycidas"; "the Adonis myth is the structure of *Lycidas* . . . the connecting link between what makes *Lycidas* the poem it is and what unites it to other forms of poetic experience."[9] What does it mean to say this?

For Frye, myth constitutes the structure of (all) literary works—in distinction to their content—and understanding literature entails grasping the underlying *mythos* just as understanding painting depends on grasping relations of proportion, color, and so on and not just what is represented.[10]

I have alluded to myth throughout as a way of characterizing the normative conditions to which we are educated in the process of reading reflecting on literature. Frye's account, which finds an intrinsic connection between myth and literature and conceives myth not just as particular stories of one culture or another but as fundamental structures of sense, will help me to give further substance to this term.

A BRIEF EXCURSUS ON MYTH

Myth, for Frye, is first of all what we commonly understand by the term, that is, traditional and paradigmatic stories involving supernatural beings, divine or demonic. But Frye's analysis implies that these stories derive from or reflect something more fundamental, the basic structures of intelligibility of human experience. This is not to deny that myths are also *constitutive* of experience—that is, that human beings make sense of what they do with conscious or unconscious reference to myth—nor to deny that our deep structures of understanding are significantly formed by our specific culture and historical period. It is only to insist that myths are not arbitrary, that mythical stories "take hold" because they respond to fundamental human problems and correspond to basic material, psychological, social, and moral realities.

Frye characterizes the most basic underlying mythical structure in terms of a fundamental divide. On the one side there is heaven or the divine, representing the total fulfillment of human desire.[11] On the other side is hell or the demonic, representing the undesirable and all that denies human desire, largely in the imagery of "the vast, menacing, stupid powers of nature" (the untamed forest or barren heath as opposed to the garden; wild and dangerous animals as opposed to the domesticated sheep; the wasteland as opposed to the city). What these images represent or manifest is "inscrutable fate or external necessity," that which thwarts human will or desire.[12]

With the exception of pure depictions of one or the other of these extremes (of which there are relatively few in literature), Frye argues that literary works derive their structure and power from the paradigmatic conflicts between "heaven" and "hell"—the ultimately desirable, or good, and the ultimately undesirable, or evil—as played out in the human realm (or in a nonhuman realm with distinctively human characteristics, like that of the Greek gods or Aesop's animal fables).

Frye notes that the underlying structure of literature—that is, myth—is, or has been, fundamentally cyclical, reflecting the cycles of nature, human life, and civilizations, each of which have their "light" and "dark" sides—spring and summer versus fall and winter, birth and youth versus old age and death, the rise and fall of civilizations. The broadest literary genres are defined by which part of the cycle they describe: tragedy is about the downward movement of the cycle, comedy about the upward movement. Elegy could be said to make the downward movement tolerable by looking forward to, or affirming, the upward movement, as is explicit at the end of "Lycidas": Lycidas's death is the setting of the sun, implying the morning sunrise.

But myth is not—for Frye, I think, and certainly in the way that I understand it—merely consoling fantasy, a story laid on top of, and possibly distorting or obscuring, the way things really are so as to make them bearable, inventing meaning for what is "really" meaningless. Andrew Von Hendy distinguishes between "constructive" and "ideological" theories of myth that emerged in the modern period, the former seeing myth as an essential source of value and meaning which is in some sense *true* or at least an indispensable ground, the latter seeing it as falsifying, whether in the interests of a particular group vis-à-vis another or simply as therapeutic protection against nihilism.[13] One might see these not as mutually exclusive alternatives but as different aspects of or ways of seeing myth: particular historical mythologies may have ideological determinants and a social functional role, but in its basic narrative and imagistic components myth is also an essential way of making sense of reality as human beings encounter it.

To return to Milton and to Frye's claim that the Adonis myth is the "structuring principle" of "Lycidas," then: to put it simply, this means that the narrative or arc of the poem is one of death to rebirth as part of the cyclical order of things. The dominant imagery is pastoral, the imagery of classical antiquity, but these images are ultimately images of Christian salvation. As Frye argues, the poem reflects four orders of existence: (1) that of Christian salvation, (2) that of perfected human nature, "represented by the Garden of Eden in the Bible and the Golden Age in Classical myth," (3) that of physical nature, "morally neutral but theologically fallen," and (4) that of disorder and sin.[14] Milton's poem acknowledges all of these levels, but the redemptive myth, or myths—Christian and Classical—encompass the orders of the merely natural or the threatening chaos. This is what constitutes its elegiac effectiveness, its capacity to give sense and consolation.

Elegy as a form of intelligibility or understanding, however, is not timeless but historical. Just as Maclean, in seeking to make sense of the deaths of the Smokejumpers, has to depart from traditional tragic form, modern elegists have had to depart from the pastoral form of "Lycidas" and other earlier elegies—as the old myths have lost their power to compel conviction, poets have had to find new ones. (One might say that the poet's search for literary form *is* the search for the myth adequate to the present reality.) The elegy develops historically in ways that are not merely a matter of formal changes but reflect a changing historical reality.

Ramazani shows how poets since the nineteenth century have used and transformed the conventions of the traditional elegy to create "anti-elegiac elegies" that reflect "the acid suspicions of our moment."[15] In particular, he notes, modern elegists take issue with "the psychological propensity of the

genre to translate grief into consolation."[16] Whereas traditional elegies per-
form the work of mourning successfully, achieving a detachment of the ego
from the lost object, modern elegies tend to be "melancholic" in Freud's sense,
reflecting a thwarted mourning, an inability to fully move beyond the loss.

At its basis this "melancholia" may be attributed to the degeneration of
belief in the old structures of order according to which people could find consolation for the loss of their loved ones—the belief that the deceased lives on
in the Christian afterlife, for instance. One might object that there is little to
suggest that people living in modern society are on the whole less able to cope
with the deaths of loved ones than people living in traditional societies—even
atheists, for instance, are able to find consolation in secular "myths" of the
persistence of their loved ones in their offspring, in memory, in their accom-
plishments, even in the energy and matter of the universe which as we now
know can be neither created nor destroyed.[17] Yet if we take modern(ist) poetry
to reflect the acute edge of modern consciousness—the most extremely individual and historical consciousness, the consciousness of the individual for
whom social institutions are the least solid—there is reflected in this poetry a
disintegration of any firm ideal or normatively structured reality within which
to make sense of loss.

It historicizes not only the particular loss (the death of an individual)
but this loss of stability and ground that the modern elegy often deals with,
more or less explicitly. Elegy has perhaps always been about the death of a
world and not only the death of an individual within that world; Frye characterizes the subject of the traditional pastoral elegy as "a representative of
the dying spirit of nature."[18] In traditional elegy, though, there is some kind
of resurrection or renewal, whereas in modern elegy the loss seems not to be
just one phase of a cycle, the coming of winter that only precedes the coming of spring, but a loss without redemption, one which simply leaves the
world emptier, or—in the "apocalyptic elegies" I will discuss—figures the
end of the world itself. Modern elegies mourn, in Ramazani's cataloging, the
deaths of "ritual, God, of traditional consolation, of recuperative elegy, of the
sanctity of the dead, of 'healthy' mourning, and even perhaps—in the age
of the visual media and psychology—the death of the poet."[19] In traditional
elegy, beneath the death of the individual or the ending of a season is a deeper
and persistent reality that is not lost. In modern elegy, one might say, the
world itself dissolves, and what is left is a kind of consciousness—the poem
as the form of the consciousness of the poet. While traditional elegy could
still rely on underlying shared collective myths, particularly religious beliefs,
modern elegy lacks that (relatively) stable foundation.

Among the modern "anti-elegiac" elegies, I want to focus on two American
poems that could be called apocalyptic in the two dimensions I have explored,
that is, revelation and catastrophic ending, revelation *through* catastrophic

ending. Robert Lowell's "The Quaker Graveyard in Nantucket" and Wallace Stevens's "The Auroras of Autumn" do not only struggle with grieving absent the traditional consolations; they confront the very disintegration of the human world. And they are not merely skeptical and recriminatory, calling into question the order of things, debunking the old consolations; beyond the disillusioning there is some kind of revelation. (Perhaps the apocalyptic retains something inherently modernist rather than postmodernist, not merely deconstructive and disillusioning but constructive, if only of a transcendent perspective.)

Lowell's and Stevens's poems are not just elegies for an individual but for a world. Both works were written shortly after the end of World War II and the dropping of the atomic bomb, and they suggest, more or less explicitly, that the catastrophes of the first half of the twentieth century can only be comprehended by reconceiving the character of human history in light of an end that is at the same time a revelation—a revelation of ultimate tensions within the conditions of modern human life, and perhaps of the possibility of a transformed humanity.

"THE QUAKER GRAVEYARD IN NANTUCKET" AND THE CLASH OF MYTHS

I begin with Robert Lowell's "The Quaker Graveyard in Nantucket," which also, in a very different way from *Fire*, aims at transforming catastrophe into art, occasioned as it was by the death of Lowell's cousin Warren Winslow.

Allusions to "Lycidas" pervade "Quaker Graveyard." Lowell's elegy is also dedicated to an acquaintance who died at sea—Winslow was a Navy sailor who died in the apparently accidental explosion of his ship in port during World War II.[20] It has, furthermore, a similar structure to Milton's poem, with almost the same number of lines (194 to Milton's 193), likewise loosely rhymed and divided into stanzas of varying length; Hugh Staples therefore argues that the poem "implicitly invites" the comparison to Milton.[21]

If so, the effect is to emphasize how otherwise unlike "Lycidas" Lowell's poem is—that is, in alluding to this paradigmatic and traditional elegy, Lowell summons up a set of expectations which he will then defy. In dramatically departing from the conventions embodied by Milton's poem, Lowell implies that the conditions of traditional elegy—the persistence of a stable order which the bereaved can accept, if not welcome—no longer hold. As William Doreski writes, in keeping with the general critical consensus, "Lowell's poem represents . . . a questioning of the very roots of th[e] tradition" of English elegy.[22]

Opinions on the nature and outcome of that questioning are more diverse. Doreski argues that "Lowell rejects all the possible consolations that tradition offers, including the consolations of religion and literature."[23] Other critics find, if not consolation, at least an austere religious affirmation; as Robert Hass puts it, "the poem imagines the whole of human life as sterile violence . . . and it identifies finally with the inhuman justice of God,"[24] whether the God of "the traditional Christian mystic," as Staples claims,[25] or some less orthodox divinity. Marjorie Perloff finds this attempted identification to fail aesthetically, leaving us only with the poem's "merciless invective against man-made violence and horror, a horror never really transcended within the limits of the elegy."[26] If Lowell's poem does fail, however, I will argue that it is a "successful" failure like Maclean's, one that in its reaching toward an impossible reconciliation reveals an insuperable tension in our current condition.

The poem begins with an account of the discovery of an anonymous "drowned sailor," "bloodless, a botch of reds and whites," whose "open staring eyes / Were lustreless dead-lights." Already there is a contrast with traditional elegy, both in the anonymity of the dead and in the hideous description of the corpse, the emphasis not on the dearly departed soul but on the already decaying flesh. The poet-prophet then admonishes the sailors (or himself) to "ask for no Orphean lute / to pluck life back"—explicitly rejecting one of the fundamental myths underlying "Lycidas," the recovery of the dead from the underworld through song—figuratively, the possibility of a meaningful immortality through memorialization in poesy. This suggests an extreme materialism—that despite the classical allusions, this world is all there is. The sea is a "hell-bent deity" but only by analogy, because of its overwhelming violent power.

As the poem proceeds, it implies that human beings themselves—including the drowned sailor—are responsible for this world of force and violence through making war on nature and on one another. The drowned sailor is the victim of this violence but was also a collaborator in it. (As Alan Williamson asks rhetorically, "Where is there another elegy which concludes that its subject died partly because he deserved to?"[27]) The first stanza begins with reference to "our North Atlantic Fleet," and ends with the fleet firing its guns in "hoarse salute" to the dead—this is a world of war, a world at war, and the first stanza already suggests that it is a world of pure force if one sees it truly, stripped of any idealistic veneer. We have the instruments of war—"the guns of the steel fleet"—but no reference to their purposes. There is the sense, then, of the absence not only of one soul but of the "soul" of things generally, of ideal (that is, nonmaterial) ends and intentions.

The dominant historical imagery of the poem, however, is not of war but of whaling, and in the subsequent stanzas the poet identifies the Sailor—and also himself and his fellows and perhaps all of us readers as well—with the Quaker whalers of Nantucket and particularly their famous literary representatives, Ahab and the crew of the *Pequod*, hunters of the White Whale.

What does the poem intend to evoke with these associations?

The whale is most obviously the force of nature with which men are in fatal combat, killing and being killed—pursuing the whale for profit, howling for revenge when it lashes back at them; twice Lowell refers to "the bones" of the drowned whalers "cry[ing] out" for the sea beast that stove their boats. But the whale is also associated with God—it is "IS, the whited monster," the capital "IS" suggesting God's statement to Moses, "I AM THAT I AM" (Exodus 3:14).[28] In the fifth section the whale is identified with Christ and the whalers with his crucifiers, as Lowell gives a gruesome description of the killing and rendering of the whale, merging this with a description of the *Pequod*'s sinking:

> The gun-blue swingle . . . hacks the coiling life out: it works and drags
> And rips the sperm-whale's midriff into rags,
> Gobbets of blubber spill to wind and weather,
> Sailor, and gulls go round the stoven timbers
> Where the morning stars sing out together
> And thunder shakes the white surf and dismembers
> The red flag hammered in the mast head. Hide
> Our steel, Jonas Messias, in Thy side.

In addition to the references to Jonah and Jesus there is the echo in these lines of God's challenge to Job out of the whirlwind: "Where wast thou when I laid the foundations of the earth? declare, if thou hast understanding. / Who hath laid the measures thereof, if thou knowest? . . . or who laid the corner stone thereof; / When the morning stars sang together, and all the sons of God shouted for joy?"[29] This stanza thus evokes the appalling sinfulness of human beings and human nullity in the face of divine might and glory; it summons all the catastrophe of the crucifixion, man's ignorant destruction of his own salvation, and his belated recognition and repentance—or at least the poet-prophet's recognition and repentance on mankind's behalf.

"Quaker Graveyard" is thus rightly read as a jeremiad lambasting humanity's violence and greed, evoking our judgment and repulsion with its assaulting diction. This could still be leading to an elegiac affirmation of the divine order according to which the souls of the dead are saved by grace. If the structuring principle of "Lycidas" is the Adonis myth, the crucifixion at the end of the fifth section of "Quaker Graveyard" leads us to expect that the structuring myth of Lowell's poem is the Resurrection. This would be similar to the

Adonis myth in offering the consolation of rebirth, and of course in Milton's poem the ultimate myth *is* Christian—Lycidas's Adonisian "resurrection" is explicitly underwritten by Christ's ("So Lycidas sunk low, but mounted high / Through the dear might of him that walk'd the waves"). Arguably, emphasizing the Christian, historical narrative, as Lowell does, rather than the pagan, cyclical one suggests that what is at stake in "Quaker Graveyard" is not only one immortal soul which is assimilated to the ongoing rhythms of nature, but the fate of humanity as a whole, a humanity desperately in need of redemption. We might then expect the poem to metaphorically deliver and affirm that collective redemption as the only possible redemption of Winslow's death, the only possible consolation for any individual's death.

But the vision of "Quaker Graveyard" is far from traditionally Christian, both in its depiction of God and of "man" (as in McCarthy, this is a vision of humanity as defined by the destructive masculine which drives the course of its history), and the poem radically questions the possibility or character of "salvation."

If the whale is God, this suggests not the personal savior represented by Christ but the God of Job who identifies himself with the Leviathan, forbidding and finally beyond human comprehension—the God whose "answer" to Job's question of why he must suffer is not an answer but a display or assertion of power.

Other figurations of the whale-God of "Quaker Graveyard" evoke not even the temperamental father figure of the Old Testament but some more alien deity. IS instead of I AM implies a power that is not a humanlike intelligence but something blind and brute; this god is a monster—a "whited monster," which suggests the "whited sepulchre" of Isaiah, shining and pure on the outside but horrible and corrupt within. As in *Moby-Dick*, the whale in Lowell's poem is an ambivalent figure. Killing it is monstrous, but the whale is also a monster (even if only made so by man's own pursuit), responsible for countless human deaths. If nature is a manifestation of God's law on earth, then this suggests that God may be malevolent or, perhaps worse, wholly indifferent to human welfare. (This is, again, the "naturalistic sublime.")

Moreover, the poem suggests that it is the essential spirit of humankind that has brought us to this point—that human spiritedness is intrinsically bound to transgression and to violence and thus our end is either annihilation—if we fulfill that spirit—or exhaustion—if we relinquish it. This human striving, which at times takes the form of domination and violence, could be seen as a response to the perception of an indifferent universe. Ahab's pursuit of Moby Dick is arguably the insistence on some kind of sense and purpose as against the possibility that "there's naught beyond" the mask of the material world. As Nietzsche says of the human will, "it will rather will *nothingness* than *not* will."[30] If Ahab is from one perspective the villain of *Moby-Dick*, he is also its tragic hero, its towering figure, and in "Quaker Graveyard" alongside the obvious critique of Ahab and the whalers I read a subtle tone of mourning for their spirit:

> This is the end of running on the waves;
> We are poured out like water. Who will dance
> The mast-lashed master of Leviathans
> Up from this field of Quakers in their unstoned graves?

"Mast-lashed master" also evokes Odysseus and Dante's ambiguous portrayal of the Greek hero in the *Inferno*, a "false counselor" but one whose words seem truly to speak to the highest aspirations of humanity: "Call to mind from whence ye sprang; / Ye were not form'd to live the life of brutes, / But virtue to pursue and knowledge high."[31] This thread is thus in tension with the idea that the poem presents human violence and overreaching simply as a moral error to be renounced—perhaps it is; certainly it has led to the present situation and to the Sailor's death, but it is also constitutive of human being and even of human greatness.

Lowell's own commentary on *Moby-Dick* corroborates an interpretation of Ahab in "Quaker Graveyard" as a figure of double aspect. "Ahab . . . is apocalyptic," he writes in an essay on epics he was working on in 1977, the year of his death, "with a rage that drowns ship, shipmates, and himself. His destiny is analogous to heroes in Norse Saga, Wagner's *Götterdämmerung*, and, in real life, Adolf Hitler."[32] The *Pequod*'s captain is likened to Hitler, but also to epic "heroes." In Lowell's experience of Melville's novel, the story "tells us not to break our necks on a brick wall. Yet what sticks in the mind is the Homeric prowess of the extinct whaleman, gone before his prey"[33]; the moral or pragmatic message is overwhelmed by the exhilarating spectacle of man tragically confronting the forces that dwarf him. (I do not mean to suggest that Lowell was ambivalent about actual violence—he was imprisoned as a conscientious objector during World War II and protested against Vietnam, and he went on public record in 1962 with a statement that "No nation should possess, use or retaliate with its bombs. I believe we should die rather than drop our own bombs."[34] But he evidently felt the pull of images of extremity and transgression which he recognized as continuous with the violence he abhorred.)

At the end of Section V, then, the structuring principle of "Quaker Graveyard" appears not as a single myth but as the competition between two myths, which might be characterized as tragic humanist on the one hand and Christian on the other. The allusions to Ahab and the *Pequod* suggest the myth of the quest—the quest against the monster, in this case ending in catastrophic defeat. There is also the resonance with Dante's Ulysses and with Icarus, both of whom transgress human limits and are consequently destroyed, but destroyed as heroes, or at least exceptional figures, figures whose pursuits define the limits of human striving.

This myth is in competition with the myth of the Resurrection, of penitence and salvation. The two myths could be seen to jostle for control of the poem until the end of Section V and the cry of repentance. But there is then a stark break and discontinuity between Sections V and VI, after which arises a new set of images.

After the almost hysterical crucifixion, the poem does seem temporarily to move toward the implied salvation through penitence, shifting to a dramatically different register—Section VI is separately titled "Our Lady of Walsingham" and describes pilgrims to a shrine of the Virgin in England. The setting suddenly becomes pastoral, and instead of "fighting Quakers" we have barefoot penitents and a memory of the deceased Sailor in peaceful harmony with the divine order, having once "whistled Sion by that stream." But this vision, like the previous representations of the divine, remains ambivalent, the penitents walking "Slowly along the munching English lane, / Like cows to the old shrine, until you lose / Track of your dragging pain." This bovine humanity hardly seems a compelling alternative to the Quaker whalers in their "mad scramble" (one thinks of Nietzsche's "herd" and the "Last Men" whose greatest wish is to eliminate suffering from human life), and while the sea may be a place of terror and violence, these lines suggest the inadequacy or diminishedness of landedness—the obverse of the fraught heroism of the seafaring life.

Here, too, we get a very different vision of God in the description of the statue of the Virgin, a statue "too small for her canopy" with "no comeliness / At all or charm in that expressionless / Face with its heavy eyelids," a face that "Expressionless, expresses God." Lowell concludes the stanza:

> She knows what God knows,
> Not Calvary's cross nor crib at Bethlehem
> And the world shall come to Walsingham.

Much of this section is quoted from E. I. Watkins's description of the shrine in *Catholic Art and Culture*, which laments the decline of religiosity in fragmented, secular modern culture and expresses the hope and need for a renaissance, and the description can be taken as characteristic of a Catholic mysticism, the figure of the Virgin inscrutable and inaccessible to this-worldly perception.[35] But Lowell, as I read it, gives us not a mystical vision but the perspective of someone thoroughly outside of the union with God. Albert Gelpi calls this description "Gnostic," wholly otherworldly and incomprehensible, in opposition to this wholly corrupt world which cannot be redeemed, only escaped. "God here is all inscrutable transcendence and no tormented immanence."[36] Whatever the world shall get from coming to Walsingham, it is not the redemption from a personal savior which would be the hoped-for response to the plea to "Jonas Messias," but rather a radical unselfing, even an annihilation. As Gelpi puts it, "the way to Walsingham presages not a redemption *of* the human but a redemption *from* the human."[37] This is the utter negation of Ahab, defined in relation to a god "whose right worship is defiance,"[38] "striking through the mask" in order to know the truth of this god and to avenge himself and humanity. Here instead we have a humanity prostrate before a divinity that is to remain ever mysterious and unmovable—or even before a vacant idol, since an impenetrable and unresponsive divine will is difficult to distinguish from no God at all.

The drastic departure in style and tone in this section is part of what led Perloff to criticize the poem for its failure of coherence,[39] and other critics have struggled as well to find the unifying principle of Lowell's diverse and divergent images and perspectives. Yet the conclusion of the poem suggests to me that this difficulty or impossibility of integration is part of its form and intention.

In the final stanza the troubling ambiguity of the vision, or visions, of God reaches a catastrophic dénouement. We are returned to Nantucket and to a seascape empty of the divine, though filled with the ghosts—or perhaps just the corpses—of humankind's turbulent history; the ocean is "fouled with the blue sailors, / Sea-monsters, upward angel, downward fish." The image of human beings as monstrous hybrids of angel and fish is striking, conveying the sense that humanity is fundamentally conflicted, in tension with itself. I am reminded of Richard Goldschmidt's conception of "hopeful monsters," new species that emerge as "macromutations," most—but not all—of which are nonadaptive. The connection to evolution is, I think, justified, even if Lowell was unaware of Goldschmidt's hypothesis,[40] as the remainder of the stanza offers a Darwinian retelling of Genesis that upends the idea of man's "dominion" over nature, concluding:

> When the Lord God formed man from the sea's slime
> And breathed into his face the breath of life
> And blue-lung'd combers lumbered to the kill
> The Lord survives the rainbow of his will.

The famous last line refers, of course, to God's promise to Noah never to flood the earth again—that is, that he will never again wipe out humanity. Yet here, God's promise proves hollow—humanity is doomed; the Lord "survives" his creation, that is, outlives it, whether because humanity is destroyed by the nature it insists on dominating or because it brings on itself its own destruction, which may finally amount to the same thing.

One could therefore say that the myth that structures "Quaker Graveyard" is, finally, the gnostic myth, as in McCarthy (if not with McCarthy's conscious intentionality)—a modern gnostic myth in which the essential corruption of this world issues forth or is manifested in historical forces that move human history inevitably toward a violent end, and salvation is attained only through an escape from history—a salvation of consciousness that comes from identifying from a perspective outside of human history, in this case, with that of the God who remains after his human creation has perished.

Such a myth would constitute a radical departure from the myth of death to rebirth that structured "Lycidas," and perhaps the departure is even more radical than that, if Frye is correct to see the myth underlying premodern, or premodernist, literature generally as that of a cosmic cycle. As Mircea Eliade observes, Christianity already represents a linearization of myth, "from cosmos to history,"[41] from recurrent cycle to teleological movement, though Milton is able to reconcile the seasonal cycle of death and rebirth with the final eschatological Rebirth. Apocalypse in the catastrophic rather than apotheistic sense, however, can be seen as the breaking of the cycle at the point of death rather than life. The myth of apocalypse is the myth of the end of humanity, the end of history, which as figured by Lowell is not the arrival of God's kingdom but a wasteland in which only the Lord survives.

It may in fact be more accurate and revealing to say that the poem is structured not by a single myth but by the competition between its myths—naturalistic, Christian, and gnostic—and that this very ambivalence and competition and arguable "triumph" of the latter is, in a sense, its "structuring myth." The loss it figures and mourns is not just the loss of the deceased but of a certain conception of salvation and of human progress, or of any assured human future whatsoever.

Thus in Lowell's poem redemption and the promise of resurrection are thwarted or at least called radically into doubt.[42] God's existence is not foreclosed, but the loss of Lowell's cousin and all the human loss Winslow's death represents and forecasts resists final reconciliation with the myth of divine salvation. God's part in all this remains unsettled, hence the poem's kaleidoscopic aspect. The myth that does command conviction is a new history of humankind—a history whose logic is not the logic of progress, the Hegelian movement toward the realization of reason and freedom, but the unfolding of perhaps irreconcilably conflicting human imperatives and inhuman forces. This is again the apocalyptic sublime, and the consolation of this elegy is only the consolation of consciousness, of comprehending human life and history in the blinding light of this terrifying trajectory.

This encompassing perspective is embedded in Lowell's very language. The incantatory cadence gives the sense of an inevitability that is exhilarating even as it is terrible, barreling toward the final lines, a perfectly rhyming couplet in iambic pentameter. This is a thunderous consummation and therefore a kind of consolation, but at the cost of a tremendous dispossession, the acceptance not only of the individual's end but of the possibility—the probability—of humanity's. We can make sense of the human trajectory, "Quaker Graveyard" implies, only by imagining it from the standpoint of a time when even God, if there is a God, cannot or will not help us.

END AND REVELATION WITHOUT END: WALLACE STEVENS'S SEARCH(ES) FOR THE "SUPREME FICTION"

In "The Auroras of Autumn," Wallace Stevens suggests that even the austere consolation of "Quaker Graveyard" might be a fiction if not a falsity—a distinction with a real difference for Stevens. While "Auroras" does not so much imply the end of the species or of civilization as Lowell's does, it is nonetheless pervaded by a strong "sense of an ending"—suggesting, both though its themes and its highly ambiguous and often obscure form, the utter insubstantiality of all prior foundational myths of human life and the ungroundedness of any sense we make. The poem, and Stevens's poetry and poetic theory generally, at the same time argue in both substance and form that poetry is essential to revealing or creating a new ground of sense. Stevens's work thus thematizes the fundamental process of poetic sensemaking, its difficulties and its possibilities, and suggests that an awareness of this fundamental process is essential to a distinctively modern apocalyptic consciousness.

Stevens's Antiapocalyptic Apocalyptic Poetics

Stevens's use throughout his poetry of themes and images of endings and revelations has provoked a substantial critical discourse on whether he is an apocalyptic or antiapocalyptic poet—or both.[43] Harold Bloom claims for Stevens an "apocalyptic impulse" that had been "dismissed" in his early poems but "begins to break in upon his reveries in *An Ordinary Evening in New Haven* and *The Rock* and then . . . dominates" in his poems thereafter.[44] Bloom seems to mean "apocalyptic" in the positive sense of the original genre, a transcendental fulfillment that constitutes a radical break with the exhausted past—though here, the fulfillment is not that of the Christian Kingdom of God but rather a realization of and through the imagination out of and against the corrupted and unmeaningful "real" world. Charles Berger finds Stevens's late poetry apocalyptic (also) in the sense of anticipating imminent worldly catastrophe, seeing the northern lights in "Auroras" as evoking the sublime terror of the atomic bomb (a reading I shall not endorse).[45] Eleanor Cook, on the other hand, characterizes "Ordinary Evening" (at least) as "antiapocalyptic,"[46] not seeking a New Heaven but rather embracing the commonplaceness of New Haven, though Cook seems to allow this resistance to eschatological rupture is ambivalent, as she characterizes Stevens's "Puella Parvula," published in the same volume, as "an apocalyptic poem [that] dissolves the world in biblical language."[47] Malcolm Woodland notes with respect to the latter poem that "its antiapocalyptic stance proves difficult to distinguish from an apocalyptic one," juxtaposing its imagery of the End with an expressed "opposition to the idea of any preordained end of history, and in particular to the biblical language in which that idea has been embodied."[48] Woodland suggests that ambivalence regarding apocalypse may indeed be encoded in Stevens's poetry generally, thus eliciting these divergent readings.[49]

A largely parallel but related critical debate has addressed the extent to and way(s) in which Stevens wrote in awareness of historical (political and social) crisis and did or did not see (his) poetry as having a public and political role to play in addressing such crises. In 1989, Jacqueline Vaught Brogan could observe that "with only a few exceptions . . . there is an unbroken tradition regarding Stevens' poetry as socially irrelevant, socially unconcerned, and even (most damningly) socially irresponsible."[50] Since that time, Brogan and other critics have successfully made the case for Stevens's poetic concern with the ills of his times and his intention to respond to those ills.[51] As the earlier consensus indicates, though, it is far from obvious what kind of a response his poetry represents, and it would seem not to be an ideologically committed one endorsing some specific politics or social program.

These discourses intersect in the question of whether Stevens, insofar as he did perceive his time as a time of crisis and his poetry as a response to that crisis, conceived of that crisis apocalyptically. James Longenbach argues that Stevens's engagement in the extrapoetic world through his profession as an surety lawyer educated him to the necessary imperfections of practical and political life, "his refusal of utopian seductions sav[ing] him from apocalyptic despair"[52] and rooting him in a commitment to "the plain sense of things," the title of one of Stevens's later (and grimmer) poems. Yet as Longenbach acknowledges, the plain sense of things "is never plain for long," and Brogan argues that Stevens's poetics were in fact "revolutionary,"[53] though not utopian.

In calling "Auroras" an apocalyptic poem responding to a collective crisis, I am not aligning myself precisely with or against any particular camp in this debate but rather arguing that the poem is apocalyptic in the sense used throughout this book—namely, in apprehending a catastrophe which calls into question the former sense of things and calls for a new kind of sense, a sense which the poem itself instantiates. This means, too, that "Auroras" intends to be "efficacious," if not (necessarily) politically in the conventional sense. My reading ought to be compatible with much of both the apocalyptic and antiapocalyptic interpretations of Stevens (which Woodland already suggests could be reconcilable) and will perhaps shed new light on Stevens's apocalyptic antiapocalypticism, or antiapocalyptic apocalypticism, as well as on the relationship between his perception of historical calamity and his sense of a need for a new imaginative vision. Most importantly for the purposes of this book, I hope to elucidate what the subtle and tensive relationship between catastrophe and revelation in Stevens's poems suggests about the conditions of sensemaking in our own precarious present.

Crises Modern and Contemporary

The central preoccupation of Stevens's poetry is often characterized as "the relationship between imagination and reality." For Stevens, this is not an idle intellectual exercise but a response to a deeply felt problem, a problem which is, at least in part, the crisis first deeply registered in the nineteenth century—the loss of traditional religious faith and the need for a new way of conceiving the transcendent basis of human life. Thus Stevens's oeuvre as a whole could be considered elegiac, an act of mourning. Stevens is a Romantic in that he believes that the only way to find such a ground is through "the imagination," the individual's capacity to apprehend structures of meaning in the world beyond what is visible or given.[54]

Fundamentally, Stevens sought to find or to create "a poem equivalent to the idea of God,"[55] a "supreme fiction," a myth in the sense articulated above: a narratively structured and imagistically embodied reflection of the fundamental reality in relation to which human beings ought to live. Assessing what he achieves or fails to achieve in his poetry, how he goes about searching for or trying to write such a poem, ought therefore to direct us to the core of the problem of finding a ground of sense adequate to the modern situation.

While Stevens claims for poetry a role analogous to that of religion, he acknowledges that the "God" one finds through poetry is substantially different from the God of traditional religion. We have lost or are losing the latter, a crisis which at the same time creates the possibility of a new consciousness. As Stevens writes in one of his essays, "To see the gods dispelled in mid-air and dissolve like clouds is one of the great human experiences," an experience that leaves us bereft and yet with a new independence and sense of our own powers: "There was always in every man the increasingly human self, which instead of remaining the observer, the non-participant, the delinquent, became constantly more and more all there was or so it seemed; and whether it was so or merely seemed so still left it for him to resolve life and the world in his own terms."[56] Without the gods—which is to say without traditional religion, in a society in which the gods or God are no longer a part of the shared social reality—the individual becomes newly responsible for the discernment of ultimate value. This allows for a kind of freedom, but it also creates the danger of nihilism.

The other contemporary crisis as Stevens conceives it, or other fundamental component to the present crisis, belongs distinctively to the twentieth century: what Stevens calls the "pressure of the contemporaneous" or the "pressure of reality," which is "the pressure of an external event or events on the consciousness to the exclusion of any power of contemplation."[57] Stevens's comments on this "pressure" are written in the 1930s and early 1940s, and their proximate referent is the tumultuous events of the period—the aftermath of World War I, the Depression in America, the outbreak of World War II. But it is not just the fact of war and social distress, which have obviously been part of the human situation throughout history. It is, it would seem, the way in which these events create a fundamental uncertainty, the sense that "the end of civilization . . . is not merely possible but measurably probable" and indeed that it has already happened: "If you are not a communist, has it not already ended in Russia? If you are not a Nazi, has it not ended in Germany? We no sooner say that it never can happen here than we recognize that we say it without any illusions."[58] The fact that Hitler would be defeated, then, does not negate a lasting change in the historical situation, the fact that stability and progress are not given, that we now live in the shadow of the ongoing possibility of an "end of civilization." This is one element that makes Stevens's poetry "apocalyptic" in the sense considered here.

Stevens sees poetry as the essential response to both of these crises, or both of these aspects of the historical crisis, and thus he can deepen our understanding of the role of literature in our sensemaking, and particularly sensemaking under conditions of crisis, terminal or perpetual. Stevens sees poetry's response to crisis as a reconciliation of "reality" and "the imagination"—a reconciliation that takes the form of a kind of elegy.

Poetry and the Death of God

With respect to the departure of the gods—or the "death of God" in the indelible formulation of Nietzsche, a major influence on Stevens: Stevens muses in one of his adages that "After one has abandoned a belief in god, poetry is that essence which takes its place as life's redemption."[59] In one of his early and most famous poems, "Sunday Morning," Stevens describes a woman resisting the austere and (as she and, it would seem, Stevens experience them) life-denying demands of Christianity—lazing at home instead of attending church, she dreams of "silent Palestine / Dominion of the blood and sepulchre" and asks "Why should she give her bounty to the dead?" protesting that "Divinity must live within herself," in her emotion-laden experiences, particularly of the beauties of the natural world. But she is troubled by the transience of earthly life, the lack of transcendent meaning—"But in contentment I still feel / The need of some imperishable bliss."

The poem seems to reject the possibility and even the ultimate desirability of such transcendent assurance; the narrator proclaims twice that "Death is the mother of beauty" (the first time, perhaps, too facilely, but the second with seemingly greater conviction) and laments the projection of earthly delights into a fantasized unchanging paradise, suggesting such a heaven could not have the piquancy of life on earth—"Alas, that they should wear our colors there, . . . / And pick the strings of our insipid lutes."

Stevens claimed in a letter that "the poem is simply an expression of paganism" and agreed with an interpreter that it described "a naturalistic religion as a substitute for supernaturalism,"[60] and, unlike most of his later poetry, it does not directly reflect on poetry or the imagination and their role in the redemption of reality. But arguably the poem enacts what Stevens would later make explicit in both his poetry and his prose—that "divinity" lies not only in the keen perceptions of all the meaningful-seeming nuance of inner and outer reality—"Passions of rain, or moods in falling snow; / Grievings in loneliness, or unsubdued / Elations when the forest blooms; / Gusty emotions on wet roads on autumn nights"—*but in their articulation in poetry.* (Indeed, can the perception be separated from the articulation?) The poem concludes:

> We live in an old chaos of the sun,
> Or old dependency of day and night,
> Or island solitude, unsponsored, free,
> Of that wide water, inescapable.
> Deer walk upon our mountains. . . .
> And, in the isolation of the sky,
> At evening, casual flocks of pigeons make
> Ambiguous undulations as they sink,
> Downward to darkness, on extended wings.

Paraphrased, these lines articulate our existentially lonely position in the universe, and essentially assert that there is no reality beyond this world. Yet that is not, I think, what most readers find conveyed by this passage—rather, the poetry of the passage itself, its beauty and suggestiveness, convey a deep meaningfulness, if a bittersweet one. The poem itself enacts the "new paganism" it proposes: "paganism" because in it divinity is to be found not in a single transcendent being but in nature (and in the self), "new" because there is no definite or reified belief in spirits here, no theology or ritualistic practice beyond the writing and reading of poetry, only the discernment and poetic evocation of some beyond, some horizon of meaningfulness beyond the visible or experiential but graspable only through the visible or experiential. The poem thus at once both registers the loss of the old "imperishable bliss" but at the same time finds the spirit of what was lost within the perishable. It describes the perishable in a way that evokes that spirit, that divine, now transformed from a personalized God—"Jove in the clouds" with "his mythy mind"—to something only evoked or suggested by our emotions or perceptions.

In the poem, one might say, reality changes "from substance to subtlety," a phrase Stevens uses in characterizing the transformation of "reality" generally in the modern period:

> The theory of poetry, that is to say, the total of the theories of poetry, often seems to become in time a mystical theology or, more simply, a mystique. The reason is the same reason why the pictures in a museum of modern art often seem to become in time a mystical aesthetic, a prodigious search of appearance, as if to find a way of saying and of establishing that all things, whether below or above appearance, are one and that it is only through reality, in which they are reflected or, it may be, joined together, that we can reach them. Under such stress, reality changes from substance to subtlety.[61]

This statement itself is somewhat mystical, but that is consistent with its claim that the theory of poetry (or art) becomes in modernity a "mystical theology"—that is, the very characterization of what art does must refer to a reality that can only finally be known through the experiential union with the divine, or its analogy. Stevens is reflecting here on the movement toward abstraction in modern art, and he connects this movement to the diminishment of religious belief and a correspondingly increasing sense that "this world"—the phenomenal reality of our experience and our scientific knowledge—is all that there is. Yet at the same time this "all" is felt, at least by the poet, not to be merely material, and many of the phenomena of our experience and of nature strike us as symbolic (the magnitude of a mountain or roaring waterfall as conveying some more-than-natural greatness) or archetypal (the aura of the mother as reflecting a not merely psychological attachment but a deep condition of sense). Like the Transcendentalists, Stevens finds the phenomenal world as symbolic of the spiritual. (In Emerson's words, "Every natural fact is a symbol of some spiritual fact."[62]) This is not necessarily to claim that the natural world was created by some supernatural power *as* symbolic, but that the natural world (and perhaps the artificial world as well) is an inexhaustible source of images according to which we make sense of our experience—especially, I would add, when that experience resists conventional categorization.

The Transcendentalists as well as the earlier Romantics had, on the whole, a far greater degree of conviction than later thinkers about this relationship between the phenomenal world and spiritual reality, a conviction that there *was* some transcendent reality or order there to be known. One can see this reflected in eighteenth- and nineteenth-century Romantic art, in which natural scenery clearly represents or manifests an ideal order, and especially the sublime. But even for Melville by 1850 this symbolic interpretation of the world has become problematic; one has to choose between fixing upon and reifying meaning like crazy Ahab, who "pile[s] upon the whale's white hump the sum of all the general rage and hate felt by his whole race from Adam down,"[63] or reveling in polysemy like passive Ishmael. In either case the ontology is called into question, and it is further troubled by the various developments in the late nineteenth century and first half of the twentieth— among others, the "hermeneutics of suspicion" of Freud and Nietzsche, the emerging relativism of early sociology and anthropology, the ever-increasing pace of technological and social change, the political and cultural clashes bursting out into two world wars.[64]

There is consequently a shift, as Charles Taylor describes, from Romantic art portraying "unspoilt nature, human emotion . . . in such a way as to show some greater spiritual reality or significance" to nonrepresentational modern art in which "the locus of epiphany has shifted to within the work itself," an awareness of the mediating work of human subjectivity and a focus on the medium itself as the source of "epiphany." The epiphany now "can only be brought about through the work, which remains a 'symbol' . . . we can't understand what it is qua epiphany by pointing to some independently available object described or referent."[65] The work still is still "referential," but its referent must now be evoked rather than depicted.

A naturalistic painting of a mountain, if it is a great one, is necessarily a painting of sublimity or beauty. But in modern abstract art, the physical and visible object, the "tenor" or symbolic referent of the visual metaphor, so to speak, becomes progressively difficult to precisely or definitively articulate, and the "vehicle" correspondingly becomes indeterminate or elusive.[66] One might say that there is a shift from attention to the tenor of the metaphor to the creation of the metaphor as a whole, the imaginative apprehension and artistic creation of some sensible representation of an intelligible reality. In Romantic paintings one looks "through" the mountain, which is clearly a mountain, to the sublimity it symbolizes. In the art of the late nineteenth and early twentieth centuries, Stevens argues, the object becomes progressively less "objective." This abstraction disrupts our reduction of the object to the concept under which we usually classify it, and thereby have done with it.[67] Rather than a "realistic" depiction of Mount Saint-Victoire, which we simply identify as such, Cezanne gives us, as Stevens quotes the artist, "planes bestriding each other . . . planes in color . . . the colored area where shimmer the souls of the planes, in the blaze of the kindled prism, the meeting of planes in the sunlight."[68] What the picture depicts is no longer the mountain but something evoked by the abstracted visual components, the colors and angles of the planes comprising the landscape. As Cezanne's quote implies, with its personification of the planes and its reference to their "souls," this is not a shift to sheer aesthetic or visual play, either; the "planes bestriding each other" still depict something. But that referent—the reality depicted by the modern painting or, analogously, by the modern poem—shifts from substance to subtlety, from some object visually depicted to something spiritual evoked or suggested by the visual.

Stevens links this abstract transcendent referent to the Platonic good:

> Pure poetry is both mystical and irrational . . . While it can lie in the tempera-
> ment of very few of us to write poetry in order to find God, it is probably the
> purpose of each of us to write poetry to find the good which, in the Platonic
> sense, is synonymous with God. One writes poetry, then, in order to approach
> the good in what is harmonious and orderly. Or, simply, one writes poetry out
> of a delight in what is harmonious and orderly. . . . The poets who most urgently
> search the world for the sanctions of life, for that which makes life so prodi-
> giously worth living, may find their solutions in a duck in a pond or in the wind
> on a winter night.[69]

So in writing (and perhaps reading) poetry, one seeks and finds harmony and order, that which makes life worth living, and it does this through occasioning an immediate, if temporary, grasp of transcendent meaning—"a momentary existence on an exquisite plane."[70]

The poetic approach to the good goes by way of poetic "resemblance." In another essay Stevens writes that "the resemblance between things" is "one of the significant components of reality."[71] By this he seems to be referring to an essential quality of the world as we find it. Resemblance is "the base of appearance," and Stevens's first example is that of color: "There is enough green in the sea to relate it to the palms . . . the light alone creates a unity." As I look at my desk, my first impression is in fact of chaotic dissimilarity, but soon I see the kinds of relationships Stevens means: the horizontal of the desk echoes the horizontal of the stacked books and of my laptop, and so on, and one book is like another. This is another aspect of resemblance: simple categorization, which allows us to recognize a thing for what it is—"each man resembles all other men, each woman resembles all other women, this year resembles last year."[72] It is only against these kinds of likenesses that one apprehends the unlikenesses that are equally essential to our experience (a point Stevens does not make).

These are examples of resemblance in "nature," which are resemblance between "two or more of the parts of reality." But there are also metaphorical resemblances, and these include resemblances "between something imagined and something real as, for example, between music and whatever may be evoked by it" or "between two imagined things as when we say that God is good."[73] These latter examples imply that "reality" for Stevens means the visible, sensible world, and that what is not visible or sensible is "imagined."

Yet the division is not so simple. Resemblances involving what is imagined are, or become, part of "reality" too, as Stevens says when speaking of the way in which an object may "resemble" its (former) owner[74]:

> One may find intimations of immortality in an object on the mantelpiece; and these intimations are as real in the mind in which they occur as the mantelpiece itself. Even if they are only a part of an adult make-believe, the whole point is that the structure of reality because of the range of resemblances that it contains is measurably an adult make-believe.[75]

It would seem that there are two meanings of "reality" at work here. In the first instance, "reality" as "nature," as the visible, sensible world, is opposed to what is imagined. But in the second instance, as in this passage, reality is the world as we inhabit it and that world is inextricably structured by the imagination as well as by physical objects.[76] In the latter case reality is not simply equivalent to "nature"; it includes nature but also what we apprehend through metaphor.

Everyone's world is therefore structured by the resemblance of the real to the imagined, but poetry intensifies these resemblances and thereby "enhances the sense of reality, heightens it, intensifies it. . . . In short, a sense of reality keen enough to be in excess of the normal sense of reality"—that is, poetry or the poetic sense of reality—"creates a reality of its own. Here what matters is that the intensification of the sense of reality creates a resemblance: that reality of its own is a reality."[77] Stevens does not elaborate on the difference between the "normal sense of reality" and the poetic, heightened sense that is "in excess" of the normal sense, but I think the idea of "social reality" is clarifying here. In our ordinary mode of apprehending the world, we operate according to conventional resemblances or what Peter Berger and Thomas Luckmann call "typifications."[78] We recognize a woman as like other women according to the relevant characteristics (which is, by definition, what makes her a woman); a classroom as like other classrooms, and so on. And of course the example of gender indicates how these conventional structures of resemblance can be distorting—how they can prevent us from recognizing what's really there, the individuality or reality of a person or a situation. They reduce the world we inhabit to something flatter and more simplistic than it really is.

Poetry, on the other hand, evokes or draws our attention to resemblances that are not typical. Keats finds a resemblance between a Grecian urn and an "unravished bride of quietness / . . . foster-child of silence and slow time." And the commonality between these two dissimilar things is not to be found in or at the level of everyday, mundane (or profane), pragmatic, typified social reality. It is difficult to characterize the level at which that commonality *is* to be found, which is perhaps precisely the modern problem. Formerly it might have been characterized as the sacred; for the Romantics, the sublime. The mythical, the transcendent. In the twentieth century perhaps one can say little more than that it is the *relatively* transcendent, that is, whatever belongs or ought to belong to our ground of apprehension or judgment that goes beyond everyday social reality.

The "adult make-believe" that poetry creates or enables is thus one in which some depth dimension of reality is made present and real. The reality created or evoked by poetry "resembles" reality proper—poetry (and ultimately by this Stevens means all art) shows reality transformed into something harmonious and ordered, or one might say reality given *form*.

In premodern(ist) poetry, at least in Stevens's view, there is some definite or agreed-upon character to the common ground of resemblance. As his poem "Of Modern Poetry" begins:

> The poem of the mind in the act of finding
> What will suffice. It has not always had
> To find: the scene was set; it repeated what
> Was in the script.
>   Then the theatre was changed
> To something else. Its past was a souvenir.
>
> . . . It has
> To construct a new stage.

This suggests that premodernist poetry could rely on a certain common background of that ultimate source of value and meaning to which poetry is supposed to point—it had only to find new metaphors by which to convey it. Modern poetry, on the other hand, must find its own basis for resemblance, and this basis is always provisional.

> It has to be on that stage
> And . . . speak words that . . .

In the delicatest ear of the mind, repeat,
Exactly, that which it wants to hear, at the sound
Of which, an invisible audience listens,
Not to the play, but to itself, expressed
In an emotion as of two people, as of two
Emotions becoming one.

What is essential here, and essentially modern, is that the poem does not simply describe or evoke some realm of transcendent value, which the reader might just take as a fantasy. What the audience hears is *itself*, its own response to the play, and this is not a shortcoming of the poem but its purpose: through its multiplicity and ambiguity, to turn its readers back toward themselves so that they recognize what the poem evokes to correspond to and awaken some essential quality of their own consciousness. The figure of "an emotion as of two people, as of two / Emotions becoming one" suggests that the meeting of poem and reader is like a meeting of two subjectivities. Just as we only come to know ourselves in dialogue or in relationship to another, the encounter with the poem is the condition for the reader's access to their own deepest sensitivity—"the delicatest ear of the mind."

The title of this poem—"Of Modern Poetry"—in combination with its first line—"The poem of the mind in the act of finding"—implies that all of modern poetry *is* that poem. For Stevens, a poem is fundamentally a metaphor (for reality). Thus modern poetry as a whole is a metaphor for modern reality, which is "a prodigious search of appearances" for a principle of unity, or rather, prodigious *searches.* It is essential that Stevens's poetry finds myriad figures for reality and poetry or the imagination's relation to it. Poetry constructs the theater and acts out reality upon the stage. A feminine figure, "the maker," walks along the shore and sings a song that echoes or mediates or creates the song of the sea. Reality is a dump, a heap of broken images, and poetry sits on it and tries to create something from the rubbish. Even within a single poem the representation of this relation shifts: in "The Man with the Blue Guitar," reality, "Things as they are" are at one point "changed upon the blue guitar"; at other points what the guitarist plays is counterposed to reality. There is always some tension, but the relationship ranges from strict dichotomy to productive interdependence. But the fact that this myth must be expressed in these diverse figures is essential to the myth itself and its distinctiveness from traditional myths: not just its content but its form, its character, has changed, has become subtle, shifting, and a co-creation between poet and reader.

Hence the elegiac sense to Stevens's poems—a sense of the loss of sure transcendental sanction—which manifests itself in hesitations, expressed uncertainty, recurrent deflationary moments—at the same time as the poems

continue to affirm the continuance, in a different, more modern, form, of what
has been lost.

Stevens remains largely within the tradition of Romantic poetry as Von
Hendy describes it, which, though preoccupied with finding a new mythology
to replace the traditional religious belief that can no longer compel conviction,
"does not produce any new mythology except the 'reflexive' sort that consists
of celebrating the power of the imagination *to* produce a new mythology."[79]
Stevens's claims for poetry are no more modest than the nineteenth-century
Romantics'—seeking through it the Platonic Good analogous to God (or
"to integrate the mind and the world within a sentient unity of being," as
Joseph Carroll puts it[80]). Malcolm Woodland characterizes Stevens's primary
concern as "whether the world contains a teleological principle that would
give shape and meaning to the spectacle of phenomenal change."[81] But as
that "whether" indicates, these grand ambitions are counterbalanced by deep
doubts as to whether their fulfillment is possible—doubts as to the capacities
of the limited and mortal poet, and doubts as to whether there *is* such a good
or a unity there for poetry to find that is not sheer subjective fantasy. This
ambiguity is captured in the ambivalently apocalyptic "An Ordinary Evening
in New Haven":

> . . . the theory
> Of poetry is the theory of life,
>
> As it is, in the intricate evasions of as,
> In things seen and unseen, created from nothingness,
> The heavens, the hells, the worlds, the longed-for lands.[82]

On one reading, Stevens seems to suspect that the figurative language of
poetry—which is also the figurative language of myth and religion—is mere
construction ("the intricate evasions of as") out of "nothingness" to satisfy
our longing for absolute meaning, the standards of good and evil embodied
in heaven and hell. What we are evading is the knowledge that there is no
such meaning, there are no such objective standards. Yet this is also life "as
it is," and these "longed-for lands" do exist, even if it is we who have created them—and we need them, or something like them, if we are to respond
adequately to our situation.

This ambiguity is the problem that Stevens's poetry takes up as an unending preoccupation. Stevens gives us, over and over, the image of a mind
searching and sometimes finding a reality outside of itself which is not mere
material reality. This, I think, *is* the "supreme fiction": the myth of the imagination, which is a myth of consciousness—and the myth of the poet, perhaps
the myth of himself as the poet. Stevens's myth cannot be the myth of any

supernatural beings, in which he thinks we can no longer believe. As the headings of the three sections of his poem "Notes toward a Supreme Fiction" assert: "It Must Be Abstract"; "It Must Change"; "It Must Give Pleasure." To the first: the modern myth must not be a particular story which is obviously an invented *story*, like Blake's or Yeats's elaborate mythologies—these may in fact seem to convey deep truths about our situation, but only in the way that few if any would take them as sacred; it must rather seem to refer to the deep *realities* of our situation. To the second: those realities are both historical, changing over time, and aspectual, appearing now one way, now another, and dependent on the individual's capacity for reading. And finally, it must have erotic power, must compel an aesthetic and sensuous response and connect to our deepest interests and loves.

The elements of the supreme fiction appear early, in poems such as "Sunday Morning," as well as "The Snow Man" and "The Idea of Order at Key West," which in different ways describe the mind's construction of a world, but a constrained construction—the creation of a world that is not just subjective fantasy, but whose meaningfulness only emerges through the apprehension and articulation by the imagination—an activity that is at once creation and discovery. At the same time the myth is the myth of the uncertainty, provisional character, and failures of this attempt (which is why it is, as in the subtitle of Carroll's book, a *new* Romanticism, chastened by the critiques of the eighteenth- and nineteenth-century Romantic project and the failures of that project to achieve its aims).

It is essential that the supreme fiction is articulated in *poetry*—or rather, it *is* poetry, and difficult poetry. Stevens could have added "It Must Be Difficult" to his qualities—and it must be difficult, ambiguous, because it must direct our attention to the horizon of sense—to the margins of our own tacit knowledge of a reality and a ground of judgment beyond the conventional.

Poetry and the Pressure of the Contemporaneous

Now to return to the second moment of the modern crisis for Stevens, the "pressure of the contemporaneous" and the specter of the "end of civilization." To some degree poetry responds to this aspect of the crisis by responding to the aspect just discussed, the crisis of meaning—poetically transforming the world to make possible a reconciliation with it. However, in the context of Stevens's prose writings on this "pressure," poetry's role sounds more oppositional, or even escapist: the poet "resists" or "evades" the pressure of reality. Stevens meets the anticipated charge of escapism directly, asserting that "There can be no thought of escape," that "the poet who wishes to contemplate the good in the midst of confusion is like the mystic who wishes to contemplate God in the midst of evil"[83]—that is, the realities of the contemporary world are there whether one likes it or not, and the question is the direction of one's attention, the quality of one's consciousness, the reality one inhabits. He goes on to claim that the poet's resistance cannot simply be a matter of going off on flights of fancy; it must begin from and transform the situation in which it finds itself: "Resistance to the pressure of ominous and destructive circumstance consists of its conversion, so far as possible, into a different, an explicable, an amenable circumstance."[84] These two characterizations seem initially at odds with one another—the mystic, it would seem, does not *convert* the evil reality into good; he lives in reality exactly as it is and his achievement is to focus his attention on the (transcendent) good. But, to invoke the ambiguity of "reality" considered earlier, one might say the mystic *does* inhabit a different reality simply by virtue of seeing the world around him ("reality") in light of the "imagined" absolute reality and standard of judgment that is God.

We can (only) get a sense of what this "conversion" looks like by looking at Stevens's poetry. It certainly does not mean writing only of the beautiful and the good. As Longenbach observes, "Stevens began his adult career as a war poet" with "Phases," written in 1914 for a *Poetry* magazine issue on the Great War, and the poem's depiction of war is grim and unromanticized, indeed aimed against the idealization of war[85]:

> This was the salty taste of glory,
> That it was not
> Like Agamemnon's story.
> Only, an eyeball in the mud,
> And Hopkins,
> Flat and pale and gory!

War, dictators, and other evils of contemporary reality remain a persistent presence in the poetry thereafter. When such facets of the contemporary "pressure" appear, their representation is often abstracted, though still excoriating, as in the description of some fascist or demagogic figure in "The Man with the Blue Guitar": "the beautiful trombones behold / The approach of him whom none believes, / Whom all believe that all believe, / A pagan in a varnished car," a figure of "petty misery" destined to be "toppled." Here the description of the demagogue, the evocation of his "resemblance" to a drum rolling over the subtle pickings of the blue guitar, summons the reader's attention to a standard by which the false loudness of political rhetoric can be *seen*, understood, judged. It seems to me that it is this evocation of the standard of judgment that is the poet-mystic's achievement, and this is continuous with Stevens's observation in a letter of 1946:

If people are to become dependent on poetry for any of the fundamental satisfactions, poetry must have an increasingly intellectual scope and power. This is a time for the highest poetry. We never understood the world less than we do now nor, as we understand it, liked it less. We never wanted to understand it more or needed to like it more. These are the intense compulsions that challenge the poet as the appreciatory creator of values and beliefs. That, finally, states the problem.[86]

For Brogan, the conception of poetry expressed here "makes the poet . . . intensely political, though not [a] politician."[87] It is worth noting, though, that Stevens does not here affirm that the poet will necessarily succeed in enabling us (or himself) to understand or to "like" the world—this is just the *problem* that compels him.

Alongside Stevens's poems of war and social crisis, though, the majority of his poetry seeks the extraordinary dimension in the ordinary, in what is perennially around us. This is true before, during, between, and after World War I and World War II, raising the question of whether and how this apparently more general dimension of his poetics figures into Stevens's poetic response to more concrete social and political realities.

There does seem to be a general if uneven shift in the character of Stevens's poetry, specifically in the way in which reality and the imagination's relationship to it are figured, and I think we can see this shift as importantly intertwined with the vicissitudes of "the violence without"[88] and Stevens's response to it. In the later poems, the affirmations of the imagination's power that we see in "The Idea of Order" and "Sunday Morning" and even in "The Snow Man," austere but crystalline, give way increasingly to moments of extreme doubt or else to affirmations that are more severely restrained, qualified, or self-subverted. This movement is neither linear nor total. Even in the early poetry the affirmations are often subdued or hedged; and there are later poems of affirmation, like "Final Soliloquy of the Interior Paramour," "The Rock," and "Of Mere Being." But the latter tend to be hemmed in by poems intimating a drafty, threatening, and threatened world. There are early poems too which are less sanguine, such as "Comedian as the Letter C," but here the failure seems contingent, an individual failure in light of grand unrealized possibilities (the possibility of creating a new world—"founding a colony"—or saving this world). The later Stevens seems, conversely, to limit the redemptive possibilities to finding some space, a still point, a momentary epiphany, while all around the world continues in its terrifying cycles, and the failure seems not the failure of the individual but rather fated by the very character of (modern) reality. The recognition or fear seems to emerge that poetry, as Wittgenstein says of philosophy, "leaves everything as it is,"[89] that at most it can offer a temporary refuge, a "rendezvous."

The relation between these two moments of crisis—the disappearance or death of the gods and the threat to civilization—might be conceived as follows. In the first, there is "just" the threat of meaninglessness, the "indifference" of the phenomenal world, the loss of "some imperishable bliss"; the poetic reconciliation in this case is to show us that "the indifferent experience of life is the unique experience, the item of ecstasy which we have been isolating and reserving for another time and place, loftier and more secluded."[90] With the contemporary social and political upheaval, however, even this "perishable bliss" becomes threatened; it is no longer adequate simply to find some inner prerational source of meaning—or rather, this may be all that one has, but the salvation of the individual soul is not the salvation of the world, and therefore the individual's salvation is itself imperiled, since for the modern individual this "salvation" is bound up with the fate of this world. I think this is at least implicit in Stevens's later poetry.

Conversely, the contemporary crisis might be seen as emerging from the crisis of meaning, the breakdown of consensus about the ideal ends of human life and even the loss of conviction that there are such ends, leading to fragmentation and erosive and destructive conflict.

For Stevens, under these conditions the modern poet does become a mystic contemplating good or God in the midst of evil. Poetry creates a still point, a "place of communion"[91] with the transcendent ground of our being, but the storm rages without. The question can then be raised whether, or in what sense, this meets the challenge to meaning posed by our historical situation.

CONTEMPLATING THE GOOD (APOCALYPTICALLY) IN "THE AURORAS OF AUTUMN"

Although Stevens himself elaborated his theory of poetry and poetic "redemption" extensively in prose, the fact and nature of that redemption can only be fully grasped and made persuasive through reading and inhabiting the poems themselves. "The Auroras of Autumn" is one dramatization of Stevens's search for the supreme fiction, and could be characterized at the same time as aspiring to *be* (part of) what it narrates the search for—and, written in 1947 after the "pressure of reality" and the specter of the "end of civilization" have thoroughly pervaded Stevens's consciousness, it reveals something of the fate of the search for meaning in light of some threatened End.

The poem begins with a contemplation of the heavens—of what would seem to be the constellation Draco and the canopy of stars, although it could also describe the sinuous form of the northern lights of the title:

> This is where the serpent lives, the bodiless.

His head is air. Beneath his tip at night
Eyes open and fix on us in every sky.

Or is this another wriggling out of the egg,
Another image at the end of the cave,
Another bodiless for the body's slough?

The poet seems to ask whether there is any reality to what we think we see in the lights in the sky—whether they are as they look to be, the sign of some meaningful structure to the world, divine eyes that watch us, or whether rather such visions are merely like one of the shadows seen by the deluded prisoners of Plato's cave.

It is striking and essential that from the very beginning the poem resists easy understanding and determinant paraphrase. Why "wriggling out of the egg"? The syntax of the sentence implies an interpretation opposed to what has gone before ("Or"), implies that that the previous vision is deluded and redundant ("another"), just one more fantasy among all the ways in which human beings try to escape "the body's slough." But on the other hand, eggs are *meant* to be wriggled out of, and to fail to do so would mean eternal juvenility or death. Thus there is an immediate ambiguity about the character of human entrapment in our immediate world, the world of the material and social. And this ambiguity is the ambiguity of the poem itself (this poem, and perhaps poetry generally): is the suggestiveness and power of an image the real intimation of something outside or beyond the enclosure of our ordinary understanding, or is that very image—the picture of an "outside" or "beyond" the shell—false, illusory?

Stevens does not answer the question directly but instead gives another image of "where the serpent lives," literally a more grounded one of the snake's earthly habitat, of which he then says:

This is the height emerging and its base
These lights may finally attain a pole
In the midmost midnight and find the serpent there,

In another nest, the master of the maze
Of body and air and forms and images,
Relentlessly in possession of happiness.

This seems first to describe the serpent as human beings have come to know it, as part of the shared environment. The next stanza alludes to the auroras, suggesting that the celestial emerges from the terrestrial, perhaps acknowledging that our myths arise from our experience of the material world, but also proposing that they have some independent status or reality—the

Platonic form of the serpent, our concept of the serpent, may not precede its earthly instantiations (existence precedes essence), but the symbolic meaning or significance of the serpent is not simply invented or arbitrary.

But then comes another disillusionment:

> This is his poison: that we should disbelieve
> Even that. His meditations in the ferns,
> When he moved so slightly to make sure of the sun,
>
> Made us no less as sure. We saw in his head,
> Black beaded on the rock, the flecked animal,
> The moving grass, the Indian in his glade.

These final lines describe only "nature," but suggest a subtly Romantic view of nature, ordered and harmonious, human beings (the "Indian") in harmony with animals in harmony with the sun. It is ambiguous whether this final image is what we are left with *after* our disbelief, or whether it is a continuation of the earlier description of what we can now no longer believe (that is, that the serpent is "master of the maze" and "relentlessly in possession of happiness"), but perhaps that ambiguity is the point. The snake on the rock is surely real; its significance is what is in question.

Marie Borroff construes this first canto as proceeding through three myths, from cosmic and abstract to progressively more local, concrete and particular,[92] but in this progression I see also a movement of disenchantment, or at least increasing uncertainty about any reality or order beyond the immediate and concrete. At the same time, the poetry itself seems to continue to attest to some such order, which comes through in these lines by way of little more than an exquisite precision of description—not the prophetic musicality of Lowell but apt and balanced phrases which conjure the sunlight reflecting on the shining black scales, the rustling of the grass in otherwise silence, the sense of perfection one sometimes gets when observing the natural world, which then makes the return to the social world jarring in its noisiness. The lines depart just enough from prosaic diction and syntax (the alliteration of "black beaded," the internal alliteration of "rock" and "flecked," the subtle quasi-iambic pentameter of the final line) to become more than just the effective mimesis of a natural scene and to suggest an *image*, that is, an image *of* something beyond itself. (Perhaps little more of an image than the natural scene itself may be, as the Romantics saw nature as an image of the transcendent—the poetic rendering simply constituting the imagined natural scene as an object of aesthetic contemplation.)

Yet Stevens cannot let even this ever-so-subtly romanticized nature stand unironized. The next canto, as well as the following two, begin (elegiacally)

"Farewell to an idea," which Borroff interprets as Stevens taking leave, at least temporarily, from the foundational myth described in the previous canto; she characterizes the first canto as describing a cosmic myth, and, I would add, the myth of nature.

The second canto proceeds by describing a white cabin, "deserted on a beach," with white flowers on a white wall,[93] flowers that remind the poet "of a white / That was different, something else, last year / Or before, not the white of an aging afternoon . . . " The poet does not make explicit what was "different" about last year's white, and thus the desired and absent whiteness seems less like something real in the poet's past and more like a transcendent ideal, like the magic that seems to imbue remembered childhood—more keenly, perhaps, with the poet's own aging: As Merle Brown has written, this canto, and the poem as a whole, suggest approaching death.[94] (In the next stanza, the mother "has grown old," and more drastically, "The house will crumble and the books will burn.")

Borroff characterizes the myth of this canto as the myth of the changing of the seasons, which is of course symbolically significant; the encroachment of winter is, as Stevens's diction suggests, the encroachment of emptiness, darkness, fading, dying.

But then the auroras make their appearance as the antithesis of the whiteness and of the chilled, static nothingness—they are spectacular, brilliantly colored, "change" (which is, relevantly, one of the requisites of a supreme fiction) made enormously visible:

> The man who is walking turns blankly on the sand.
> He observes how the north is always enlarging the change,
>
> With its frigid brilliances, its blue-red sweeps
> And gusts of great enkindlings, its polar green,
> The color of ice and fire and solitude.

This is a sublime image analogous to the end of "Quaker Graveyard," an evocation of a cosmic perspective, an austere beauty that relativizes human endings. The auroras here—and throughout the poem—are, as I read them, an image of what transcends and outlasts individual human life and perhaps all human life. But they are an ambiguous image, searingly beautiful but mute, fluctuating, remote. (Perhaps surprisingly, given my apocalyptic reading of the poem, I resist Berger's interpretation of the auroras as evoking the atomic bomb—in part because, for me, "frigid" and "polar green" work strongly against a connection to a weapon of unimaginable heat[95]—but the reading is a plausible one, and would obviously make the imagery even more radically ambiguous.) While the auroras evoke the transcendent horizon of meaning, then, at the same time they provoke the question of whether they are just a human projection or the reflection of something real and external—that is, whether they are in fact an *objective* correlate. To answer in the negative would be to find the conditions of human life and sense unraveled, and the poem could be characterized as the drama of the poet's search for the answer. Throughout "Auroras," Stevens calls into question the suggestiveness of language and image as manifested at the end of the second canto, vacillating throughout the poem as to whether what the imagination imagines has any enduring reality or referent.

If Canto I is a series of images of meaning as immanent in the cosmos or in nature, the heavens dotted with "eyes that watch us," Canto II conversely imagines the world as without any inherent human meaning (thus it is white, a "heartless void" or "dumb blankness" upon which nature "paints like the harlot,"[96] color belonging only to the brilliant but ephemeral spectacle in the sky, which may well be meaningless itself). Here again is the naturalistic sublime, and one might call the corresponding myth Nietzschean or existentialist—that modern myth with its roots in Lucretius and the Epicureans that the world is fundamentally atoms and void and that what meaning there is must be imposed by human beings on meaningless natural phenomena, with no transcendent sanction or objective reality. As in "The Snow Man," however, even this utterly objective vision, the vision seen by the observer who is "nothing himself," still seems to have some inherent significance, if only the significance of beauty—"the junipers shagged with ice, / The spruces rough in the distant glitter / Of the January sun." The vision of the auroras at the end of this canto is similar—they are silent, distant, indifferent to the fate of the man "walking blankly on the sand," but they still figure as an image of something humanly significant—if an image of something in light of which individual human beings may be utterly *in*significant.

These first two cantos therefore dramatize the problem of finding a myth adequate to the modern situation. We cannot believe, at least literally, in stories of divine beings like the cosmic serpent; on the other hand, the world still seems imbued with some order, but how to tell if that order is not just our own projection? The image of the auroras suggests the kind of order we might legitimately find—one which, again, demands a kind of dispossession—and from this point forward Stevens seems to grapple with this idea, both directly and obliquely, retreating and evading it before it returns in the later cantos.

Cantos I and II each refer to an impersonal cosmos. Cantos III and IV (each also beginning "Farewell to an idea") turn from the myths of an individual alone in such a cosmos to those fundamental and archetypal relationships that structure the human world: the myths of mother and father. "The mother's face" is described as "the purpose of the poem"; the children "possess" her and she "gives transparence to their present peace" and "makes that gentler that can gentle be." The mother is warmth, protection, comfort; she is, as Simone de Beauvoir would put it, "pure immanence" (that which *can* be possessed, the woman who will reassure and love absolutely), that into which the poet, facing the terrifying aloneness conjured in the previous canto, would like to sink. But as every grown child discovers, she cannot fulfill this fantasy of total refuge, in part because she is only another human being; in part because she is impermanent: "And yet she too is dissolved, she is destroyed. / She gives transparence. But she has grown old." The mother here is associated to the house which is "half dissolved"; both are terrifyingly impermanent. This is all the more devastating as the mother is connected too with the supreme fiction Stevens seeks in "Notes," of which he says, "The vivid transparence that you bring is peace." The mother is, one might say, the primal supreme fiction, that matrix into which each of us is born. The dissolution of this perfect wholeness is essential to individuation and consciousness, but here it would seem we have something more than the ordinary trauma of separation and disenchantment. The mother is the house and beyond the house there is only unsheltered expanse, the sandy waste of the beach beneath the fluctuating sky; there is the sense that whatever myth one might inhabit after her passing, it will not be one of any encompassing security.

After another "Farewell to an idea," we are told, "The negations, the cancellations are never final / The father sits in space, wherever he sits, / Of bleak regard." Beyond the comforting circle of the mother's embrace there is the father, native not of the hearth but of the less-homey sky. The father, like the poet, "says farewell," and in general the father occupies a special position vis-à-vis myth—he is a mythical figure but also source of myth. He is judge, creator, patriarch, but he is also the encompassing consciousness, a figure for the imagination. He seems, finally, the personified predecessor of the auroras: "He assumes the great speeds of space and flutters them"; he is "seated by the fire / And yet in space and motionless and yet / Of motion the ever-brightening origin"—a striking abstract image of some absolute condition of being.

All this suggests a myth of individuation or of the development of human consciousness, the differentiation from the primal unity with the mother and the identification with that already-individuated figure, the father. This identification seems to be the necessary alternative after the devastating recognition of the previous canto of the mother's aging and death, and more generally the facts of transience and destruction.

But the father's throne is somehow beset, and the canto concludes again in a menaced tone: "What company / In masks, can choir it with the naked wind?" This transcendent imagination's "actors" are "masked," patently false, and therefore (or somehow) insufficient to contend with or withstand the gusts of naked reality. Here the myth of individuation and of the powers of the human imagination run up against the earlier annihilating vision of Canto II.

The following canto develops this disillusionment with the father and his imaginative constructions. It describes the mother and father throwing a party in which "the father fetches tellers of tales," musicians, "negresses to dance," "fetches pageants out of the air," "fetches his unherded herds," orchestrates a party that the poet eventually calls "a loud, disordered mooch." The image is one of artificiality, indulgence, and meaningless fantasy, an attempt at "escape" that is repulsive and ultimately ineffectual: "These musicians dubbing at a tragedy . . . which is made up of this: That there are no lines to speak[.] There is no play. / Or, the persons act one merely by being here." This seems an aporia, similar to Stevens's characterization of arriving at "the plain sense of things" in the poem of that name: it is "as if / We had come to an end of the imagination."

The recovery from this disaster of sense comes from a return to the auroras, a stunning description of the spectacle as "a theatre floating through the clouds," purposeless and magnificent. Against and despite the degradation of humanity and the failure of the human artifices, there is the magnificence of indifferent and inhuman nature, a beautiful sublimity incommensurate with the human scale. By contrast, the human world comes and goes: "A capitol / It may be, is emerging or has just / Collapsed." Here too is the suggestion of that "pressure of contemporary reality," the chaotic flux of current events and the threat of the end of civilization, relativized by the enormous and ethereal image of the lights in the sky.

Yet it is not enough for this spectacle just to *be*. The poet then pronounces, in what is perhaps the poem's emotional climax:

> This is nothing until in a single man contained,
> Nothing until this named thing nameless is
> And is destroyed. He opens the door of his house
>
> On flames. The scholar of one candle sees
> An Arctic effulgence flaring on the frame
> Of everything he is. And he feels afraid.

The first stanza suggests that this immense inhuman horizon must somehow still be made part of human consciousness, part of an *individual* human consciousness. And it must be there transformed, made "nameless" and "destroyed." This at first defies sense—how can "nothing" become something by being *un*-named and, even more paradoxically, destroyed? Un-naming is a common theme in Stevens; "do not use the rotted names" the poet enjoins

in "The Man With a Blue Guitar," and "The sun / Must bear no name, gold
flourisher, but be / In the difficulty of what it is to be" in "Notes Toward a
Supreme Fiction." Un-naming would thus seem to be the fundamental poetic
act, or at least the essential condition to a poetic re-naming. And destruction
must come first; the condition of a new creation is the breakdown of the old
edifices. As Stevens write elsewhere: "The mind is the great poem of winter,
the man, / Who, to find what will suffice, / Destroys romantic tenements / Of
rose and ice."[97]

Yet this does not entirely resolve the difficulty. The auroras have *already*
been poetically transformed, renamed—must *this* poetic construction be
(again) unnamed, destroyed? This perhaps too-comforting, too-human image
of the auroras as a "theatre"? It is unclear, but what is unambiguous is the
terror of the man, his sense of the inadequacy and insignificance of the "one
candle" of an individual human consciousness in the face of an annihilating
immensity—whether it is the annihilation of one's own death or of the collapse of a civilization.

In Canto VII, Stevens wonders whether there *is* an imagination capable of
an objective perspective, an imagination of which the auroras are objective
correlate. He begins by powerfully describing such an imagination, which
identifies itself no longer with the father but with the auroras:

> Is there an imagination that sits enthroned
> As grim as it is benevolent, the just
> And the unjust, which in the midst of summer stops
>
> To imagine winter? When the leaves are dead,
> Does it take its place in the north and enfold itself,
> Goat-leaper, crystalled and luminous, sitting
>
> In highest night? . . .
> It leaps through us, through all our heavens leaps,
> Extinguishing our planets, one by one,
> Leaving, of where we were and looked, of where
>
> We knew each other and of each other thought,
> A shivering residue, chilled and foregone
> Except for that crown and mystical cabala.

But the poet cannot help but then belittle this grand vision—a belittlement
that is at the same time a recovery from the reduction of the self to "shivering
residue" in the face of the inhuman eternity:

> But it dare not leap by chance in its own dark.

> It must change from destiny to slight caprice.
> And thus its jetted tragedy, its stele
>
> And shape and mournful making move to find
> What must unmake it and, at last, what can,
> Say, a flippant communication under the moon.

This is both the fate and the prerogative of the modern consciousness that is driven to seek truth which it equates with a skeptical questioning of everything. The imagination cannot take itself too seriously, it must ironize itself, and the poem here enacts that ironization, leaping in the final two stanzas of this canto "from destiny to slight caprice," from "jetted tragedy" to "flippant communication." Critics have called Stevens a comic poet and here his comedy emerges with a double edge, both assertion of human life and joyousness despite the threats of meaninglessness or inhuman circumstance, but also ironization that undercuts the meaningfulness that potentially comes from facing those circumstances.

The belittlement is transformed into acceptance in the final canto. Stevens begins by calling us "an unhappy people in a happy world," which Borroff interprets to mean that "we live in a world in which there is splendor and vitality and the sun is like a jungle tuft of feathers and like an animal eye, but we're unhappy because we lack the faculty of imagination."[98] Stevens then exhorts the "rabbi," apparently a figure of the poet himself, to save these unhappy people, to allow them to see what their own imaginations fail, without the poet, to apprehend:

> Now, solemnize the secretive syllables.
>
> Read to the congregation, for today
> And for tomorrow, this extremity,
> This contrivance of the spectre of the spheres,
>
> Contriving balance to contrive a whole,
> The vital, the never-failing genius,
> Fulfilling his meditations, great and small.
>
> In these unhappy he meditates a whole,
> The full of fortune and the full of fate,
> As if he lived all lives, that he might know,
>
> In hall harridan, not hushful paradise,
> To a haggling of wind and weather, by these lights
> Like a blaze of summer straw, in winter's nick.

On one level, this canto profoundly affirms the power of poetry to convey a "whole" within which human life appears intelligible. On the other, it ironizes this power: the heavy alliteration calls attention to the artificiality of the language, and Stevens calls the "spectre of the spheres" a "contrivance," diminishes it into "a blaze of summer straw / In winter's nick," a fire we build to warm ourselves. As Bloom writes, "All that the flash reveals to Stevens is change and ourselves as the origin of the meaning of change."[99] If in Lowell we see the world end with a bang, Stevens confronts us with the possibility that it might end with a transient flicker and a poignant irony regarding our apprehensions of anything transcendent.

But even so, the transcendent abides in the poem, beside the belittlement. Even the unsatisfactory character of the final stanza could be felt as provocation, leaving a longing for the intimations of transcendence earlier in the poem, a longing that suggests, even if it cannot prove, that there is some object to which it is correlate. As Malcolm Woodland argues, "Stevens reads the aurora borealis as the harbinger of a postapocalyptic apocalypse, of an 'apocalypse *without* apocalypse,' of an end that transcends and exceeds the narrative of teleological fulfillment inscribed in the apocalyptic tradition, and his elegiac *mourning* of this end inscribes a certain *resistance* to that situation within the poem."[100] "The Auroras of Autumn" thus elegizes what is perhaps the most fundamental myth—the myth of the very possibility of making mythical sense, sense that is more and other than utilitarian. The consolation, then, in "Auroras" is in a sense even more austere than in "Quaker Graveyard"—it is the consolation of a *double* consciousness, the recognition that the question of the reality of what the imagination grasps cannot finally be resolved with respect to any particular, given mythical structure of sense (so the archetypal mother and father figures that appear in the middle of the poem must fall by the end, or at least lose their solidity).

This does not mean that the poem asserts that there *is* no such possibility or such sense. As I have said, elegy *mourns* the lost object, which means not only recognizing the loss but also affirming the value of what is lost, a value that persists. The elegy transforms the object. In this case, one might say the transformation is "from substance into subtlety." The poem affirms through its very ambiguity and suggestiveness the existence of *some* order which exceeds our consciousness and must be known. That is the essence of the myth that remains for Stevens when the other myths have been mourned—the myth of the imperative for consciousness to discover and articulate its own conditions.

That is not *all* that remains, such that all we come to know through Stevens's poetry is that there is an imperative to consciousness, but nothing of this elusive object of consciousness itself. In "Auroras" we are referred to the archetypal figures of mother and father, not only persons but bearers of two fundamental aspects of the individual's relation to the world, essential realities of our constitution, and the poem also compels us to come to terms with their limitations and their transience and the need to find some ground beyond them, which is to be found in relation to something transcendent, figured in inhuman nature and its "innocence," which becomes a recurrent theme of the last few cantos. The poem is a modern elegy, elegizing the ground of sense, but there is also something of the traditional elegy in it, elegizing the aging poet facing extinction, personal or collective, and affirming something that will abide, perhaps not temporally, if whatever abides can only abide in human consciousness, but nonetheless in a significant way, through our imagination of the personal or the human arc, which becomes part of our current reality.

But "Auroras" suggests that only the (myth of the) imperative to consciousness is global—other orders are or may be local. The particular myths of the poem are represented as dissolving and recondensing, as ethereal and elusive. What is mourned, then, is not myth or foundational sense *per se*, but the determinacy of myths and our certainty about them.

If Stevens is indeed an "apocalyptic" poet, not in the sense of counseling despair or political quietism but nonetheless responding to the perceived possibility of the "end of civilization," then his poetry suggests that the response to the apocalyptic situation must include the recognition of the way in which we are co-creators of the reality (the world) we inhabit. We are partners with others—poets and artists co-creating with other makers past and present, readers and viewers co-creating with artists past and present—and with our own imaginative subjectivity, with all its external conditions.

BEYOND STEVENS: "IT MUST BE HISTORICAL"

At the same time there is something not finally satisfactory to me about "Auroras" as a response to historical crisis. As Joseph Carroll characterizes one interpretive viewpoint, for Stevens as for all modern poets "'the central concern' . . . is 'the quest for wholeness' and . . . this quest always, necessarily, fails"[101]—and, one might argue further, wholeness or meaningfulness or belief in our own creativity is not what is needed. The supreme fiction that we need is not just the myth of our capacity and responsibly for creative consciousness, "the poem of the mind in the act of finding," but a way of understanding the historical conditions of that consciousness, one that takes up the historical human situation, the human destiny in relation to economic and political and social and cultural realities. While Stevens's poems do engage with historical conditions, "understanding" those conditions seems, at least in "Auroras," finally secondary to finding a way to "like" them, the fundamental project one of poetically constituting a world that one can "celebrate," a world in which our deep need for meaning can be reconciled with the reality of the external world. Stevens keeps his poetry from becoming sheer fantasy or escapism by its continuous dramatization of the struggle for sense, the acknowledgement that sense *is* a struggle, but ultimately he seems to me what I might call a "therapeutic" poet. His poetry provides perhaps the most austere therapy possible; light, joy, meaningfulness must be found in flashes of aesthetic perfection in the midst of war, depression, and banality, and sometimes the imagination cannot even manage that, its only remaining achievement to imagine—or cognize—the world unvarnished by imagination, and affirm the "necessity" of such a cognition, as in Stevens's late poem "The Plain Sense of Things." The question is whether one can be a therapeutic poet of any kind in an untenable historical situation.

This limitation, if it is one, may stem from the fact that Stevens does not see the cataclysmic trajectory itself as the *result* of our failure to grasp reality. Rather, the evils are simply there, and poetry appears as a symptomatic treatment, a means of continuing to bear and to find meaning amongst them. But I would argue—based in part on works such as Maclean's, McCarthy's, Lowell's—that our problem is not "just" nihilism, not just whether we can find a myth to believe in, a reenchanted world to inhabit, a way to stage comedy in the midst of tragedy (which is not to say Stevens does these things blithely or facilely). Our problem is to see the real conditions of our lives.

Stevens enjoins us, I think rightly, to recognize the reality we inhabit to be a function of our capacity to read, and to work to discern/create the ulterior depths of that world. We must recognize reality to be not "substance" but "subtlety," not *things* but aspects, and poetry can convey this. If the task requires more than what his poetry offers us (and doubtless no single poet can provide the vision we now need), it pertains to Stevens's way of conceiving that depth, insofar as there is something ahistorical about his conception—not that he fails to engage with the problems of his historical moment, but that he seeks a solution or salve for those problems outside of history. If Stevens recognizes that God can no longer be found in the phenomenal world, he still seeks some analogue in a much-chastened imagination inhabiting a much-diminished world.

Lowell and McCarthy, however, suggest that the conditions we would need to grasp in order to redeem, or at least to make sense of, the apocalyptic situation, are those of humanity's historical development—including the moral and ethical dimensions of that development, both what we have realized and what we have violated. Arguably humanity's destructive trajectory is a result of the failure to grasp that very reality. To the extent that history appears in Stevens's poetry, it is part of the nightmare from which we must awaken, the reality to be transformed by the imagination, subordinated within a supreme fiction to something that transcends it. But the specter of the "end of civilization" makes our problem not finally one of meaning(fulness) but of consciousness of our true situation. We need also "the poetry of history," an adequate historical consciousness. What we need, one wants to say, is not a myth, or a supreme fiction; what we need is reality.

(I would note that my criticism indicates an important aspect of our education by literature—that we need not find a poet or author to be wholly "right" in order to be educated by reading and reflecting on their work. What the work must do is refer us to real problems, and show sufficient honesty, integrity, and insight to elicit some deeper tacit knowledge of our own in judging it, and stimulation to, if necessary, go beyond it.)

Lowell and McCarthy are perhaps such "poets of history." Yet their works read differently, and necessarily so, in light of what Stevens shows and tells us so thoroughly and variedly: that our fictionalizing is essential to our knowledge of the conditions of sense, which is to say our knowledge of reality, and the kind of fictions required are *poetic* fictions; only through poetic resemblance can we become aware of a certain dimension of the ground of intelligibility. On the other hand, we come to see the necessarily provisional character of all these fictions.

Stevens and Lowell—along with the other works treated—therefore collectively suggest that the apocalyptic consciousness is a double, or multiple, and multiply ironic consciousness. First there is the recognition that our construals of the character of the end we face are constructions, but constructions that we cannot do without, and constructions that are not free but are ways of groping toward, bumping up against, the "limits of reality" which for us human beings include the limits of sense. And then, more wrenchingly, there is the tension between the imperative to consciousness in an apocalyptic world and the need to live in that world—between the imperative toward goodness and the recognition of its inefficacy; the need to be oriented toward a proximal future and the very real possibility of futurelessness; the burden of responsibility and the feeling of powerlessness. We cannot forswear the need to "leap from destiny to slight caprice," to continue to assert what allows us to keep living—the need for joy, celebration, which I think is not just a psychological need but also a facet of consciousness, a recognition of real goods—but those goods become radically relativized and perhaps must be finally relinquished, mourned, in light of the larger and grimmer reality.

Beyond these tensions, though, there is a common orientation that these works urge upon us, an orientation urged by the tensions themselves. They press us to become conscious of and thus internalize the loss of the former certainties of humanity—to mourn and to relinquish, not our humanity, but those former certainties, and to set oneself the daily and unending task of "getting the world right"[102] through straining to the limits of our (poetic) apprehension and articulation—to become, perhaps, what Stevens called the "more than human human"[103] in a less and less human world.

NOTES

1. That is, elegy in the modern sense. The origin of the term, *elegeion*, referred to a particular meter used by Greek poets for a wide range of subjects. (See "Elegiac Distich" in Preminger, Brogan, and Warnke, *The New Princeton Encyclopedia of Poetry and Poetics*).

2. Preminger, Brogan, and Warnke, 322.

3. See Sacks, *The English Elegy*; Cavitch, *American Elegy*, 1; Ramazani, *The Poetry of Mourning*.

4. Sacks, *The English Elegy*, 7.

5. Freud, "Mourning and Melancholia," 245, 249; quoted in Ramazani, *The Poetry of Mourning*, 3.

6. Frye, *Northrop Frye on Milton and Blake*, 25.

7. As Coleridge first argued, and many after him, the poet may use fantastic characters and situations and yet "transfer from our inward nature a human interest and a semblance of truth sufficient to procure for these shadows of imagination that willing suspension of disbelief" (*Biographia Literaria*, 174).

8. Frye, *Northrop Frye on Milton and Blake*, 32.

9. Frye, 32.

10. " . . . the primary business of the critic is with myth as the shaping principle of a work of literature. Thus for him myth becomes much the same thing as Aristotle's mythos, narrative or plot, the moving formal cause which is what Aristotle called the 'soul' of the work and assimilates all details in the realizing of its unity" (Frye, 33).

11. Frye, *Anatomy of Criticism*, 141.

12. Frye, 147. I find it curious that Frye rarely uses "good" on the one hand or "evil" or "bad" on the other in the descriptions of these worlds, for it seems to me that this division could equally, perhaps more satisfyingly, be reformulated in those terms which are ideal rather than ambiguously empirical like desirable and undesirable. Frye resists this equation on the basis that "morality" often acts as external constraint in conflict with desire. But human beings so often desire what would ultimately result in undesirable outcomes, and at least the Christian heaven is correspondingly associated with the proscription of certain desires. The Christian view is Platonic in that the good and the desirable ultimately coincide—since for Plato the ultimate object of our eros is the good, and as Socrates frequently insists in Plato's dialogues, we cannot really desire other than the good; if we seem to do so, it is only out of confusion or ignorance.

13. Von Hendy, *The Modern Construction of Myth*.

14. Frye, *Northrop Frye on Milton and Blake*, 27.

15. Ramazani, *The Poetry of Mourning*, x.

16. Ramazani, *The Poetry of Mourning*, 3.

17. See for instance Rizvi, "Grief Without Belief."

18. Frye, *Northrop Frye on Milton and Blake*, 25.

19. Ramazani, *The Poetry of Mourning*, 8.

20. I am aware of no evidence that Lowell was close to Winslow; the only reference to him in Lowell's letters comes in a discussion of "Quaker Graveyard" in which he refers to Winslow as "the one the poem's about" (Letter to Shozu Takunaga, January 10, 1969, in *The Letters of Robert Lowell*, 510).

21. Staples, *Robert Lowell*, 45.

22. Doreski, *Robert Lowell's Shifting Colors*, 54; Hugh Staples is a nominal exception, claiming that "Lowell has made only one radical departure from the old tradition [of pastoral elegy]: He has omitted any expression of personal grief and he has made no allusion to his personal career as poet" but arguably one "radical departure" is sufficient to call the genre into question (*Robert Lowell*, 46).

23. Doreski, *Robert Lowell's Shifting Colors*, 54.

24. Hass, "Lowell's Graveyard," 57.

25. Staples, *Robert Lowell*, 69.

26. Perloff, *The Poetic Art of Robert Lowell*, 145.

27. Williamson, *Pity the Monsters*, 35.

28. Stephen Gould Axelrod has also linked it to Christ as characterized in Gerard Manley Hopkins's poem "That Nature is a Heraclitean Fire": "I am all at once what Christ is, | since he was what I am, and / This Jack, joke, poor potsherd, | patch, matchwood, immortal diamond, / Is immortal diamond" ("Robert Lowell and Hopkins," 64).

29. Job 38:4–7, King James Version.

30. Nietzsche, *On the Genealogy of Morals and Ecce Homo*, 97. This interpretation of Ahab comes from Charles Thomas Elder.

31. Canto XXVI, trans. Henry F. Cary.

32. Lowell, *The Collected Prose*, 218.

33. Lowell, 221.

34. In a *Partisan Review* symposium on the Cold War, quoted in Hamilton, *Robert Lowell*, 295.

35. Hobsbaum, *Reader's Guide to Robert Lowell*, 42–43. See also Ross Labrie, *The Catholic Imagination in American Literature*, 169.

36. Axelrod and Deese, *Robert Lowell*, 63.

37. Axelrod and Deese, 63, my emphasis.

38. Melville, *Moby-Dick*, 367.

39. Perloff, *The Poetic Art of Robert Lowell*, 142. Indeed, this section was printed as a separate poem in Jonathan Raban's 1974 selection of Lowell's poetry, though it was restored to "Quaker Graveyard" in later publications.

40. Put forth in *The Material Basis of Evolution*, published in 1940, so it is not inconceivable that the idea might have influenced Lowell at least via cultural osmosis, but I'm not aware of any evidence that he was familiar with it.

41. Eliade and Smith, *The Myth of the Eternal Return*.

42. Alan Williamson "wonders if the move toward the greater abstractness of Christian Existentialism" he finds in "Quaker Graveyard," from Lowell's earlier

"desire to see the world reshaped by the force of his visions," represents "the beginning of deconversion" (*Pity the Monsters*, 47).

43. For thorough discussions of Stevens's (anti)apocalypticism, see the special issue of *The Wallace Stevens Journal* on "Approaching the Millennium: Stevens and Apocalyptic Language" (vol. 23, no. 2, Fall 1999) and Malcolm Woodland's *Wallace Stevens and the Apocalyptic Mode*.

44. Bloom, *Wallace Stevens*, 298.

45. Berger, *Forms of Farewell*, 35–36.

46. Cook, *Poetry, Word-Play, and Word-War in Wallace Stevens*, 269.

47. Eleanor Cook, "Introduction," 120.

48. Woodland, "Wallace Stevens' 'Puella Parvula' and the 'Haunt of Prophecy,'" 99.

49. Woodland, *Wallace Stevens and the Apocalyptic Mode*, xiii.

50. Brogan, "Stevens in History and Not in History," 168.

51. For two detailed studies of Stevens's "worldly" engagements, see Longenbach, *Wallace Stevens*; Brogan, *The Violence Within/The Violence Without*.

52. Longenbach, *Wallace Stevens*, vi.

53. Brogan, *The Violence Within/The Violence Without*.

54. Though he descries Romanticism insofar as it seeks "minor wish-fulfillments and is incapable of abstraction" whereas the imagination "is intrepid and eager and the extreme of its achievement lies in abstraction" (Stevens, *Collected Poetry and Prose*, 728).

55. "Three Academic Pieces," in *Collected Poetry and Prose*, 686.

56. "Two or Three Ideas," in Stevens, 843.

57. "The Noble Rider and the Sound of Words," in Stevens, 654.

58. "The Irrational Element in Poetry," in Stevens, 788.

59. "Adagia," in Stevens, 901.

60. Stevens and Howard, *Letters of Wallace Stevens*, 1996, 250, 464.

61. "The Relations Between Painting and Poetry," in Stevens, *Collected Poetry and Prose*, 750.

62. Emerson, *Nature*, 13.

63. Melville, *Moby-Dick*, 148.

64. For a thorough and illuminating analysis of the cultural conflicts leading to the two world wars, see Eksteins, *Rites of Spring*.

65. Taylor, *Sources of the Self*, 419.

66. This is not necessarily true of all modern art. Some German Expressionism, for instance, could be said to make its meaning *more* explicit through its departures from naturalistic depiction. On the other hand, Cubism understood itself as concerned with visual appearance and not symbolic or expressive meaning.

67. Compare Horkheimer and Adorno's critique of Enlightenment reason and their argument for the need to rehabilitate the nonlinguistic from the tyranny of conceptualization, as in *Dialectic of Enlightenment*.

68. Stevens, *Collected Poetry and Prose*, 750.

69. "The Irrational Element in Poetry," in Stevens, 786.

70. Stevens, 786.

71. "Three Academic Pieces," in Stevens, 686.

72. "The Irrational Element in Poetry," in Stevens, 786.

73. "Three Academic Pieces," in Stevens, 686–87.

74. It would seem that resemblance can be of one of two kinds, similarity or contiguity. Stevens does not make this explicit in the essay, but it accords with Roman Jakobson's assertion that these are the two fundamental possibilities of relationship and form the basis for metaphor and metonymy, respectively ("Two Aspects of Language," in Jakobson, *Language in Literature*).

75. "Three Academic Pieces," in Stevens, *Collected Poetry and Prose*, 688–89.

76. Compare Heidegger's description in *Being and Time* of human beings, Dasein, as Being-in-the-World.

77. "Three Academic Pieces," in Stevens, *Collected Poetry and Prose*, 690–91.

78. In *The Social Construction of Reality*; see my discussion in the Introduction.

79. Von Hendy, *The Modern Construction of Myth*, 42.

80. Carroll, *Wallace Stevens' Supreme Fiction*, 47.

81. Woodland, *Wallace Stevens and the Apocalyptic Mode*, 250.

82. Stevens, *Collected Poetry and Prose*, 415.

83. "The Irrational Element in Poetry," in Stevens, 788.

84. Stevens, 789.

85. Longenbach, *Wallace Stevens*, 46.

86. Stevens, *Letters of Wallace Stevens*, 526.

87. Brogan, "Stevens in History and Not in History," 185.

88. Discussing "nobility," which he connects to the imagination and poetry, Stevens characterizes it as "a violence from within that protects us from a violence without" ("The Noble Rider and the Sound of Words," in Stevens, *Collected Poetry and Prose*, 665).

89. Wittgenstein, *Philosophical Investigations*, §124.

90. "Two or Three Ideas," in Stevens, *Collected Poetry and Prose*, 848.

91. Thanks to Liam Maguire for this formulation.

92. Borroff, "Wallace Stevens' 'The Auroras of Autumn' (Lecture 20, ENGL 310, Yale Open Courses)." This lecture is the source of subsequent references to Borroff's reading of this poem.

93. This also evokes the terrifying nullity of whiteness described in "The Whiteness of the Whale" in *Moby-Dick*.

94. Brown, *Wallace Stevens*, 195.

95. "Nuclear winter" was not hypothesized until decades later and is unlikely to have been at work in Stevens's imagination.

96. Melville, *Moby-Dick*, 195.

97. "Man and Bottle," *Collected Poetry and Prose*, 218.

98. Borroff, "Wallace Stevens' 'The Auroras of Autumn'" (Lecture 20, ENGL 310, Yale Open Courses).

99. Bloom, *Wallace Stevens*, 280.

100. Woodland, *Wallace Stevens and the Apocalyptic Mode*, 139.

101. Carroll, *Wallace Stevens' Supreme Fiction*, 2.

102. One of Stevens's "adagia": "Poetry is a response to the daily necessity of getting the world right" (*Opus Posthumous*, 201).

103. Stevens and Howard, *Letters of Wallace Stevens*, 1996, 434.

Conclusion

Reading At and Against the End of the World

So we come to the end, if not (yet) the End.

I have tried to show that the works I have read educate us to our apocalyptic situation, not through making claims but through what they compel us to consult as we read and try to make sense of them. They do not *tell* us that the developments of the last century put our humanity into question, but they dramatize that destabilization in its various aspects. In trying to understand the drama and the images, we necessarily draw upon and draw together our existing knowledge, both tacit and explicit, and that knowledge is transformed: deepened, sharpened, corrected, made conscious, perhaps in some instances wholly overhauled. If we read these works and others like them with attention and openness, we may quite literally come to inhabit a different world—the conditions of our humanity and the threats to those conditions both become clearer and more palpable to us.

I came to these works, as my readers likely have as well, already bearing some sense of both material and (for lack of a better word) spiritual threats to humanity, a sense derived not only from the news but from the political and social theory, history, and philosophy of the crisis of late modernity. As I sum up what I take to be the collective implications of my readings, I want to consider what literature, as distinct from such theoretical treatments, contributes to our understanding of and response to this crisis in its present manifestation(s).

In his influential if controversial book *The Myth of the Eternal Return,* Mircea Eliade argues that human life is lived in flight from the "terror of history"—the sense that there is no logic or meaning to the course of events, and therefore that the suffering wrought by war, famine, natural disaster, oppression, exploitation and so on is without reason or justification. In Eliade's account, premodern peoples evaded this terror through interpreting extreme suffering as the result of an incursion into the mundane realm of the divine or supernatural, giving it meaning and thereby making it (more) tolerable.

Modern humanity, Eliade argues, has lost this sacred ground of justification and intelligibility and the buffer it provided against the terror of history.

> [I]n our day, when historical pressure no longer allows any escape, how can man tolerate the catastrophes and horrors of history—from collective deportations and massacres to atomic bombings—if beyond them he can glimpse no sign, no transhistorical meaning; if they are only the blind play of economic, social, or political forces, or, even worse, only the result of the "liberties" that a minority takes and exercises directly on the stage of universal history?[1]

Like Wallace Stevens, Eliade argues that the "pressure" of the events of the early twentieth century challenged both the sacred meaning of history and its secular reformulations, such as Hegel's view of history as proceeding toward the realization of reason and freedom, or Marx's interpretation of history as class struggle culminating in a classless, egalitarian and truly human society. History becomes merely the "blind play of economic, social, or political forces."

This is bad enough—to see the sufferings, unfulfilled lives, and and unfulfilled deaths of human beings throughout the ages as simply waste or the wreckage of market forces or struggles for power. But the works I have read suggest an arguably more terrifying terror—the prospect that history is not an arbitrary sequence of contingencies but in fact follows a logic proceeding toward dehumanization, the destruction of civilization, and possibly the extinction of the species. This represents a different threat to sense, analogous to the threat that death poses to the sense of an individual human life, though even more radically, since one way we make sense of the death of the individual is to see them as a part of a larger whole—be it a family, society, or the species—that persists both materially and as the bearer of human culture and value. The persistence of the whole becomes uncertain on a global level in the twentieth and twenty-first centuries.

The present book and the works considered in it could be understood as responses to the "terror of history" as it developed in the last century and as we now feel it in this one. I have chosen these works because I believe that they acknowledge that terror and attempt, more or less directly, to come to terms with it, and that engaging with them illuminates whether and how it is possible for us to inhabit an apocalyptic reality: whether there is an alternative to fleeing into denial, dissociation, and fantasy, and what that alternative might be.

My texts suggest that there is and must be such an alternative, a way to make sense of our situation that still affirms the possibility of living toward a human end, even independently of the hope of salvation, divine or secular. They indicate that there is a way to construe and construct the human meaning of history, even a history apparently tending toward human destruction. I have read Maclean, McCarthy, Lowell, and Stevens as referring us to this ground of sense—this myth, in the sense in which I have used the term—through more or less explicit representations of a radically endangered or untenable human situation that seems to threaten all sense. This may seem paradoxical, but, as I have argued, they do this by finding literary form for their catastrophic subjects, representing them so as to make the meaning of those subjects manifest.

Of course, literature is not the only medium in which such an effort has been attempted. Perhaps the more obvious efforts would be those of historians and social and political theorists—the direct and expository attempts to make sense of the facts of the past and present by analyzing their causes. Simone Weil's *Oppression and Liberty* and Hannah Arendt's *The Origins of Totalitarianism*, both foundational for my own understanding of the crises of the twentieth century, aim to discern and articulate the human meaning and underlying causes of events that each saw as manifesting a fundamental breakdown or undermining of the conditions of human civilization. These and other such treatises form the historical and theoretical background of my readings, and I think that some such background is necessary; literature alone cannot educate us to our historical situation, and the works themselves refer us to this kind of empirical and theoretical background.

But the "imaginative" literature of apocalypse is also necessary to comprehension. The works discussed do something analogous to, and at the same time distinct from, historical and theoretical tracts such as Arendt's and Weil's. The latter are explanatory and analytical and directly tackle the contemporary historical catastrophes; they explicitly articulate the ethical and political conditions that come into view as those conditions are shockingly violated, as well as articulating those characteristics of our time that make such a violation possible and perhaps even inevitable. By contrast, the works I have discussed are narrative or poetic and only obliquely touch upon twentieth-century history, but their form similarly refers us to certain deep conditions of the modern—apocalyptic—situation. These apocalyptic literary works at once refer us to a catastrophic human trajectory driven by unconsciousness, ignorance, violence, impotence, and the disintegration and failure of traditional grounds of meaning and judgment; at the same time they imply through their mode of representation a different and transcendent perspective from which to see and judge, and perhaps allow us to momentarily inhabit that perspective. I conclude with a pointed summarization of my readings that reemphasizes and elaborates how these and other literary works can distinctively, in complement to discursive works, suggest and, at least temporarily, reorient us toward that horizon of judgment and compel us to probe the depths of our tacit knowledge of the conditions of our humanity. This suggests that the imperative to consciousness that comprises the core of an apocalyptic ethics takes the form, in part, of an ongoing practice of reading.

In his search for a tragic form adequate to the shocking and terrible deaths of fourteen young men in the Mann Gulch forest fire, Maclean saw and represented his Smokejumpers as tragic heroes, representative of a kind of beautiful hubris, a human confidence and greatness that transgresses against some order of the universe and thereby provokes its nemesis. But as the distinctly modern and nontraditional form of his work indicates, he also saw the need to find a different way of understanding that order, which could no longer be conceived as divine, and yet still seemed to encompass more than just the purely physical laws of nature. Ultimately, the Smokejumpers' battle with and ultimate defeat by an overwhelming conflagration becomes an image of each human life and death and finally of the career of the human species as a whole, so the search for sense is generalized. *Young Men and Fire* reflects and, to some degree, transcends two threats to the task of making sense of catastrophe in modernity—first of all, the absence of some collective religious or mythical way of construing human experience and especially human suffering, and second, at the end of the work, the prospect of human extinction.

Fire suggests that "the universe," that great Other to humankind, that which is not humankind, is still imbued with human meaning, that confronting the Universe still has meaning—not because there are supernatural beings that declare and underwrite that meaning but because all that we know and experience of human life can only be comprehended with reference to this background of immensity which is an object both of terror and of a kind of eros, a source of imperatives and constraints which cannot be derived from utility or moral rules. There is no "external" argument to be made for this, but only the evocativeness of image—the temporal and spatial geological vastness of the Western landscape, the beauty and terror of fire which Maclean paints with his strange poetry.

Maclean's immediate concern is not the end of civilization but the deaths of individuals, and yet the specter of the End haunts his work—as it must, to some degree, haunt the consciousnesses of all who lived through the dropping of the atomic bomb and the terrifying instability of the Cold War. Maclean uses the figure of "the end of the world" to characterize the terror of the historic 1910 wildfire, and at the end of the book, in his final description of the conflagration that killed the Smokejumpers, he invokes the Bomb, and images of immensity give way to the grotesque and the apocalyptic, a breakdown of sense in the face of individual and collective death.

Ultimately, Maclean suggests the analogy of the collective end to an individual end and finds the sense of both in a type of Stoicism—defeat by such implacable forces is a part of the human condition, at some level inexplicable but also the condition for a compelling heroism. He surmises that, for his Smokejumpers, fear is burned away in the last moments and what is left is only a kind of pity: not self-pity but some "divine bewilderment" that something so valuable could be extinguished, a grief that "finds its answer, if at all, in its own final act" which is simply an insistence on a continued striving to live humanly in the face of all that would deny and annul that human life. This is what he finds in the image of the Smokejumpers who "after [they] had fallen, had risen again, taken a few steps, and fallen again, this final time like pilgrims in prayer," expressing "some firm intention to continue doing forever and ever what we last hoped to do on earth." He sees this courage too in his wife "on her brave and lonely way to death,"[2] and in his work he manifests his own intention to live and die similarly, expending the energy of his last years clambering the steep sides of Mann Gulch, struggling to master the complicated mathematics of fire science, and *writing*, grappling with a subject whose weight and complexity resisted but did not finally defeat his attempt to find its form. The imperative he reads in the Smokejumpers' struggle for life, however futile, becomes his own imperative toward consciousness and articulation, and in the questions it raises, its loose ends and provocations and failures, it becomes ours as well. All of this is something that can only be conveyed literarily, narratively, because the sense that Maclean finds cannot be extricated from the struggle and uncertainty necessarily involved in the modern search for sense.

Maclean's figure of apocalypse is wildfire, a natural disaster, and in *Fire* defeat and death appear as disasters that come upon humans from the outside or from nature, though such disasters are of course an essential feature of the human condition. This may be continuous with Maclean's final retreat from the apocalyptic vision, his descent from the towering inferno back to the ground, to the realm of individual death and the Forest Service's pledge to maintain the grave markers of the men, which reintroduces the assumption of a human future, at least a proximal one. Humanity in Maclean's vision has its failings and tragic flaws as well as its lesser and occasionally downright-bad specimens, but our basic humanity is something fundamentally good—as Maclean himself conveys as narrator, with his humor, humaneness, integrity, and tenacity, as well as the appealing and varied humanity of the characters he describes.

Lowell and McCarthy, on the other hand, emphasize that that the threat to humanity is internal as well as external. "The Quaker Graveyard in Nantucket" and *Blood Meridian* confront the apocalypse as something seemingly intrinsic to human history which humans bring upon themselves—as the historical development of human nature. Central to both of their visions is an inherent and determinative violence in humanity, which both authors saw magnified into globe-spanning war in the twentieth century. McCarthy

tells a historical tale of human depravity, of a band of mercenary scalphunters who somehow manage by the end of the book to yet further lose their
humanity, and Lowell turns an elegy for his dead Navy sailor-cousin into a
jeremiad conflating the war of his time with the gory slaughter perpetrated in
the nineteenth-century whaling trade.

But neither of these works is simply a polemic against violence or an argument that human beings are violent animals. In both, the violence is represented as bound up with a modern crisis of sense, of which it appears as both
cause and symptom in a kind of vicious cycle. On the one hand, the fact of
force as the dominating determinant of human life and human history seems
to call into question the liberal ideals—peace, progress, utility, humaneness—
that we see, convincingly, dismantled and trampled in both works. On the
other hand, force and violence gain all the more ascendancy as all forms of
legitimate authority, both traditional and modern, seem to lose their sanction.
This loss is exemplified in the judge's exchange with the scalphunters after
he lectures them on geology and prehistoric time:

> A few would quote him scripture to confound his ordering up of eons out of the
> ancient chaos and other apostate supposings. The judge smiled.
>
> Books lie, he said.
>
> God dont lie.
>
> No, said the judge. He does not. And these are his words.
>
> He held up a chunk of rock.
>
> He speaks in stones and trees, the bones of things.
>
> The squatters in their rags nodded among themselves and were soon reckon-
> ing him correct, this man of learning, in all his speculations, and this the judge
> encouraged until they were right proselytes of the new order whereupon he
> laughed at them for fools.[3]

Modern science has challenged the authority of religion, but, the passage
parabolically suggests, modern science cannot serve as the new authority
either. Its truths are not moral truths and thus it places no constraints on those
who wield it, and they can use or not use it as it serves their ends. I argued that
the judge identifies himself with history, and here the judge mimics history in
wielding science as a corrosive of traditional forms of belief and then denying
even its objectivity or the reality of anything except what he himself declares.

What he declares is constrained by one thing only—the brute reality of force, the only constraint remaining after all ideals have been denied.

And it is not just that force breaks the bounds of weakened ideal constraints. The sheer exercise of power becomes dangerously compelling when other beliefs and motivations wane, and we as readers at times experience a kind of exhilaration in the violence. In Yeats's famous lines, "The best lack all conviction, while the worst / Are full of passionate intensity." The "best" in *Blood Meridian* scarcely rise above an impotent mediocrity, while the judge dominates gloriously. The passion and the intensity—the sheer fact of the judge's undivided, confident exertion of power; the annihilating descent of the Comanches upon the filibusters; Glanton's unrepentant end—hold, I think, a certain disturbing attraction. Lowell's poem provides a similar contrast between the Quakers' bloody hunting and evisceration of the whales, described in his pounding, inexorable rhythms, and the docile penitents under the opaque and perhaps blind gaze of the Virgin. The works compel us to acknowledge this attraction to the exertion of power, the expression of will, and not, I think, simply to have us ward against it. This too is part of what it means to be human, this terrible striving, and the ambiguous aspect of this striving, because it is ambiguous, can, again, only be presented through literary means: character, story, image, figure.

The standard according to which we would resist and judge against such power cannot, these works suggest, be only that of enlightened self-interest or empathy or the moral law, Kantian or Christian or otherwise, none of which are finally adequate to withstand the power of force—including its aesthetic or erotic power. But the forms of the works do nonetheless evoke a standard of judgment and resistance and the knowledge of a need for such a standard. The narrative or poetic voice of each imagines and allows us to inhabit an impersonal consciousness which stands outside and above the figures of violence and even outside and above this humanity so constituted, since we see it from a perspective beyond its end. And yet this perspective is not "inhuman" but some "more than human human": things seen from this angle, from this extreme distance, have value still, but a value the basis of which is not yet fully known or grasped, a value derived not from the happiness of the individual and not even from the collective well-being of the species but from an intimation of a humanity defined in relation to some absolute.

McCarthy and Lowell are not prophets; they do not know what "humanity" is or ought to be any more than their readers (or at least their more sensitive, intelligent and educated readers). But if their works, as well as Maclean's and Stevens's, have some compelling power and continued interest despite their limitations, it is because, and insofar as, their vision resonates with our own tacit knowledge of certain conditions of human life—not just confirming what we already know, but compelling us to see how, disturbingly, our experience and knowledge gain a new coherence when seen from this perspective, and also making the demand for an ongoing effort of understanding. These authors put before us narratives and images that seem right, the source of that rightness only partially known to the authors themselves, and we must take up the task of discerning that source. Their works can be seen not as definitive pronouncements but as struggles to come to some further comprehension of the twentieth-century trajectory which can, they implicitly argue, only be arrived at through narrative and image and difficult literary form.

Stevens, finally, helps us to understand why the difficulty, ambiguity, obscurity might be necessary to the fundamental task of representing the crisis. In "The Auroras of Autumn," as well as in his prose reflections on the relation of poetry and reality, Stevens reflects a concern with a different but in some sense encompassing aspect of the End. The historical catastrophe, the catastrophe that is history, that Lowell and McCarthy figure in their works, depends upon and in part *is* the catastrophe of a collective (and for many, also an individual) failure to be able any longer to conceive and experience a normatively structured and meaningful human reality, to inhabit a world in which human imperatives and constraints can still compel conviction and stand athwart the sweep and the lure of force. Some new basis of judgment must be apprehended, and Stevens suggests that it is poetic resemblance that can evoke and orient us toward and even in some sense constitute this basis of judgment; in "Auroras," the shifting images—from cosmic serpent to transient parental home to the awesome beauty of the Northern lights— "resemble" the succession of myths and the desperate, interminable, necessary quest for a supreme fiction adequate to our contemporary pressures.

In these works of apocalyptic literature, history becomes the revelation of the inhuman as it works itself out within human endeavors, and of an inhuman background that conditions and will outlast human life—but it also becomes the revelation of some transcendent standard of judgment, which the works suggest both negatively, through the reaction the spectacle of destruction provokes in us, and positively, through images of austere sublimity. The suggestion is that only through the identification with something far, far larger than ourselves might we adequately comprehend and judge our situation.

I have offered an interpretation of these works, but the interpretation is not the same as the reality to which they refer us. The strangeness, difficulty, and ambiguity of narrative form and images is essential to the distinctive way that literature might be revelatory. The work, being a fiction and the creation of a limited human consciousness, is not divine revelation but the expression of an intuited coherence dramatically different from the whole as we typically conceive it, that is, stable and abiding, with ourselves at the center. In trying to make sense of these works, not in order to reduce them to some literal statement but in order be able to grasp and inhabit them, our perspective is shifted and our very sense of reality changed. In discerning the ground of "resemblance" (what have nineteenth-century scalphunters to do with twentieth- and twenty-first-century crises? What does the white cabin on the beach evoke? Why do these things seem *right*?) we are educated to that ground, *and* to the fact that there *is* such a ground, that reality—in the only humanly meaningful sense—is such that this is how we must come to know it.

These authors' ideas and visions are of course not authoritative, nor is this the only way that the themes they address could be imagined or dramatized. But in the effort to attribute sense to their works, we are referred to our experience and our educated intuitions. We draw on these and test what literature presents against them, and on the other hand test our own previous manner of comprehending our experience against these new visions, and perhaps find that they allow a greater comprehensiveness, if also a more disturbing one.

Thus I believe that our reading finally educates us to the need for an ongoing practice of reading, and a kind of reading aimed at attending to those realities to which literary works refer us. There is, obviously, much more to be said than I have been able to say about the conditions of humanity as revealed through apocalyptic works—more that would emerge from the consideration of other works, of more contemporary works that deal with the ever more pressing ecological crisis and other material and nonmaterial threats to the human, and with the intertwinement of those threats with racial, economic, and other forms of social injustice. This practice of reading is a matter of widening and deepening consciousness but perhaps most fundamentally a matter of direction: the point is not just to know something but to be continually reoriented, made aware of a different ground of judgment. Of something called "humanity," which we only have some chance of preserving if we come to a far deeper understanding than we yet have of what it is and what threatens it. The imperative of reading is the imperative to make humanity conscious: to articulate and therefore to bring to consciousness—to bring into being—what humanity is, which would maybe allow it to be something else. Even a conscious humanity would be something different from an unconscious one, and would perhaps—if anything can—make it possible to tell a different story of ourselves.

NOTES

1. Eliade and Smith, *The Myth of the Eternal Return*, 151.
2. Maclean, *Young Men and Fire*, 299–301.
3. McCarthy, *Blood Meridian, Or the Evening Redness in the West*, 116.

Bibliography

Abbott, H. Porter. *The Cambridge Introduction to Narrative*. 2nd ed. Cambridge: Cambridge University Press, 2008.

Arendt, Hannah. *The Origins of Totalitarianism*. New York: Harcourt, Brace, Jovanovich, 1973.

Aristotle. *Nicomachean Ethics*. Translated by Roger Crisp. Cambridge: Cambridge University Press, 2014.

———. *Aristotle's Poetics*, edited by Gordon M. Kirkwood. Translated by James Hutton. New York: W. W. Norton & Company, 1982.

———. *Poetics*. Translated by Malcolm Heath. New ed. New York: Penguin Classics, 1997.

Arnold, Edwin T. "Naming, Knowing and Nothingness: McCarthy's Moral Parables." In *Perspectives on Cormac McCarthy*, edited by Edwin T. Arnold and Dianne C. Luce. Jackson: University Press of Mississippi, 1999.

Atnip, Lindsay. "From 'Meaning' to Reality: Toward a Polanyian Cognitive Theory of Literature." *Tradition and Discovery: The Polanyi Society Periodical* 46, no. 1 (January 30, 2020): 40–54.

Axelrod, Steven Gould. "Robert Lowell and Hopkins." *Twentieth Century Literature* 31, no. 1 (1985): 55–72.

Axelrod, Steven, and Helen Deese. *Robert Lowell: Essays on the Poetry*. Cambridge: Cambridge University Press, 1989.

Balthaser, Benjamin. "Horror Cities: Contesting the Ruins of Capitalism in Contemporary Genre Cinema." *Camera Obscura: Feminism, Culture, and Media Studies* 35, no. 1 (103) (May 1, 2020): 139–59.

Barthes, Roland. *S/Z*. New York: Macmillan, 1974.

Bell, Vereen M. *The Achievement of Cormac McCarthy*. Baton Rouge: LSU Press, 1988.

Berger, Charles. *Forms of Farewell: The Late Poetry of Wallace Stevens*. Madison: University of Wisconsin Press, 1985.

Berger, Peter L., and Thomas Luckmann. *The Social Construction of Reality: A Treatise in the Sociology of Knowledge*. New York: Anchor, 1967.

Bloom, Harold. *How to Read and Why*. New York: Scribner, 2001.

————. *Wallace Stevens: The Poems of Our Climate*. Ithaca: Cornell University Press, 1977.

Boone, Joseph Allen. *Queer Frontiers: Millennial Geographies, Genders, and Generations*. Madison: University of Wisconsin Press, 2000.

Booth, Wayne C. "The Struggle to Tell the Story of the Struggle to Get the Story Told." *Narrative* 5, no. 1 (1997): 50–59.

Borroff, Marie. "The Achievement of Norman Maclean." *The Yale Review* 82, no. 2 (1994): 118–31.

————. "Wallace Stevens' 'The Auroras of Autumn' (Lecture 20, ENGL 310, Yale Open Courses)." Accessed May 6, 2018. https://oyc.yale.edu/english/engl-310/lecture-20.

Brogan, Jacqueline Vaught. "Stevens in History and Not in History: The Poet and the Second World War." *Wallace Stevens Journal* 13, no. 2 (Fall 1989): 168–90.

————. *The Violence Within/The Violence Without: Wallace Stevens and the Emergence of a Revolutionary Poetics*. Athens: University of Georgia Press, 2003.

Brooks, Peter. *Reading for the Plot: Design and Intention in Narrative*. Revised ed. Cambridge, MA: Harvard University Press, 1992.

Brown, Merle E. *Wallace Stevens: The Poem as Act*. Detroit: Wayne State University Press, 1971.

Bultmann, Rudolf. *History and Eschatology: The Presence of Eternity*. Waco: Baylor University Press, 1957.

Carroll, Joseph. *Wallace Stevens' Supreme Fiction: A New Romanticism*. Baton Rouge: LSU Press, 1988.

Cavitch, Max. *American Elegy: The Poetry of Mourning from the Puritans to Whitman*. Minneapolis: University of Minnesota Press, 2007.

Chamberlain, Samuel. *My Confession*. New York: Harper, 1956.

Coleridge, Samuel Taylor. *Biographia Literaria: Or, Biographical Sketches of My Literary Life and Opinions*. London: Leavitt, Lord and Company, 1834.

Collins, John J. *The Apocalyptic Imagination: An Introduction to Jewish Apocalyptic Literature*. Third ed. Grand Rapids, MI: Eerdmans, 2016.

Cook, Eleanor. *Poetry, Word-Play, and Word-War in Wallace Stevens*. Princeton, NJ: Princeton University Press, 2014.

————. "Introduction." *Wallace Stevens Journal* 15, no. 2 (Fall 1991): 115–25.

Cooper, Lydia R. *No More Heroes: Narrative Perspective and Morality in Cormac McCarthy*. Baton Rouge: LSU Press, 2011.

Crews, Michael Lynn. *Books Are Made Out of Books: A Guide to Cormac McCarthy's Literary Influences*. Austin: University of Texas Press, 2017.

Daugherty, Leo. "Gravers False and True: 'Blood Meridian' as Gnostic Tragedy." In *Perspectives on Cormac McCarthy*, edited by Edwin T. Arnold and Dianne C. Luce. Jackson: University Press of Mississippi, 1993.

De Cristofaro, Diletta. "'Time, No Arrow, No Boomerang, but a Concertina': *Cloud Atlas* and the Anti-Apocalyptic Critical Temporalities of the Contemporary Post-Apocalyptic Novel." *Critique: Studies in Contemporary Fiction* 59, no. 2 (March 15, 2018): 243–57.

Doreski, William. *Robert Lowell's Shifting Colors: The Poetics of the Public & the Personal.* Athens: Ohio University Press, 1999.

Dreyfus, Hubert, and Sean Dorrance Kelly. *All Things Shining: Reading the Western Classics to Find Meaning in a Secular Age.* New York: Free Press, 2011.

Duff, Nancy J. "Christian Apocalyptic." *Theology Today* 75, no. 1 (April 1, 2018): 5–8.

Eagleton, Terry. *Sweet Violence: The Idea of the Tragic.* Malden, MA: Wiley-Blackwell, 2002.

Eksteins, Modris. *Rites of Spring: The Great War and the Birth of the Modern Age.* Boston: Mariner Books, 2000.

Elder, Charles. *The Grammar of Humanity: The Sense and Sources of the Imperative to Consciousness.* Manuscript in preparation, 2021.

Eliade, Mircea, and Jonathan Z. Smith. *The Myth of the Eternal Return: Cosmos and History.* Translated by Willard R. Trask. Reprint ed. Princeton: Princeton University Press, 2018.

Emerson, Ralph Waldo. *Emerson: Essays and Lectures: Nature: Addresses and Lectures / Essays: First and Second Series / Representative Men / English Traits / The Conduct of Life.* New York: Library of America, 1983.

———. *Nature.* CreateSpace Independent Publishing Platform, 2012.

Felski, Rita, ed. *Rethinking Tragedy.* Baltimore: Johns Hopkins University Press, 2008.

Freud, Sigmund. "Mourning and Melancholia." In *The Complete Psychological Works of Sigmund Freud,* edited and translated by James Strachey, 14: 243–58. London: The Hogarth Press, 1957.

Frye, Northrop. *Northrop Frye on Milton and Blake,* edited by Angela Esterhammer. 2nd ed. Toronto: University of Toronto Press, 2005.

———. *The Anatomy of Criticism: Four Essays.* Princeton: Princeton University Press, 2000.

Future of Life Institute. "Existential Risk." Accessed February 27, 2019. https://futureoflife.org/background/existential-risk/.

Gallie, W. B. *Philosophy and the Historical Understanding.* New York: Schocken Books, 1968.

Hamilton, Ian. *Robert Lowell: A Biography.* London: Faber and Faber, 2011.

Harrington, Michael. *Socialism: Past and Future.* New York: Skyhorse Publishing Inc., 2011.

Hass, Robert. "Lowell's Graveyard." *Salmagundi,* no. 37 (1977): 56–72.

Hay, John, ed. *Apocalypse in American Literature and Culture.* Cambridge: Cambridge University Press, 2021.

Heidegger, Martin. *Being and Time.* Reprint ed. New York: Harper Perennial Modern Classics, 2008.

Hobsbaum, Philip. *Reader's Guide to Robert Lowell.* New York: Thames & Hudson, 1988.

Homans, Peter. *The Ability to Mourn: Disillusionment and the Social Origins of Psychoanalysis.* Chicago: University of Chicago Press, 1989.

Horkheimer, Max, and Theodor W. Adorno. *Dialectic of Enlightenment,* edited by Gunzelin Schmid Noerr. Translated by Edmund Jephcott. Stanford: Stanford University Press, 2007.

Hughes, Robert. *American Visions: The Epic History of Art in America*. New York: Alfred A. Knopf, 1999.

Hurley, Jessica. *Infrastructures of Apocalypse: American Literature and the Nuclear Complex*. U of Minnesota Press, 2020.

Hurley, Jessica, and Dan Sinykin. "Apocalypse: Introduction." *ASAP/Journal* 3, no. 3 (2018): 451–66.

Jakobson, Roman. *Language in Literature*, edited by Krystyna Pomorska and Stephen Rudy. Cambridge, MA: Belknap Press, 1990.

James, Henry. *The Tragic Muse*. New York: Penguin Classics, 1995.

Jonas, Hans. *The Gnostic Religion*. 2nd Revised ed. Boston: Beacon Press, 1963.

Kermode, Frank. *The Sense of an Ending: Studies in the Theory of Fiction*. 2nd ed. Oxford: Oxford University Press, 2000.

Librett, Jeffrey S., ed. *Of the Sublime: Presence in Question*. Albany: SUNY Press, 1993.

Literary Hub. "The 50 Greatest Apocalypse Novels," October 27, 2020. https://lithub .com/the-50-greatest-apocalypse-novels/.

Longenbach, James. *Wallace Stevens: The Plain Sense of Things*. New York: Oxford University Press, 1991.

Longinus. *On the Sublime*. Translated by H. L. Havell. London: Forgotten Books, 2018.

Lowell, Robert. *The Collected Prose*. Farrar, Straus and Giroux, 1990.

———. *The Letters of Robert Lowell*, edited by Saskia Hamilton. New York: Farrar, Straus and Giroux, 2007.

Maclean, Norman. *The Norman Maclean Reader*, edited by Alan O. Weltzien. Chicago: University of Chicago Press, 2008.

———. *A River Runs Through It, and Other Stories*. Chicago: University Of Chicago Press, 1976.

———. *Young Men and Fire*. University of Chicago Press, 2010.

———. "Episode, Scene, Speech, and Word: The Madness of Lear." In *Critics and Criticism*, edited by R. S. Crane. Chicago: University of Chicago Press, 1952.

———. "From Action to Image: Theories of the Lyric in the Eighteenth Century." In *Critics and Criticism*, edited by R. S. Crane. Chicago: University of Chicago Press, 1952.

McCarthy, Cormac. *Blood Meridian, Or the Evening Redness in the West*. New York: Vintage Books, 1985.

McFarland, Ron, Hugh Nichols, and Norman Maclean, eds. "Montana Memories." In *Norman Maclean*. American Authors. New York: Confluence Press, 1992.

McMurry, Andrew. "The Slow Apocalypse: A Gradualistic Theory of the World's Demise." *Postmodern Culture* 6, no. 3 (1996).

Melville, Herman. *Moby-Dick*, edited by Hershel Parker. 3rd ed. New York: W. W. Norton & Company, 2017.

———. *Moby-Dick*, edited by Alfred Kazin. Boston: Houghton Mifflin, 1956.

Mundik, Petra. "'Striking the Fire Out of the Rock': Gnostic Theology in Cormac McCarthy's *Blood Meridian*." *South Central Review* 26, no. 3 (October 29, 2009): 72–97.

Newton, Isaac. *The Principia: Mathematical Principles of Natural Philosophy.* Translated by I. Bernard Cohen, Anne Whitman, and Julia Budenz. Berkeley: University of California Press, 1999.

Nietzsche, Friedrich. *On the Genealogy of Morals and Ecce Homo.* Translated by Walter Kaufmann. New York: Knopf Doubleday Publishing Group, 2010.

———. *Saemtliche Werke: Kritische Studienausgabe,* edited by Mazzino Montinari and Giorgio Colli. 2nd ed. München: Walter de Gruyter, 1999.

Novak, Barbara. *Nature and Culture: American Landscape and Painting, 1825–1875, With a New Preface.* 3rd ed. New York: Oxford University Press, 2007.

Nussbaum, Martha C. *Love's Knowledge: Essays on Philosophy and Literature.* Revised ed. New York: Oxford University Press, 1992.

Owens, Barcley. *Cormac McCarthy's Western Novels.* Tucson: University of Arizona Press, 2000.

Perloff, Marjorie. *The Poetic Art of Robert Lowell.* Ithaca: Cornell University Press, 1973.

Phillips, Dana. "History and the Ugly Facts of Cormac McCarthy's *Blood Meridian.*" *American Literature* 68, no. 2 (1996): 433–60.

Pinker, Steven. *Enlightenment Now: The Case for Reason, Science, Humanism, and Progress.* Illustrated ed. New York: Viking, 2018.

Polanyi, Michael. *Personal Knowledge: Towards a Post-Critical Philosophy.* Chicago: University Of Chicago Press, 1974.

Polanyi, Michael, and Amartya Sen. *The Tacit Dimension.* Revised ed. Chicago: University of Chicago Press, 2009.

Potolsky, Matthew. *Mimesis.* New York: Routledge, 2006.

Preminger, Alex, Terry V. F. Brogan, and Frank J. Warnke, eds. *The New Princeton Encyclopedia of Poetry and Poetics.* 3rd ed. Princeton: Princeton University Press, 1993.

Ramazani, Jahan. *The Poetry of Mourning: The Modern Elegy from Hardy to Heaney.* Chicago: University of Chicago Press, 1994.

Ray, Gene. *Terror and the Sublime in Art and Critical Theory: From Auschwitz to Hiroshima to September 11.* London: Palgrave Macmillan, 2005.

Redfield, James M. *Nature and Culture in the Iliad: The Tragedy of Hector.* Durham, NC: Duke University Press, 1994.

Rizvi, Ali A. "Grief Without Belief: How Do Atheists Deal With Death?" *Huffington Post* (blog), October 22, 2013. http://www.huffingtonpost.com/ali-a-rizvi/atheists -death_b_4134439.html.

Sacks, Peter M. *The English Elegy: Studies in the Genre from Spenser to Yeats.* Baltimore: Johns Hopkins University Press, 1987.

Shaw, Philip. *The Sublime.* London: Routledge, 2005.

Staples, Hugh B. *Robert Lowell: The First Twenty Years.* London: Faber and Faber, 1962.

Steiner, George. *The Death of Tragedy.* New Haven: Yale University Press, 1996.

Stevens, Wallace. *Letters of Wallace Stevens,* edited by Holly Stevens and Richard Howard. Berkeley: University of California Press, 1996.

————. *Wallace Stevens: Collected Poetry and Prose*, edited by Frank Kermode and Joan Richardson. Reprint ed. New York: Library of America, 1997.

Taylor, Charles. *Sources of the Self: The Making of the Modern Identity*. Cambridge, MA: Harvard University Press, 1992.

Thomas, Alan. "The Achievement of 'Young Men and Fire.'" *Los Angeles Review of Books*, September 10, 2015. https://lareviewofbooks.org/article/the-achievement -of-young-men-and-fire/.

Toole, David. *Waiting For Godot In Sarajevo: Theological Reflections On Nihilism, Tragedy, And Apocalypse*. Boulder: Basic Books, 1998.

Von Hendy, Andrew. *The Modern Construction of Myth*. Bloomington: Indiana University Press, 2002.

Wagar, Warren. *Terminal Visions: The Literature of Last Things*. Bloomington: Indiana University Press, 1982.

Weil, Simone. *Oppression and Liberty*. Amherst: University of Massachusetts Press, 1978.

————. *The Notebooks of Simone Weil*. London: Routledge, 2013.

White, L. Michael. "Apocalyptic Literature in Judaism & Early Christianity," November 1999. https://www.pbs.org/wgbh/pages/frontline/shows/apocalypse/ primary/white.html.

Williamson, Alan. *Pity the Monsters: The Political Vision of Robert Lowell*. New Haven: Yale University Press, 1986.

Wittgenstein, Ludwig. *Philosophical Investigations*, edited by Joachim Schulte. Translated by P. M. S. Hacker. 4th ed. Malden, MA: Wiley-Blackwell, 2009.

Wood, James. *How Fiction Works*. New York: Macmillan, 2008.

Woodland, Malcolm. *Wallace Stevens and the Apocalyptic Mode*. Iowa City: University of Iowa Press, 2005.

————. "Wallace Stevens' 'Puella Parvula' and the 'Haunt of Prophecy.'" *Wallace Stevens Journal* 23, no. 2 (Fall 1999): 99–110.

Wallace-Wells, David. "The Uninhabitable Earth." *New York Magazine*, July 10, 2017. https://nymag.com/intelligencer/2017/07/climate-change-earth-too-hot-for -humans.html.

Index

World Wars: 117, 125, 141n63; First,
114; Second, 21, 103, 107, 114

Young Men and Fire
(Maclean): catastrophe in, 38–40;
heroism in, 89–90; humanity in, 67;
magnitude in, 47–51; scholarship on,
ix, xi, 3–4, 69, 148; sense in, 60–62;
struggle to write, 30–31, 63n3,
65n48; total conflagration in, 56–59;
tragedy in, 12–14, 27–30, 33–38;
tragic form in, 30–33, *32*, 62–63;
tragic inevitability in, 44–47; tragic
sense in, 40–44

About the Author

Lin Atnip is Tutor at St. John's College in Santa Fe. She also teaches in the University of Chicago Graham School's Basic Program of Liberal Education for Adults. She also teaches in the University of Chicago Graham School's Basic Program of Liberal Education for Adults.